So You Think You
Know Me?

Allan Weaver

So You Think You Know Me?

Published 2008 by
WATERSIDE PRESS LTD
Sherfield Gables
Sherfield on Loddon
Hook
Hampshire RG27 0JG

Telephone 01256 882250
E-mail enquiries@watersidepress.co.uk
Online catalogue www.WatersidePress.co.uk

ISBN-10: 190438045X
ISBN-13: 9781904380450

Cataloguing-In-Publication Data A catalogue record for this book can be obtained from the British Library.

Cover design © 2008 Waterside Press Ltd.

Front cover photograph © Tom Gibson Photography. Rear cover photograph shows Allan Weaver with his sons, Paul (22) and Allan (21).

North American distributor International Specialised Book Services (ISBS), 920 NE 58th Ave, Suite 300, Portland, Oregon, 97213-3786, USA
Telephone 1 800 944 6190 Fax 1 503 280 8832 orders@isbs.com www.isbs.com

So You Think You
Know Me?

Allan Weaver

About the author

Allan Weaver was born and raised in the Ayrshire town of Saltcoats. He began offending at the age of 12 and subsequently spent more than a decade steeped in an offending lifestyle. This culminated in years of detention in various reformatory and penal institutions. After 'returning to school' at the age of 31 and successfully obtaining the necessary higher qualifications, he attended the University of Strathclyde where he was awarded his Diploma in Social Work. He has been employed as a criminal justice social worker for the past 13 years and has been a team leader for the past five, during which time he also completed an MSc in Criminal Justice and obtained a Practice Award in Advanced Criminal Justice Studies. He has also supported a number of social work students through their practice placements. *So You Think You Know Me?* is his first book.

The authors of the Foreword

Mike Nellis is Professor of Criminal and Community Justice in the Glasgow School of Social Work, University of Strathclyde. He is a former social worker with young offenders, trained at the London School of Economics in 1977/8 and between 1990-2003 was closely involved in the training of probation officers at the University of Birmingham. He was awarded his Ph.D by the Institute of Criminology, University of Cambridge in 1991. He has written extensively on the changing nature of the probation service, the promotion of community penalties, the significance of electronic monitoring and the cultural politics of penal reform (including the educational use of prison movies and the autobiographies of offenders). His most recent book (edited with Eric Chui) was *Moving Probation Forward* (Longmans, 2003) and he is currently editing a book, with Belgian colleagues, on electronic monitoring around the world.

Fergus McNeill worked for several years in residential drug rehabilitation and as a criminal justice social worker before taking up a lecturing post at the University of Glasgow in 1998. Since then his teaching, research and writing have examined crime and criminal justice issues including sentencing, community penalties, resettlement of prisoners and youth justice. He is a regular contributor to public debates and has acted as both witness and expert adviser to committees of the Scottish Parliament on these issues. Latterly, his work has focused on how practice with offenders is changing and how it should change in the light of research evidence about desistance from crime. *Reducing Reoffending*, his first book, co-authored with Bill Whyte was published by Willan in 2007.

CONTENTS

Foreword

Mike Nellis and Fergus McNeill

Glasgow School of Social Work

Academics like us long ago learned to take good offender autobiographies seriously; by dint of their obvious 'human interest' they tend to get the attention of the public in a way that our books don't, no matter how similar our concerns. Clifford Shaw, a social worker turned criminologist in 1920s Chicago famously persuaded a young thief he knew to write out his life story and the resulting account, *The Jackroller* (Shaw 1930), remains a classic to this day, still culled for insights into criminal behaviour and lessons for criminal justice, though surrounded on the bookshelves by many more recent examples from around the world. In Britain there is a long history of ex-prisoner autobiographies making serious—if all too often short-lived—contributions to debate on penal reform and the rehabilitation of offenders. This one will be no exception, and its influence deserves to last. The genre of offender autobiography has been somewhat degraded in recent years by a certain type of 'true crime' book in which maybe-former gangsters recycle and celebrate their former misdeeds as entertainment for impressionable young men. The newer genre of 'painful lives'—usually stories of abusive childhoods, some of which propel their victims into crime, 'care' and imprisonment—is often touching and less exploitive of public gullibility, but can veer towards the mawkish. In some shops at least *So You Think You Know Me?* will suffer the indignity of being marketed as 'true crime', but actually it restores one's confidence in what good offender autobiographies can achieve—*and* what social work can achieve—and it could just as easily, and more intelligently, be shelved under social science, criminology or even Scottish literature.

Scotland—and Glasgow in particular—has produced more than its fair share of offender autobiographies. Jimmy Boyle and Hugh Collins come to mind, but they are not the only ones. Allan Weaver's story is mostly set in Saltcoats, a small town 30 miles west of Glasgow on the Ayrshire coast, but in its wry and evocative depiction of truancy, of early rebellion against authority, of peer pressure to be a 'hard man', of drinking, constant thieving and fighting, of the failings of the care system and of the inevitable, criminality-confirming imprisonments, it has recognisable affinities with the offender autobiographies that preceded it. The reason is simple—though we are talking about different generations, the lives and prospects of the men who wrote them barely changed. A culture was handed down. Allan even writes at one point that as a teenager 'Jimmy Boyle was my hero and I wanted to be like him'—a simultaneously dismal and exhilarating thing for a boy when you look back upon it, but an aspiration in which Allan would not have been alone.

Glasgow's apparent flair for producing offender autobiographies constitutes a literary legacy about which—despite the various writers' emphases on overcoming adversity—respectable elements in the city are understandably ambivalent, often embarrassed and sometimes angry, fearing the effect on municipal reputations. It is a commonplace of the genre for writers to point out that given the circumstances they were born into, their lives up to early adulthood, and sometimes beyond that, could hardly have been different. Conservatively-inclined commentators almost always baulk at this, insisting that there is always choice, that not everyone who grew up in violent families or gang-ridden schemes went to the bad themselves, not realising that while this is true, it is these exceptions who need special explanations, not the many who became hard and cruel because this is what survival and status-seeking amidst poverty and disadvantage demanded of them.

The steel and stone of HM Prison Barlinnie figures prominently in parts of *So Think You Know Me?*, as it has in so many Scottish offender narratives, but the first Glasgow connection here comes in the form of Allan Weaver's father, a violent man who beat his wife and traumatised his children, instilling the resentments in which his son's rage festered, flourished and eventually became a core ingredient of his identity. But Weaver senior was himself the son of a violent, slum-born man, and, without education, no more able to free himself from tradition or imagine himself to be different than Allan himself initially was. Writing of the era when Allan's father was a boy, with an uneasy mix of sympathy and despair, socialist Edwin Muir (1935) had famously lamented the milieu in which such viciousness arose:

These people are [not] a special class outside the bounds of humanity, but merely ... ordinary men and women in a hopeless position, who have been placed there by the operation of a process over which they have no control.

That being so, it would surely be inhuman to grudge them what enjoyment they can get, whether in drink, love or fighting, and stupid to complain, as the benevolent sometimes do, that the hearts of these people are not at once softened by a smile or a few kind words. A natural impulse is to snatch every child away from such places, but even if that could be done the slums would fill up again: the system under which we live forces people into them with a continuous mechanical pressure, and once they are there they may give up all hope; they will become like their neighbours. The sufferings of an ordinary healthy child brought up in the slums are dreadful beyond imagination. The terror and corrupt knowledge of these children can be heard in their voices, the most desolate and discordant sound in creation. This terror breaks out in early youth, that is as soon as these boys are strong enough to fight for themselves, in revengeful violence and cruelty. This process coincides with puberty: it is automatic, and kind words and boys' clubs will never have more than a passing effect of on it.

Muir, 1935: 118-119

The slums of the 1930s and the schemes of the 1960s and 1970s were not exactly the same as each other, but it is impossible to read this book without seeing dispiriting continuities. The streets of Saltcoats were not slums as Muir described them but the taint of that harsh world marked Allan and his young friends from the start. Some of those friends are marked by it still and have never escaped it. As a youth Allan became what pride and adverse circumstance required him to be and took all the painful consequences, but he sensed always, deep within, that he was never fully given over to it, that there was more to life, and to him, than this world had allowed him to see. One of the greatest pleasures of this book, and its most hopeful aspect, is undoubtedly his account of the tortuous processes by which he extricated himself from a criminal lifestyle, began to imagine a different life for himself, and to break the cycle for his own two sons. The determination was all his; but as he is the first to admit, the opportunities he availed himself of were created by others—teachers who had laid the foundations, social workers who had faith in him, a mother who never gave up on him, as well as a wise friend on the prison landing—and one key lesson of books such as this is that 'desistance '—giving up crime—requires structures, cultures and kind, supportive people who first make it seem conceivable and then work to make it possible. Periodic spells of work outside Scotland enabled Allan to break old ties and habits, but, as is often the way with desisting individuals, he developed an appetite for education and giving back to the community from which he had come, and in doing so he found his vocation; in 1995 he graduated, with a full degree, from the University of Strathclyde social work programme, and has worked for local government ever since, currently as a criminal justice services team leader. Ultimately this was how he fought and won his toughest fight; to see himself and to compel others to recognize him as something more than just another 'offender'.

Allan Weaver is not the first ex-offender to have become a social worker, just the first to have published a book about it—but the kind of transition he made remains all too rare, and the case for creating frameworks which permit and encourage it can never be made too often. Allan is living proof that it can be done successfully, and one very welcome consequence of the debate his book will stimulate might be a renewal of interest in the now almost forgotten 'new careers movement'. This began in the 1960s in the USA as a means of offering people from disadvantaged backgrounds—including (eventually) offenders—the chance to train as professional social workers, utilising their distinct and hard won experience to work with clients whom social workers from more conventional backgrounds would otherwise find hard to reach. The movement never made a big impact in the UK, but the Bristol New Careers project which ran in England between 1973 and 1992, achieved some success in this respect. It was initially run by Nacro, and a significant number of ex-offenders did become social workers. Paradoxically, after it was taken over by the probation service, fewer of the ex-offenders who joined it found it congenial: their distinct experiences of desistance were simply not 'accorded any operational value in [the] agency's aims, purposes or practices' (Caddick 1994: 458). Of his own experience of social work in Scotland, Allan writes:

> To my disappointment, I was never encouraged to use aspects of 'self' in a professional context and indeed if my experiences of the social work course were anything to go by, it would be actively frowned upon. As such I refrained, therefore, from overtly discussing my past with clients which I found frustrating as perhaps the use of my own experiences may have given my role, advice and understanding a degree of credibility in their eyes.
>
> (p. 208)

For those of us in social work and in social work education, these are hard but important words to read. A quarter century ago, one of us had experience of employing an ex-offender (Nick) as a volunteer on an alternative to custody programme for young offenders, prefiguring by a few years the opportunity for voluntary work that social worker

Margaret Clark gave to Allan when he came out of prison in 1985. Among the numerous inadvertent benefits Nick brought to the programme was inspiration to one particular youngster (Kevin) who had been sentenced to it, who, seeing that Nick had successfully put offending behind him, and embarked on a new life-course, resolved that he would too. And he did. It was only because Nick was known to be an ex-offender, and talked sensibly about his experiences that Kevin identified with him enough to sense that his own horizons could be extended. Kevin undoubtedly appreciated the support the programme's social workers gave him, but none of us could have inspired him in the way that Nick did, because he did not—could not, given his background—identify with us in the same way. Allan is making the same point, and it is rather sad, 25 years down the line, that the lesson has still to be learned. There is little point in academics and policy-makers seeking to develop research-based forms of effective practice in criminal justice social work if the voice of ex-offenders is not also listened to. We may think, rightly or wrongly, that we know 'what works ', but only they can tell us how and why they have changed; and in the last analysis those are surely the questions that generate the insights that we need to create better systems and practices.

Still, there are straws in the wind now—Allan's book is one more of them—and this might be a good time to rediscover 'new careers'. Currently in Scotland, the Glasgow-based Routes Out of Prison project uses trained (and paid) ex-offenders to mentor released prisoners, precisely because they have the credibility that statutory agencies don't often have. There is no reason why ex-offenders should be restricted to being mere volunteers if they want full-time paid employment in social work and show an aptitude for it; 'new careers ' once promised them the whole hog, and there is no reason why the same deal could not be engineered again, and, this time, done better. Such an option might not be to every ex-offender's taste—for some desistance means putting everything associated with their former lives behind them, burying it, and not making constructive use, even for a short while, out of having been an offender, but for those who do wish to utilise their experience in this way, the ever strengthening 'user voice ' movement in social work (and in social work education) offers interesting possibilities. Regrettably, ex–offenders, as the archetypal 'undeserving poor' have been somewhat marginal to this movement, compared, say, to mental health service users and old people. In our increasingly risk averse society, ex-*criminals*, it is said, can't be trusted, can they? In England, however, ex-offender (and businessman, courtesy of the Prince's Trust), Mark Johnson is currently acting as an adviser to the National Offender Management Service, exploring with them the possibility of getting ex-offender representation on all 42 of the Probation Trusts that manage the service at local level. It may work, it may not—but the attempt will be worth it. The new Community Justice Authorities in Scotland could do far worse than use Allan Weaver in the same way—but his fine book deserves a readership well beyond the professional networks in which he and they work. It is a superbly written, sombre and inspiring record of a Scottish life, whose lessons should be pondered far beyond the confines of criminal justice. In the ongoing conversation about this country's future, Allan's hard won insights need to be heeded, because to Scotland's shame there are in the 21st century young people still whose potential is no less great but whose prospects are no better than his once were. Somehow, sometime, that has to change.

References

Caddick B (1994), The 'New Careers' Experiment in Rehabilitating Offenders: Last Messages from a Fading Star, *British Journal of Social Work*, 24: 449- 460

Johnson M (2007), *Wasted*, London: Sceptre

Muir E (1935), *Scottish Journey*, Edinburgh: Mainstream Publishing

Shaw C (1930), *The Jackroller: A Delinquent Boy's Own Story*, Chicago: University of Chicago Press

'You never really understand a person until you consider things from his point of view … until you climb into his skin and walk around in it.'

Harper Lee, *To Kill a Mocking Bird* (1960)

Acknowledgements

Firstly, to identify the potential for change in someone requires insight; to assist them in actually realising this potential at times takes courage.

I would like to thank the staff of Waterside Press and in particular Bryan Gibson for his time and efforts and for showing faith in this book.

Amongst those with the courage to assist me in this endeavour are included my family, who persevered and stuck with me through thick and thin. Margaret Clark, my social worker, possessed that warmth and humanity and proved a lone, independent voice for many years. Likewise, Donald Lake, the man serving life imprisonment in HMP Dungavel in 1984 proved to be an inspiration and has probably no idea of the impact he made on my life during those dark days of imprisonment.

Prof. Mike Nellis and Dr. Fergus McNeill provided support and encouragement at a critical stage of my writing and reinforced to me that this was a project worth pursuing. To them I will always be grateful.

I must thank my two sons Paul and Allan for their continual encouragement during the writing of this book and, in their own separate ways, they have been instrumental in nurturing that seed of change over the years.

I am especially indebted to my wife Beth, whose love and support has been unflinching and her belief in me to finish this project unquestionable. I couldn't have completed it otherwise.

Allan Weaver

June 2008

Dedication

This book is dedicated entirely to my Mother, Ellen McMillan Weaver, who committed her life to her children and who taught me about love and loyalty. She will always be in my heart.

Publisher's note

The author has changed the names of various people in the story that follows and it is not intended that any such individuals should be recognized, criticised or otherwise referred to in a personal or real life capacity. *So You Think You Know Me?* contains a number of words that can best be described as Scottish slang, jargon or colloquialisms rather than standard English. The explanations below may assist any reader who is perplexed.

broo dole (i.e. social security or welfare payments)

crabit easily irritated, annoyed

da father (or 'dad')

doubt (or fag doubt) a cigarette end

greetin crying or moping

hamesucking 'battering' into someone else's home, what was also sometimes called 'breaking and entering'

huckle push around, especially unceremonious arrest by the police

maw mother

sciff throw

shed a wig, or hair that looks like a wig

spurtel thin or emaciated

tablet (as. e.g. in 'home made tablet') cake

weans small children

CHAPTER 1

An Education of Sorts

Life in Saltcoats for the Weavers during the 1960s, the decade in which I was born, was pretty much the same as it was for any other large working class family in the town—whilst there was never enough money to go round, to which I was reasonably oblivious due to my age at the time, periods of economic hardship appeared to be mixed with good times and bad times in equal measure.

Saltcoats is a town on the Ayrshire coast some 30 miles west of Glasgow with a population of approximately 14,000. Historically, the town derives its name from the traditional trade of boiling sea water to extract salt. There is a twelfth-century headstone in the cemetery of Kilwinning Abbey, three miles away, that refers to the neighbouring village of 'Suat Couts'.

Although the salt mines have long since gone, the town has a pedigree of sorts. Following some murderous land feuds, Saltcoats became more established in the 1500s when it was made a Burgh of Barony. Reflecting on the historical legacy and identity of the town over the years, it is nice to see that some traditions have not changed much as the murderous feuds are still re-enacted with vigour every Saturday night when the pubs are emptied.

For most of the last century, Saltcoats—with its beach, rail link to Glasgow and cheap accommodation—was one of the major holiday resorts for the city dwellers during their annual Glasgow Fair, which they affectionately termed coming 'doon the watter.' The advent of cheap package foreign holidays in the early 1980s, however, brought an end to this way of life and a further death knell to this increasingly deprived area, which had already suffered from the loss of traditional industries. Driven by sentiment, no doubt, a few hardened Glasgow punters remain loyal to their childhood resort regardless of the money, economics or weather. Fairly easy to identify, they are generally the pasty looking families running about the beach in the pissing rain stripped to their underwear.

Like most children starting school, my initial feelings were of unrestrained dread. My brother and sisters had been sent to this place and they were never the same from that point on, I thought to myself, as I was half-cajoled, half-tugged along by my maw to join that institution that would equip me to make my mark on life. As we approached the school, I noticed clusters of women congregated near the entrance, wearing faces masked by wear and tear, some showing thinly-veiled signs of relief; certain mothers were no doubt only too glad to get rid of their next batch, albeit temporarily, grateful for only having to run after the remaining two or three younger ones left in the house.

There we were, 36 weans leaving the womb for the second time— only this time there was no gas and air to ease our departure— abandoned, ignored, and deserted. Spic and span with our new-to-us, vaguely over-sized clothes which had been washed and starched, to movement-restricting dimensions, for the start of a new campaign; I was blissfully oblivious to the fact that I was sporting the second-hand clobber of my elder brother. That said, I was certainly not the worst— some weans were frogmarched into class with their clean but threadbare, non-gender-specific clothes hanging from their backs. In the coming years, I discovered that the newness of returning to school after a hot sticky summer, was a great equaliser for weans whose wee bony knees were usually sticking out of their trouser legs the rest of the year round.

Through experience, no doubt, the mothers moved slowly *en masse* towards the classroom door, waiting on permission to flee the scene as we sat rigidly on the hard wooden seats following their every move with terror. 'Come on, face the front … face the front!' the teacher shrilled in unison with her rapid hand claps. Miss Brown looked like an old witch, with her grey hair pulled tightly back against her head, emphasising her sharp features and leathery looking face, deserted by any external sign of inner warmth and compassion. 'Sit … sit … sit … come on quickly, let's all be seated …. Let's all be seated,' she again shrilled, as if addressing a disobedient Labrador, in the high pitched nasal voice that only an elderly spinster, who had long since ceased to be captivated by the wonders of children, could perfect. Unable to reach the floor, our wee legs were dangling from the seats as we shrunk into ourselves in mortal fear of this scary old woman.

Having manoeuvred herself into pole position, I caught my maw heading up the charge of adults from the classroom without looking back and I knew from that moment that she was never coming back; it was obviously a ploy she had hatched up with the rest of my family and she had no intention of returning for me. Christ, I would have to end up living with one of my grannies, or some other distant relative, or worse still, with the old witch woman! In shock, we sat rigidly, like the starched collars round our wee fledgling necks, staring at each other in horror.

'Ah want ma mammy!' snapped Nicky Hill first, abandoning all dignity in his hysteria, as he made a bolt for freedom, only to be caught at the door by the arse of his pants. Obviously prepared for such dissent, Miss Brown's steely fingers were quickly wrapped vice-like around big Nicky's throat as she ran him back to his seat, confirming everyone's silent fears that they were indeed placed here as a consequence of some misdemeanour that had gone unpunished—until now. 'Now sit and hold your tongue, boy,' she hissed as if trying to maintain an element of professional composure. 'You're no ma mammy,' Nicky gargled as he struggled to free himself from Miss Brown's tightening grip, before changing to a more familiar tack and shouting back, 'Get aff me, ya auld bastart!'

Mesmerised, we sat quietly aghast at this overt display of kamikaze rebellion as Nicky twitched and thrashed defiantly under Miss Brown's stranglehold. 'Ah want ma maw tae,' echoed wee Johnny Grant, his bravery in the face of this nightmarish scene truly awe inspiring. 'So dae ah,' cried another reckless infant, uniting the full class as it swiftly grew to a crescendo of 30-odd screaming weans. The ones who cried loudest were dragged unceremoniously by the collars and, with their sparrow-like legs in overdrive, were shunted down to the desks at the front of the class, where Miss Brown could poke at them more conveniently with her unnaturally long, and unexpectedly painful, fingers. As if on a broomstick, she singled the rest of us out, one at a time; her darting, beady eyes picked up every movement, every sound, before she swooped in on her prey, giving us all a painful introduction, if not rapid education, as to what lay ahead. Welcome to primary school; welcome to life.

Having been protected by the innocence borne of my relatively sheltered early childhood, I have little recollection of life before I started primary school other than shamelessly stumbling around the garden in my sister's ill-fitting navy knickers which gathered around my chubby, grazed knees. My maw was there to pick me up when I fell, to feed me when I was hungry, to warm me when I was cold and, of course, to love me when I needed love. I also recall being held closely to her bosom during a bout of illness, in pain, but feeling safe and secure as she rocked me back and forth to the hum of a sweet gentle lullaby. In my formative years I quickly became accustomed to the order of things and knew that younger siblings were for slapping and older ones for swearing at.

The idealism that characterises my early memories of my family does not extend to my da who, on the other hand, did not seem to show the same emotional involvement. Rather, from my earliest years he always appeared to be withdrawn and distant, offering no physical contact that I recall. I don't know whether this was just a general reluctance on his part to become involved, or whether he perceived this to be outside his masculine role or gender. Significantly, however, when I was around six years old, an older wean in the street pulled my hair and, as weans do at that age, I ran towards the house to find my maw, crying hysterically at this unprovoked act of sheer wickedness, only to be stopped abruptly and unexpectedly by my da at the front door. 'Whits the matter wi' you?' he asked grabbing my arm firmly and twisting it uncomfortably as I came to a sudden stop. 'Th ... th ... th ... that big boy keeps pullin ma hair,' I spluttered between heart-wrenching sobs, to which my da remained resistant. Turning me round and pushing me from the door he said, 'Never mind greetin like a wee fucken lassie, smash a brick ower his heed and he'll no' come near you again.' Unable to find a brick, blinded as I was through my tears, and feeling a wretched failure, I sat crying on the front doorstep until my maw returned from the local shops.

I still don't know if it was coincidental, or an executive decision, informed by some type of manly expectations, but concerted efforts were made in the following months to toughen me up. My da's Uncle Jimmy and his wife, an elderly couple from Yoker, in Glasgow, would visit us occasionally and during one such visit I was taken out to the back garden by Uncle Jimmy. He had an artificial limb as a consequence of a construction accident and to my horror he pulled his trouser leg up in front of me, exposing the unsightly wooden leg and proceeded to manipulate the knee joint to allow him to bend down on his knee. As if this sickening display wasn't enough, for my young mind to digest, he then bizarrely instructed, 'Right, punch me in the face as hard as you can.' Standing, disbelievingly, before him I could detect a foul smell from his breath which I would discover in later years was stale alcohol. 'Come on ... as hard as you can,' he repeated with an air of impatience. 'But ah don't want to,' I replied innocently confused as to the purpose of this game. 'Make a fist and smash it hard,' he repeated, 'this is how you learn to fight.' At this stage, I had no particular yen towards learning to fight but I was not openly defiant towards adults and particularly not family members, so I meekly slapped his face, which in itself felt strange and unnatural. 'Aw come on, ur you a wee lassie or somethin,' he laughed as I stood fidgeting before him, embarrassed and self-conscious. Again I slapped him. 'Harder,' slap, 'harder,' slap, 'harder,' slap. 'Make a fist ... come on harder ... hit me like a man.' Starting to cry out of frustration, but spurred on by a longing to have this whole ugly episode come to an end, I made a fist and punched him in the face as hard as I could. Punch, punch, punch, 'That's better,' he said in approval as my small fist hammered away with all its might, disappearing into the creases in his big fleshy face, as my tears made dirty tracks down my own. Although I earned approval from Uncle Jimmy, not everyone was as enamoured with my newly acquired skill which I proceeded to demonstrate with an unreserved enthusiasm. Within a short period of time, I was made to stand in the corner of the classroom many an afternoon for punching other weans during playtime scuffles.

Uncle Jimmy's form of education clearly did not lend itself to the regimented orderliness and sterility of a Catholic education and there was I, the third youngest in a family of six and fourth in line to be processed through the Catholic conveyor belt. Although my mother would classify herself as Protestant and my father as Catholic, my parents were never really religious; their classifications tended more towards a tribal division reflecting decades of inherited tradition, as both of them were non-practising. This did nothing to prevent them from putting us through the Catholic milestones of Communion and Confession, however, as a means of securing our religious identity as opposed to any internalised belief that this would ensure our salvation.

The affiliation to specific denominations did in the eyes of some people, however, serve a more meaningful and important purpose in as much as it distinguished you clearly from the other half of the sectarian divide. Living on the west coast of Scotland during this period you were either Catholic or Protestant; one or the other, which for some was less of a devout association with one religion and more a collective sense of distrust for the other and a justification for abuse and intolerance. That said, the Catholic Church was not totally without its memorable impact on me as a child, as the first adult to assault me ever was the local parish priest, when I was playing with my pal, Johnny Grant, in the chapel car park at age of seven.

Father Garland was a large ruddy faced man with snowy white hair and he had been our parish priest for as long as I could remember. As he possessed the power personally to save me from the damnation of Hell, should I warrant that journey in later life, I was always overtly courteous to him as a young child.

In quite literally glaring contrast to the vows of modesty normally associated with his ministry, Father Garland had treated himself to a brand new, bright yellow, Volkswagen Beetle car, complete with standing boards sporting from the sides, similar to the ones that gangsters hung off and shot at the police cars in hot pursuit in old American gangster movies. Despite my youth, I still considered this a strange choice of car for a priest, with its bohemian image born from its association with the hippy love generation, as it sat, dazzling, in pride of place, right in the middle of the chapel car park.

When we collided with this somewhat overindulgent display of car ownership on one of our aimless childish jaunts it was, of course, far too much to resist for Baby Face Weaver and Bugsy Grant, as we jumped onto the standing boards and began bobbing and weaving to avoid the imaginary bullets, lost in the innocent abandonment of play, only to be wrenched back into reality as fat fleshy fingers suddenly curled tightly round my neck like a coil and yanked me off the car. Before I could even begin to understand what was happening, Father Garland, who by now stood towering over me, slapped me hard across the left ear. With my ear stinging and still unable to comprehend what I had done to cause the wrath of this pious agent of the Holy Institution, I stood momentarily motionless in disbelief, as if the decision to condemn me to eternal Hell had been finalised. With the veins almost bursting from his neck he launched into a volley of abuse at our heathen behaviour in his thick Irish accent, 'You little scoundrels, do you have no sense of decency? ....
If I see you here again you'll get another belting, so help me God!'
Backing out of striking distance, Granty turned and fled for his life as I stood still, with tears in my eyes, rubbing my ear. 'Ya big fat swine!' I shouted at him, unable to control my hurt, anger and surprise any longer, at which I turned and followed wee Granty at great pace amid a rant of profanities. Anger had long since turned to fear as I lay in bed that night crying as I contemplated my mortal fate but, as this did not materialise in any concrete way in the succeeding years, my fear of damnation eventually subsided, and, some three or four years later, me and Granty settled the score with Father Garland.

CHAPTER 2

First Offence to Hangman's Noose

Although we eventually drifted apart during the early years of our secondary education, wee Granty, who lived in Anderson Drive, about 50 yards from my own house, and I were close pals throughout primary school. Like me, he came from a large family with scarcely enough money to go round; unlike me, he did seem to have some sort of a relationship with his da. His da was a long distance lorry driver and on the odd occasion he would take us on some of his shorter delivery trips. It was as if we were heroic explorers, adventurously journeying into the unknown, to seemingly exotic places like Cumnock and Dalmellington for the day. In fact, these were small rural towns set deep in the hills of South Ayrshire, where, according to Granty's da, the inhabitants were completely cut off from civilisation during the worst of winters and, in true survivors' tradition, were said to have resorted to eating their weans in a bid to fend off starvation.

Most Sunday mornings, however, Granty and I would trudge bored and grudgingly up to chapel. On one particular Sunday, when we were aged around ten, Granty, with every tensed muscle in his torso mirrored in his contorted wee face, released a well-practised roar of flatulence at the precise moment we were meant to bow our heads and individually reflect on our sinful behaviour. Despite nearly suffocating as I attempted to conceal my hysterical giggling, betrayed obviously by my shaking shoulders, I personally thought that this was an exceptional talent on Granty's part; this view was certainly not shared by the unappreciative adult members of the congregation who glared menacingly in our direction.

It was on this specific day too that we happened to notice that the collection boxes were routinely returned and left unguarded at the altar after the service. With no real intention to steal anything at this point, we agreed to assess this further and so we observed this practice closely and guardedly for several weeks, even attending the odd early evening Mass. We rapidly became regarded as the keenest chapel goers in the whole parish, even giving rise to a rumour spreading round the class that we were desperate to be altar boys.

Unable to resist the growing temptation, one Sunday after Mass, we loitered (with absolute intent) around the chapel until everyone had left and then, mirroring the commando skills Granty's da used so successfully in killing hundreds of Burmese soldiers single-handedly during the War, we slowly crawled on our bellies towards the altar where the collection boxes stood unattended. Hearts pounding loudly with fear and excitement, we quietly took a collection box each and began hurriedly filling our pockets with coins and the occasional pound note but making sure we left some money in the boxes. I remember thinking at the time that this was an extremely generous gesture on our part, which partly squared things in my mind, but if truth be told it was also a way of ensuring that the scam went unnoticed and as it happened, this proved a lucrative swindle for a good seven or eight weeks.

We became the most popular weans in school, as Granty and I would go in on a Monday morning, laden down with bags of confectionery and begin handing it out to almost anyone we came into contact with. Our philanthropic kindness knowing no limits, we would even occasionally hand out money to the deserving poor, like Tam Brown, one of 13 children, who had even less than us. 'Here, Broony, get yourself some sweeties and gie some to your wee brothers,' I thoughtfully instructed the eternally grateful Broony, as if possessing the moral authority of a local missionary.

Ironically, we would donate some of the stolen money to the 'Black Baby' fund, for the starving children in Biafra. Each class in our school had six 'Black Baby' teams and a record was maintained of each individual's donation to the black baby cause over the course of a month, their very survival apparently dependent solely on how much money we gave them. Remaining firmly within the Catholic principle of charity towards those less fortunate than oneself, those less 'charitable' towards the fund were often openly derided and berated by the teacher for their selfishness. Such was the personal guilt felt by some that at one point several weans were stealing money from the house to donate to the black baby cause. Before our entrepreneurial adventures, many a morning I would hear Granty's mother's sweet dulcet tones as I stood on the doorstep waiting on him for school, 'Ah'll black baby money you, I cannae feed ma ain weans, ya bloody half wit!' she would scream at him at the top of her voice, from which I assumed she did not wish to donate to the black babies at that particular time. It had been only a few years earlier, incidentally, that I had thought that the winner of the black baby donations actually received a black baby and I had worried for a while where I would put it if I won, which was particularly concerning as I was already sharing a room with my two wee brothers. I need not have worried, however, as the first prize was a piece of home-made tablet made by the headmaster's wife. Living on tablet for several months, Granty and I felt quite self-righteous and above any form of moral recrimination during the period of our collection-box-scam, justified in the knowledge that we donated healthily to the poor wee black babies for a while; it was a pseudo-socialist redistribution of Catholic resources if you like.

Granty was smaller than the rest of the class and cut a mischievous wee character; known to be game for a laugh, he was always involved in various trivial escapades. When I began to get into more serious trouble as we got older, wee Granty rightly distanced himself from me, becoming more studious and responsible as he matured. He joined the Army on leaving school and served for lengthy periods in Northern Ireland during the height of the 'Troubles', which appears to have had a lasting impact on him as he has suffered from mental health difficulties and an enduring drink problem ever since.

My da was born and bred in Glasgow, one of the youngest in a family of nine children; reflecting the high mortality rates of city slum life during the 1930s and 1940s, however, two of my granny's children died at birth, and another two died in early childhood. Life in Partick, an area located in the west end of Glasgow, was hard for the Weavers. It was a time and place where families lived in damp, overcrowded, rat infested tenement slums providing a grim existence for their inhabitants. Ironically, the Second World War provided a large number of families with some relief in the opportunity to escape from the squalor to outlying rural boroughs; hundreds of families, my da's included, were evacuated to the Ayrshire coast which had at that time been spared the level of deprivation apparent in Glasgow and must have been something of a godsend. Determined to maximise the opportunity afforded her during the War, my granny refused steadfastly to return to Partick after the War had ended, choosing instead to remain and leave her own indelible mark in Stevenston for decades to come, in addition to bequeathing generations of Weavers to the Three Towns area.

My memory of my granny's facial features is somewhat hazy, but I have always recalled her as a small squat woman, who was ascribed the dubious honour of being in possession of a quick tongue and quicker fists, and who in later years reminded me of an ageing Eastern Bloc female shot-putter on steroids.

The most vivid, if not the most enduring, memory I had of my granny from my early childhood, surrounded my unwelcome, if not scarring, introduction to certain parts of the female anatomy. Forced to endure one of the infrequent horrors of sleeping with my grandparents, one morning, when I must have been around eight years old, I lay awake pondering over the challenge as to how I could get out of this bed without coming into contact with my granny's snarling teeth as they sat menacingly nearby on the bedside cabinet, my pappy having long since fled the scene.

Before I had managed successfully to implement my own developing strategic exit, I heard her begin to creak and groan as she struggled out of bed, spluttering in anticipation of her morning fag. In a manner typical of her grace and elegance, her nightgown had somehow unfathomably become entangled in her hair rollers and, as I lay there rigidly peering from beneath the blanket, her big bare arse hovered horrifyingly above me. Breakfast has never been quite the same since.

That said, to be fair, I had always hated that house with its dull lighting, giving it something of a chilling, macabre appearance, and that lingering musty smell: the aroma of talcum powder won in a raffle that you could only associate with elderly grandparents. Contributing to this catalogue of repugnance, the only mode of communication appeared to be one of continuous shouting and swearing—loudly. To cap it all, they also kept greyhounds in the kitchen, who in their genetically starved appearance (somewhat ironic given their place of residence in the house) seemed to wear their ribcages over their matted coats. With their long rat-like faces, the dogs would slither towards me and sniff brazenly at my arse and crotch whenever I had the unfortunate need to go into the kitchen, which seemed to be a source of amusement to everyone as I squirmed and manoeuvred uncomfortably to avoid this gross intrusion on my privacy.

Shortly after the horrors of my granny's buttocks, my pappy, who was a placid man, and thus my granny's direct opposite, was escorting me and my brother James to the bus stop to ensure that we got on it safely. James was four years older than me and my pappy's favourite, which was startlingly apparent as I stood at the bus stop, watching them both wrestle around playfully. As they straightened up as the bus trundled along, I saw my pappy handing James a silver coin at the same time as he thrust a dull brown penny into my palm. 'It's okay, he disnae know the difference,' I heard him say to James as they both chuckled away. The irony being of course that I *did* know the difference;

unfortunately this otherwise innocent exchange stuck in my mind as a gesture of lasting disregard and my feelings of hurt ensured that there would never be a closeness between my pappy and me.

However, one particular story about him always amused me and related to my granny ridiculing him some years later for his War efforts; or rather lack of them. 'Get out of ma sight, ya dirty coward!' she screamed at him this particular day, her toothless face contorted with rage and although they were not a couple during the War, her being previously married, he was not slow to retaliate. 'I'll tell you whit, Kate darlin,' he chuckled in reply, savouring the moment somewhat theatrically, 'ah never seen any German soldiers durin' the War, but the brothels in France were somethin' else,' slapping his thigh loudly for good measure.

Like most families, dark foreboding stories of past misdeeds surrounded our older distanced relatives to one extent or another; of particular intrigue was the story surrounding my granny Weaver. It was only spoken of periodically, and then in the hushed tones usually reserved for discussing the recently departed. Unlike other families, however, *my* granny's first husband was said to have murdered a young girl many years before. It was rumoured that she had appeared unexpectedly at the door of their Glasgow tenement and that he had ultimately killed her and was subsequently hung for this offence. Always intrigued by this macabre story as a child, I had no way of knowing if it was actually true or not and despite my repeated attempts to break my maw's caginess and to entice her into embellishing the limited details I had managed to gain, she resolutely maintained the wider family party line and told us nothing, leaving me to ponder curiously over this mythical relative who by now in my mind, was nothing short of a cross between the infamous murderers Peter Manuel and Bible John.

The desire to unravel the details of this story never left me and many years later, I felt compelled to undertake my own investigation which finally unearthed the truth underpinning this dark family secret. In 1922, my granny's first husband's brother, William Harkness, and his wife Helen strangled a 14-year-old girl, who had been collecting customer instalments in relation to her father's drapery business. As she stood innocently at their front door, she was bludgeoned to death by Harkness with a blunt instrument and asphyxiated; the official motive was established as robbery. Helen Harkness subsequently, if not obviously, turned to my granny's husband, John Harkness, for assistance with removing the corpse from the house, which he duly provided. Although not specifically stated in the literature I had obtained, I later found out through further investigation (I could not let this one go) that both my granny and John Harkness helped the other two carry the dead girl's body from the house, to the back of some tenements in Whiteinch, Glasgow where they left her before disposing of her belongings.

William Harkness, Helen Harkness and John Harkness stood trial for the murder of Elizabeth Benjamin resulting in convictions for both William and Helen. Following conviction there was a unanimous recommendation of mercy for Helen Harkness who went on to spend 15 years in prison having been reprieved from a death sentence. Her less fortunate husband, William, was hung for the crime at Barlinnie Prison on 21 February 1922. My granny escaped any formal criminal proceedings. I am unsure whether it was because of his involvement in the crime committed against this young girl or not, but my granny's first husband, John Harkness, was subsequently murdered in a fight in a Glasgow pub on New Year's Eve, 1926.

Just to even things out, my maw's family, the Farrells, were a decent, hard working family. They were all Saltcoats born and bred, with far more social stability, grace and finesse than the evacuated, immigrant Weavers from the slums of Glasgow. My maw was the only daughter and the youngest in a family of three children, which meant that she was doted on by the other family members, in what was a generally protective and loving family environment.

Although they were not wealthy, my grandparents seem to have had some disposable income which afforded them a relatively comfortable existence; my maw was to tell me in later years that, such was their desperation and conviction, they offered her everything they had, even to the point of financing a period of extensive travel for her, should she agree not to marry my da. To their obvious disappointment, in her youthful innocence she declined, preferring instead to follow her heart. I don't know whether they did not like my da personally, or had perhaps just heard of the Weaver clan generally and had drawn their own prophetic conclusions, or again, maybe they had just heard of the family involvement in the murder of Elizabeth Benjamin—who knows? I certainly know that my da was totally indifferent to *them* and for whatever reason, and there seemed to be a few substantial ones, this was certainly not the marriage they had envisaged for their only daughter.

Despite the fact that I was named Allan Farrell after my maternal grandfather, which you could be forgiven for assuming would have automatically sold me to them in some kind of selfish desire to claim me, I never actually bonded with this set of grandparents either, which could have been due to my own in-built tendency to be a 'mummy's boy'. I was forever following my maw around like a wee moon orbiting the planet that enabled it to cling constantly to its own shaky position in the universe; no-one else existed for me and it was perhaps this peculiarity of mine, compounded in some way with a form of middle child syndrome, which meant that I was a relatively insignificant oddity, sealing my place somewhere below the grandparental radar of affection. Either way, both sets of grandparents appeared to have their own personal favourites within the family group, which excluded me. I, rightly or wrongly, just tended to view them all as old, decrepit people with nothing particularly interesting to say.

That said, mind you, my wee brother Jerry and I would race up to my granny Farrell's house straight after school most days to ask if she wanted anything from the shops, knowing full well that we would get coppers for our trouble. Jerry, being more forward and less self-conscious, or perhaps just more desperate, made a more frequent habit of nipping up to their house during school intervals and going into my granny's bedroom, where she lay bedridden. He would just stand there and stare at her blankly until she gave him money. In any other context this would probably have constituted demanding money with menaces, although under cross-examination from us periodically, Jerry refused to budge and steadfastly maintained that he went to visit her so often as he really loved and missed his granny Farrell. Mirroring perhaps the conniving Glasgow immigrant side of the family, our behaviour must have unsettled her at times and thinking back, she never *did* need anything from the shops, or maybe she just did not trust us to return with the goods.

The Catholic primary education system in Saltcoats spanned seven years and comprised three separate age-graded primary schools which children attended progressively on their way to the only Catholic secondary school in the area, St Andrews. St Mary's was the senior primary school, where Catholic children spent the last two years of their primary education and it was during this particular period of time that my life began to change in a number of ways and where in many respects, I began to lose forever my childhood innocence.

My teacher at St Mary's for this two year term was a Mrs Susan Wallace, a little wiry woman, aged around 50, her acne-scarred face and tightly cropped grey hair giving her a hard, masculine appearance which, as time progressed, was mirrored in her behaviour towards me. Unlike earlier primary school teachers who had been undeniably strict, Wallace had something of a sadistic streak in her and through this, I was initiated into a world in which control, enforced by principles of deterrence and retribution, was directly translated into abuse.

For the most part Mrs Wallace would, all too readily, engage in the legalised abuse of children through her constant use of the 'belt'. Although I was not the most enthusiastic pupil in an academic sense, I was never particularly disruptive in class either. Rather, most of my misdemeanours were confined to the school playground where I applied myself to honing the skills promoted by Uncle Jimmy. Nonetheless, I seemed to be singled out by Wallace at every cut and turn from the outset.

The 'belt' was a specifically designed leather strap used to violently beat the outstretched hands of delinquent pupils to enforce discipline within the school setting. Now outlawed, this was an acceptable and frequently used mode of corporal punishment of the day in schools up until the 1980s. With no safeguards or forms of regulation this punishment was used by teachers at will and many a day I would go home with inflamed welts on my hands and up my wrists from the belt. Worryingly, some male teachers would actually wear their strap over their shoulder and under their jacket, so that like ageing Western gunfighters they could quickly draw their strap on unsuspecting children—which even as a child I considered perverse. Even then, I could visualise them working on their technique and drawing out their strap meanly in front of a full length mirror at home as they fantasised about being the famous cowboy sheriff, Wyatt Earp. As I reflect on this practice, I'm sure the belt was a comfort object for some, a leathery extension to their penises, perhaps, or in Wallace's case maybe the penis she never had. The other methods in her repertoire of control were slightly less orthodox but no less painful.

CHAPTER 3

Maw, Madness, Mayhem and Me

Our primary six class consisted of 38 children, fairly evenly split across gender, with perhaps the ratio divide in terms of social status and background. Perhaps due to my fighting in the playground and definitely in relation to the boisterous behaviour of wee Granty and James McCleary at the previous primary school, we three were forced to sit under strict surveillance at the front of the class, a position which afforded us no margin for error. As the seats and desks were joined in twos, we were each made to sit beside a lassie, which at this stage of our schooling, and particularly at this stage of our development, we thought was nothing short of a moral outrage. In addition to this, it materialised, after a heated debate on the subject, that each one of us was convinced that we had the ugliest, smelliest lassie to sit beside, with perhaps my own desk mate just edging it in the horror stakes.

I cried all night after my first day at St Mary's because I was sentenced to one year's accommodation, without the possibility of parole, beside Janet Fry. Janet was a wee lassie with round National Health spectacles taped together, her teeth were brown and she always smelt of pee; she also had a terrible limp due to a road traffic accident, which, when combined with her unfortunate odour, convinced the observer that she was constantly in dire need of the toilet facilities. Although most of the class got to choose where they sat and with whom, these three innocent lassies were in some discriminating way considered by Wallace to be suitable enough horrors to act as punishment details for me, Granty and James McCleary, or Jeg as he was known.

Jeg was also brought up in Anderson Drive and lived directly across the road from Granty. Jeg was only slightly taller than me in primary school but he was utterly unique in that he was a strikingly bizarre looking figure with a set of teeth which resembled a row of condemned buildings. He also had an uncontrollable mop of bright red hair, which always looked as if it belonged to somebody else's head, or at least had leanings to do so, while his face and neck were peppered with big, dark rust coloured freckles, finished off with a prominent nose which would not have looked out of place on the face of a Roman emperor and which would later become more distinguished with every break.

Jeg would prove to be a good and loyal friend for a number of years and one of the funniest guys I have ever met. His parents tended to be quite laid back in comparison to other parents at the time, but on reflection were probably emotionally distant. As a result, Jeg and his sisters were basically allowed to do what they wanted in the house, which was a foreign concept to the rest of us. Much to our constant amusement and astonishment, from an early age, he was allowed to swear in front of his parents, take days off school and help himself to money from his mother's purse as and when the mood suited. As you would expect, schooling didn't feature on Jeg's list of personal priorities; he preferred instead to act the clown and entertain people, which he did with flair, ease and abundance.

It wasn't so much a case of 'If the cap fits', but rather that the cap was forced upon us, so we seemed to decide subconsciously between the three of us, that we would therefore wear it and with some style. Granty, Jeg and I began to become more troublesome in class, frequently ending the day with the now increasingly familiar belt welts across our hands and wrists.

Inviting yet another onslaught one day, wee Granty leaned across and sat a drawing pin on the empty chair of his seating partner, Agnes McGlynn, which, needless to say, caused an absolute uproar in class when she sat down; Agnes herself, as you can imagine, was not best pleased, although to this day I still don't know what kind of reaction Granty thought this would evoke. Trying to quell the commotion, Wallace's face was a mask of fury as she darted animatedly from one side of the class to the other in her desperation to establish what had happened, the veins increasingly protruding from her wrinkled neck. As we sat, panic stricken, she suddenly stopped in her tracks, hollered some profanity and proceeded to grab wee Granty by the throat in front of the full class. 'Right—class dismissed,' she hissed through gritted teeth. Before the emphatic hiss had concluded and whilst the spittle was still showering over Granty's face, a stampede of weans catapulted themselves across the classroom, leaving numerous jackets and schoolbags behind, pushing and shoving each other through the door.

As her grip tightened around wee Granty's throat, his eyes began to bulge; only just less than hers, mind you. Throughout the commotion, I remained rooted to my seat; although I was genuinely concerned for Granty's welfare, to be honest, it was more out of panic than loyalty. 'Leave now, Weaver!' she shouted at me. 'Ahm no leavin till wee Granty comes wae me', I said in a quivering voice which belied my forced courage. 'Leave the room—now Weaver .... Leave!' she screamed in reply. 'Naw am no goin ....,' I persisted. In a lightning move of surprising agility, she released her grip on Granty's throat and ran towards me. As I sprinted towards the door she swooped like a ravenous hawk, grabbed me by the hair and in one flowing movement, she gave me a dead leg by ramming her knee into the side of my leg and then proceeded to batter the back of my head. I remember being more fearful of her high pitched screaming voice in my ear, than the torrent of blows, as she launched into a tirade of abuse. 'Weaver, you thick layabout, you complete waste of space!' she spat out of her mouth to the same rhythm of her slapping hand clattering painfully off my head, as I cowered in the corner of the classroom. Sharing the same panic but obviously not the same loyalty, I only just managed to turn amid the blows and catch the tail end of Granty's wee spurtel legs as he sprinted, wailing like a banshee, from the classroom.

After yet another belting session, albeit partially provoked this time, Granty, Jeg and I decided that something would have to be done. 'But we'll get murdered,' said Jeg in a panic as we began to hatch a plan round the school dinner table. 'Tae hell wi her,' I said vehemently, feeling nothing but loathing now towards this woman, who incidentally, had a season ticket for Lourdes. As Jeg kept lookout, Granty and I, once again drawing on our Burmese Command skills, sneaked into the unlocked classroom during playtime and rifled through her bag quietly, until we discovered the dreaded belt. Mission accomplished! With the belt bundled up my jumper, we bolted from the classroom, still somewhat taken aback by our own audacity, and made our shifty wee way to the furnace, located in the coal room at the other end of the playground. Before we had time to reflect over the possible consequences and bottle it, I lobbed the belt with a force fuelled by rage into the searing flames. Nothing was ever said overtly, although a substitute belt was immediately obtained and her increasing use of it on the three of us left us in no doubt whatsoever that she didn't need to know the story of its demise; she knew exactly who the belt-jackers were. Despite the welts it was a price worth paying. I don't know what fate bestowed Wallace after my departure from St Mary's, but I can only hope that she got the opportunity in later life to make amends for her abusive behaviour towards children.

Exposure to this form of behaviour from adults, particularly those in authority who had a duty of care, altered the naïve and childish attitudes I had until then held about the world, prematurely invoking a more hardened and cynical view of life, in which adults could not necessarily be trusted and those with power and authority even less so. As if accelerating this pace and reinforcing this process of change within me, events on the home front were also beginning to alter and change direction.

During my last year of primary schooling, I was lying sleeping in bed one night when I was abruptly awakened by someone screaming, over the sound of loud, incessant banging noises coming from downstairs. Shocked and bewildered, I lay wide-eyed in the darkness, every muscle rigid in an instinctive fight or flight response, barely breathing as I strained to establish the source and cause of this disturbance, while my wee brothers hurled themselves into my bed beside me in a panic, having also been wakened with a start. Paralysed by fear and insecurity, we began to whimper quietly and in unison, utterly mystified as to the nature of the certain horrors that were unfolding in our house. We lay in absolute terror as the volume increased, and the sounds of thuds followed by a scuffle came from directly outside our bedroom door. Hearing the urgency of what I immediately identified as my maw's scream, I bolted from the bed without a second thought, my fear for myself now abandoned despite the pounding beating inside my chest, yanking open the bedroom door.

To my agony I saw that my beloved maw was on her knees, and my da was standing over her, holding her by the hair with one hand and slapping her in the face with the other. 'You're a fucking slut ... a dirty whore .... a prostitute!' he shouted oblivious to my presence, as he slapped her repeatedly. Momentarily shocked, I stood aghast and unable to believe what was happening in front of me; I didn't even understand half of the things he was calling her, let alone why. Within seconds, my sister Ellen had wakened and come out to the hall just as Jerry and Billy shuffled out, their eyes wide in horror. In unison, we all began to cry and scream for him to stop. 'Jerry, the weans are there,' my maw said quietly to my da, concerned only for us and trying to protect us from this sight, as he stood over her still holding her by the hair. I am still not sure whether it was from physical exhaustion, or whether he was too drunk to maintain the onslaught, or if the realisation of our presence had taken him by surprise, but he let her go, turned and staggered alone downstairs. My maw lay on the floor in a heap trying to reassure us quietly that she was okay as we all sat around her sobbing.

The vision of my maw being beaten burned like a hot poker into my memory every day for some time afterwards as I relived every word, every blow, every part of the horrid scene. I knew even then that my life could never be quite the same again. Despite being an eleven-year-old child, I experienced an overwhelming sense of guilt that I had let my mother down, that I had failed to protect her and this was perhaps for me the most difficult aspect of this situation to deal with at the time; from that moment on, I was afraid to leave my mother on her own, having decided that my presence in some way afforded her a measure of protection. Lost in our own confused, childish thoughts, we *all* struggled to deal with the traumatic events of that night, it was never referred to or discussed openly and like events surrounding the Harkness family incident, it was confined to hushed tones. I recall that Jerry and Billy seemed to become more sullen and agitated. As for me, the remainder of my primary schooling was made difficult by my increasingly troubled relationship with Wallace and in turn my hatred for her intensified with each belting and slap to the back of my head.

The summer before I started secondary school was a scorcher and the days seemed to pass agreeably slowly. I rarely saw Granty that summer, preferring instead to spend most of my time with Jeg and a new set of pals. We were all from the same area, living in the same or neighbouring schemes; Eddie and Malky attended the local Protestant school, while me, Jeg, Watty, and Auldy attended the Catholic School. During this summer we began to involve ourselves in activities which hovered, initially, somewhere between nuisance behaviour and relatively minor offending. This included raiding apple trees from gardens in more affluent areas of the town; chapping house doors and running wildly down the street before the frustrated and irritated occupant could clap eyes on us; sneaking on to trains and weaving in and out of carriages in a bizarrely choreographed routine to avoid detection by the ticket collector, which facilitated our daring excursions further down the coast where we could spread our delinquent mischievous adventures in relative anonymity. We were also breaking into the occasional garden shed ,although we had no real thought at this point of actually stealing anything.

With most of this going unchecked throughout the summer months, we unhesitatingly drifted into a more established pattern of minor offending behaviour, turning our attentions towards shoplifting and other acquisitive offences, when we were not alternatively engaged in the odd scuffle with children from neighbouring schemes. In the process, we inadvertently formed into an unorganised street gang within a relatively short period of time. Central to this was my best pal at the time, John Auld, or Auldy. He was good company, right enough, but he was also a strange kind of child. Although he was only a year younger than me, from a young age he was unusually preoccupied with the meaning of life, and what he may have lacked in depth of insight, given his tender age, he more than compensated for with his characteristic flashes of moroseness and morbidity.

In the same way that we had been rapidly seduced by the sheer thrills of shoplifting, stealing sweets and the like from local shops—even swiping ridiculous but alluringly pocket sized items, which were of no possible use to us and just as quickly discarded—we similarly progressed within a short period of time to more serious, and more economically rewarding crimes. These became a means of trying to earn money to finance yet a further number of growing diversionary activities: drinking cheap wine on the street corner, smoking, and frequenting the local fairground. Thus, when he was successfully distracted from his philosophical musings, Auldy, as much as I, was on the lookout for quick and easy money and we soon began to shoplift more lucrative items, such as clothing or small electrical goods, from shops in the town centre, which we could quickly sell to a host of willing, unquestioning buyers. One of us would create a diversion by causing a bit of a rumpus at the other end of the shop while the other one reached over the counter, pressed the till keys and made off with whatever notes were lying in the unattended till, which netted us a nice wee lift on several occasions. As you would expect however, we were hardly the master criminals and our routine was hardly artistic in form or execution; we thought we were all that, however, due to our unhindered and unequivocal success despite the occasional inconvenience of being apprehended and taken home in the back of a police van.

During such times my maw was always more worried than angry; on reflection, she was probably more preoccupied with my da's behaviour at this juncture, which basically gave me a free rein. Auldy, on the other hand, would take the most terrible beatings from his da and was warned within an inch of his life to keep back from me, which of course went unheeded at this particular time. We became firm friends over the school years although we began to drift apart naturally and through our own choosing, as we got older. Auldy is now a born again Christian, having converted to Christianity in full around the age of 34 and I am pleased to say that although still searching for the meaning of life, he is now a more settled individual, both personally and spiritually.

Perhaps the most transparently disadvantaged area in Saltcoats at this time was New England Road, known as 'The Street', and this was our main stomping ground where we could now be found most weekends and week nights, with the summer firmly behind us. The Street was part of a pre-war housing scheme situated in the top end of Saltcoats. The whole scheme was run down, but this street in particular, despite having only 20-odd houses in it, was the most deprived road in the town, housing a range of so-called problem families. Adding to its troublesome reputation, the Street and its inhabitants certainly had more than their fair share of heartache, with a horrifyingly high mortality rate. Wee Thomas Martin was from a big family in the street, but at the age of ten, he was swept into the sea while playing in the harbour during the early 1970s. Lynne Hammond, just a wee bit younger than us, was killed in a road traffic accident the following year. Tiger Stevens, the same age as us, died in a swimming accident whilst in local authority care some months later. Margaret Lee, some years older than us, died in a house fire. Alice Thomas was stabbed to death by another Street resident living at number 20 just before we started hanging around the Street. Several years later, Cathy Moore's battered body was discovered in a local field by schoolchildren, she having been apparently murdered in her house in the Street; her husband Hughie was subsequently arrested for the murder and hung himself in Barlinnie Prison whilst on remand for this crime several months later; still protesting his innocence.

Given the Street's reputation for trouble, people tended to go out of their way to avoid walking through it and even the police were reluctant to come through it at times. Of course, *we* all thought the Street was great, this was our main hangout; for us it was as legendary as New York's notorious Hell's Kitchen—we not only belonged there, we felt safe there. Initially, people were probably more concerned with their own hardships and tragedies to bother us and later, as more people got used to our almost permanent presence, the more we became as much as fixtures of the landscape as the flickering streetlights, uneven paving stones and scarring graffiti. We even provided a public service selling stolen goods; as most of the people in the street were blacklisted from the mainstream debt companies, they were only too grateful to buy a range of goods from us at ridiculously low prices, which ensured that we had a firm foothold in the Street for years to come.

Reflecting perhaps the tough façade that my own life was, at this point, beginning to form, life on the west coast of Scotland in the mid-1970s was typically patriarchal, in which men and woman had clearly defined roles. My da, like other men, was the main breadwinner, the unquestionable head of the household, returning home after his work to his own personal empire wherein his every need was catered for by my maw who, similarly, had her own clearly defined maternal and domestic role within the family, which carried with it substantially less authority. There was a chair in our house which was solely reserved for my da, where no one else dared to sit whilst he was present in the building; we had to be quiet if he was watching television; and whilst we ate cheaper brands of food, he would be partial to steaks or other expensive foods. It was through these privileges that his authority within the family hierarchy was honoured.

Picking up snippets of information here and there, I became aware that my da was also something of a big shot in the pubs, splashing his money about quite generously as he plied his cronies with drink, with what then was most of my maw's housekeeping money. With no expense spared he once went to see a live Frank Sinatra concert in London and, being quite a smart dresser, he bought himself a new silk tie for the occasion. This particular event only stuck in my mind as I remember my maw crying one night at the time as the cost of the tie would apparently have bought me and my wee brothers shoes for going back to school. On the other hand however, his trip to see Frank Sinatra was not all bad, I thought, as when he came home drunk from the pub for a time afterwards he would occasionally sing *My Way* or give an intoxicated rendition of *Little Green Apples* instead of his normal dark, morose IRA songs; the variation was nice.

Although there were a number of areas in my da's life which he bitterly resented, there was one which I felt disappointed him in particular. In 1960, he and his younger brother, Billy, went to New York to work in the construction industry with a view to emigrating. Several months into their stay however, my da was rushed to hospital and subsequently flown back to Scotland after suffering a ruptured stomach ulcer. Having heard the content of his repetitious drunken rants in later life, his bitterness at missing this opportunity to emigrate to America was unmistakeable and barely concealed, lying forever just beneath the surface of him; furthermore, it became clear, any efforts to return with the family were impeded by my maw's pregnancy with me. As time progressed I began to feel a sense of misplaced responsibility for denying all of us this opportunity to move to a new life in America, particularly as his brother Billy was successful in officially emigrating and has remained in New York ever since.

By a strange twist of fate, and in stark contrast, perhaps, to the lives of their Scottish cousins, Billy's son Walter, became a New York policeman and latterly worked in the Bronx as a member of a tactical armed response unit. Having just started duty one day, he received an emergency call to report immediately to the Twin Towers in Manhattan on 11 September

2001. With unimaginable bravery, he arrived at the scene of devastation and instinctively ran into one of the towers in an attempt to rescue those trapped in the burning building. Aged 30, my cousin, New York police officer Walter Edward Weaver's body was never recovered. Walter's brother, Brian, by all accounts, is a fairly affluent individual who has worked in or around Manhattan's Wall Street area for a number of years and the youngest brother, Michael, is a serving soldier in the US Marine Corps. When considering both sets of cousins and the 'nature versus nurture' debate, there is probably enough material here to keep any aspiring young psychologist busy for months.

CHAPTER 4

Painting Lesson, Screaming Colours

When I was aged around 13 or so, my da seemed to be drinking constantly and although we didn't witness anything overtly on the scale of my maw's earlier beating, I would still occasionally hear the isolated thump during the night and see marks on my maw's face the following day. However, I also discovered that the psychological turmoil and anguish produced by the anticipation and fear of violence was in some sense just as horrendous, if not more so, than the actual act, for my maw as well as for me. I recall endless nights lying in bed feeling utterly strained and psychologically distressed at my potential helplessness to intervene, if not prevent, any event that might unfold.

One particular night is forever etched into my memory; perhaps because of my hyper-sensitive vigilance, I had sensed the oppressive atmosphere throughout the day and almost prophetically, I lay in bed that night, almost waiting, in dreaded anticipation of my da returning from the pub. He did not disappoint. In the stillness of the night, I heard a car door slam shut outside our house and I did not need to hear my da's drunken and abusive rants towards my maw as he made his way up the garden path to know that he had returned. I was by now slightly older and with it more worldly wise; I now *knew* what these names meant, every single filthy one of them and as I lay there rigidly, silent tears of rage spilled unstoppably from my eyes, into my ears and hair; my head throbbed with anger that he would dare treat my maw in such a way. In the darkness of that moment I vowed to myself that someday I would murder him and pull out his tongue with my bare hands.

No sooner had he crashed drunkenly through the front door and staggered into the house when he launched directly into a quick and frenzied attack on my maw who was alone downstairs in the living room. Hearing her scream, I sprang from the bed and hurled myself down the stairs, alone, with no specific thought of what I could possibly say or do, other than to be at my maw's side. At least if I was there, she was not on her own, I thought. As I burst through the living room door my maw was on her knees, her face already bloodied. I stood watching as, swaying drunkenly over her, my da held on to the side of the couch with one hand to steady himself, whilst holding her by the hair with the other, and then as if in slow motion, he pulled his leg back and then swung a full force kick at my maw's face. As her head swung back, there was a loud crack and a stream of blood flew from her face as her head was flung back in a sharp, violent jolt. She crumpled to the floor and lay motionless whilst all I could do was stand in the doorway, transfixed, feeling utter revulsion and loathing for this man yet so paralysingly powerless that I remained stunned and rooted to the spot, unable to move or speak, thinking that my maw was dead.

With no concept of order or time for me, the living room became a hive of activity, a number of people were now mulling around, my brothers and sisters were clinging to each other and screaming hysterically as the ambulance men lifted my maw onto a stretcher. As she was carried past me, I could only stand and stare silently at her battered face as she lay unconscious; I didn't even notice where my da went in my ensuing state of shock.

The following few days at home had something of a surreal quality; this incident, like so many others, was never mentioned as we quietly just tried to patch up the broken furniture in an attempt to restore at least a semblance of order. My da had returned home the day after the attack and never spoke to anyone. Several days later, I went to see my maw in hospital with my sisters and brother. Although apprehensive and unsure what to expect, I missed my maw so desperately and I was so eager to see her that I stormed into the ward ahead of them and as I saw a woman sitting up in bed with a horrible, massive, blackened, purple head I hurriedly ran past in search of my maw. However, looking behind me, I saw my sisters and brother stopping to talk to this woman and as I walked back slowly towards them, with horror I realised that it was my maw.

Although I was barely in adolescence, due to my lack of understanding, which was obscured by my youth, ignorance and love for my maw, I was infuriated with her for continuing to stay with my da. In those days, however, there were no Womens' Aid or refuge hostels and on the occasions she did seek temporary respite from the abuse, it was with other family members and with six children in tow, which of course was both unrealistic and impractical. On a number of occasions, when the police were called, they would just bundle my maw and the six of us into their van, leaving my da alone in the house, as we were driven in the early hours of the morning to some unsuspecting relative; not once was it he who was removed. Oblivious to our trauma, the attending police officers would sit in the front of the van talking about football or some other irrelevant everyday matter as we huddled together, distressed, in the back of the van like criminals. 'It'll be okay tonight, Ellen, but you'll have to leave first thing in the morning ... he'll have calmed down by then,' said one aunt in particular, in her diplomatic attempt to offload and reassure us; and so the humiliating and painful cycle continued.

Police attitudes towards domestic violence in the 1970s were such that violence against women was not even really viewed as a criminal offence; rather it was accepted somewhat as a reality of life, an inevitability, and in this manner it was unquestioningly tolerated, rather than challenged. Indeed, despite an increasing emphasis on this issue, some people have argued that, in effect, attitudes haven't really changed that much over the years. Specific policies and procedures in dealing with such matters were non-existent and domestic violence was seen as rather tiresome and annoying incidents which interfered with real police matters. Had I committed my usual earlier nuisance offences in the community, however, the exact same officers would have swooped and lifted me unmercifully and I would be charged accordingly.

Several months after my maw was hospitalised, the police attended our house in response, I assume, to yet another phone call from a worried neighbour. The furniture was upturned and strewn everywhere, the house was the usual mess and my maw's nose was bleeding. As the police arrived at the door my da grabbed my maw and threw her into a small, blackened, airless cupboard just next to where the two policemen were standing and then stood with his foot against the door wedging it shut. In a panic for air, my maw began scratching and banging on the door; pleading to be let out, as my da stood unmoved. 'Shut up ya cow ye,' he shouted at her through the door as the police officers stood passively. Worried that my maw couldn't breathe in this cupboard, we began screaming for the police to do something but ignoring us completely, they tried gently to cajole my da into letting her out. 'Come on, Jerry, you're better away up to your bed, you'll feel a lot better in the morning,' suggested one sympathetically. 'Come on ... away and have a wee sleep,' said his partner in support. 'Aye ... and you're really not helping matters with all that banging and shouting, Mrs Weaver,' he rebuked my maw loudly through the door as she continued to bang and scratch for air. Seemingly satisfied in their own minds that there would be no further trouble, the police officers left the house with my maw still locked in the cupboard.

I never recalled my maw drinking much as a young child, although I noticed that she began to drink more and more as the trouble in the house intensified, which with hindsight, was obviously some form of coping mechanism on her part no doubt and given the chaos of her life at the time, was understandable to a large extent. Despite the nature of my da's drinking, my maw would conceal her drinking from him by hiding her cans in the dirty washing basket, and for years later I would tease her by saying that we were the only family ever who had a washing basket that actually clinked. Carlsberg lager was her drink of choice, referred to locally as cans of 'Callies'. Unfortunately they were widely known by younger guys as 'leg openers,' which I was to discover as I got older, deriving from their customary consumption by women who, when drunk on Callies, were rumoured to be more forthcoming sexually. However, if the truth be told this probably says far more about young men's attitudes towards women in this part of the country than it does about the mythical power of Callies and women's perceived moral conduct. Either way, I never used this derogatory term.

Although my maw, like the majority of working class women of that era, never socialised as such, she had one particular friend throughout the duration of my childhood. When the men were out drinking, they would meet occasionally in each others' houses, like a forbidden alliance, and empty the contents of their dirty washing baskets together. My maw and Margaret shared a lot of similarities; they were both local, both around the same age, both had six children and both were in extremely abusive relationships. Living only yards apart from each other, there was many a night that we would go to Margaret's with my maw as a means of escaping the madness of our own lives with my da, only to be exposed to the same violent and abusive behaviour whenever her man, Donny, fell in the door drunk. Unlike our own situation however, Margaret's two oldest sons, somewhat older than us, would just steam into him with their fists and feet whenever he became abusive. Standing quietly at my maw's side amid the pandemonium, I would marvel at their bravery whilst being equally envious of them and their ability to protect their maw in such a manly way.

Where the odd Callies afforded my maw a means and measure of escape, mine was provided by the company of the guys and our endless misadventures. As an established seaside resort, the fairground would come to Saltcoats every summer for six weeks or so but as well as providing a wide range of family entertainment; it also became a focal point for the town's young delinquent element. Not to disappoint, me and the guys would get drunk on cheap wine and gravitate towards the fairground and in particular the waltzers where the music blared loudly attracting both the lassies and the *real* hard men of the town. The real hard men were easily distinguishable; they were the ones generally spinning the waltzers with their tattoos and capped sleeved t-shirts, strategically small in size to exaggerate the size of their biceps. Much to the amusement of everyone else, I never did like the waltzers; I would hold on, white knuckled, nauseous and terrified as the posing bastards would lie sleekly over the top of the waltzer cart in show of macho bravado as they spun uncontrollably. As if to heighten the whole horror of the experience and to rob the rider of the last shred of dignity, was the fact that as well as screaming in fear, the rider was generally treated to the spinner's testicles rammed obscenely close to the back of their neck; really, for the uninitiated—it just wasn't worth the hassle, although it was through the fairground in many respects that I would embark on a darker side of life the following year.

I was also introduced to another activity around this period, around the age of 13, which I thought equally wasn't really worth the hassle: sex. Within this culture at the time we were never educated about sex or the reproduction process and in particular, none of our das would *ever* have broached the subject in any direct or honest fashion. When Granty was aged around ten he caught his wee tearaway of a mongrel dog, Candy, mating with his old next door neighbour's poodle. Of course, given Candy's social status and lack of pedigree this caused something of furore with the old neighbour. Trying to play down the incident in the mind of his young inquisitive son however, Granty's da told him that when dogs are doing this 'sex thing' they are really just giving the other dog a blood transfusion because they are either sick or due to have puppies.

Granty, Jeg and I must have been a sight to behold some weeks later when we burst into the classroom 20 minutes late one morning, breathless and somewhat dishevelled from the final sprint to school. 'And what time do you call this!' shouted Wallace rhetorically in her normal welcoming manner. 'But, Miss,' blurted wee Granty indignantly as Jeg and I nodded away in unison in confirmation of the mitigating circumstances, 'we hud to wait on ma Candy gein the dug next door a blood transfusion.'

This was shortly followed by Jeg passing his father's pornographic magazine around the playground which depicted in graphic detail the whole intercourse process; it was not so much an insightful revelation that we all gawked at wide eyed, but more a disturbing concern as to what lay ahead. And so it was within this context that we had to develop our own knowledge base in such a delicate subject matter.

Perhaps more honestly than Granty's da, but with certainly no more enthusiasm, I was afforded my first sexual experience by an older lassie in the street. At this age, however, I was never really that enamoured with the sex thing, considering it overrated and would have much preferred a game of five-a-side football to be honest; although I would never have dared tell any of the guys this. Standing against a garage wall on a drizzly summer night trying desperately to mimic wee Candy in full flight, with the guys giggling and hollering away in support nearby, just wasn't my idea of fun. In addition to this, the passion of the moment wasn't helped any by this worldly wise lassie blowing chewing gum bubbles right into my ear and asking repeatedly when I was going to be finished.

Like most pupils starting secondary school, I found the whole experience initially a bit daunting as this was a massive move away from the insular existence of primary school which, despite Wallace's' behaviour towards me, still offered an element of comfort, protection and security. Young people from Saltcoats, Stevenston and Ardrossan, known collectively as the Three Towns, tended to form tight knit cliques, developing a distrust of people from the other towns that sometimes resulted in inter-territorial disputes. There have been on-going gang fights between the various factions from the Three Towns for as long as I can remember, and possibly as far back as the Burgh of Barony days, which have resulted in numerous serious assaults and even the occasional murder over the years. It was within this mindset that I started my secondary education at St Andrew's school, particularly aware that my newly acquired reputation held less sway with the older boys.

My sister, Ellen, had started at St Andrews two years before me and due to her several suspensions for different minor misdemeanours, and no doubt due to my own problematic behaviour at primary school, my card was invariably marked before I had started. That said, with the exception of only minor hassle from certain teachers, I had a tendency to switch off at school and just go through the required motions, rendering most of my first year at secondary school rather uneventful.

However, as if making amends for this, I continued to meet the guys up in the Street after school and this remained the main focal point of our collective lives. Around this time, we progressed from the more primitive art of shoplifting to the more lucrative act of actually breaking into shops. The first shop we broke into was a local grocery store; having cased it studiously for weeks, me, Auldy, Jeg and Malky acquired a hacksaw from somewhere and crept round the back of the shops late one night, each taking turns to saw patiently through the solid metal bars on the window, until we could pull them apart. Having smashed the window, we clambered inside and grabbed boxes of cigarettes and cases of drink both for personal use and for sale locally.

With such alternative attractions monopolising my time and attention, my truanting and lack of effort at school were beginning to invite unwanted and unwarranted levels of attention from certain teachers, in particular the deputy headmaster, Martin Mullen could be a bully of a man who tried to enforce school discipline through intimidation of those who failed to conform in any way. Although it occurred somewhat later in the school year than I had anticipated, he began to pick on me relentlessly, perhaps making up for lost time, as he verbally abused and goaded me at every apparent opportunity, in the corridors or in the playground. Looking back, I can see my younger self presenting something of an disobedient nuisance to him, to be persuaded by whatever means necessary into compliance with school norms; I remain saddened that it never appeared to occur to him to consider the difficulties that I was experiencing at home or the causes of my truancy. This was, after all, a mature individual and a supposedly responsible public servant, with a duty of care, bullying a 13-year old child for nothing more than I could see but to maintain his uncompromising reputation within the school. I never could understand it and it only served to secure my increasing resentment towards him in particular. As always, I continued to seek refuge and understanding up in the Street after school.

Early into the second year of school, as a result of boredom and just looking for something to do on yet another cold and drawn out November night, Jeg, Auldy and I broke into a local car garage one night. As the premises were virtually empty of anything of value, we opportunistically lifted several cans of spray paint each on the way out of the building, with no real concrete plan other than pure mischief in our minds.

As we dawdled along the Street, passing the school, I just couldn't resist the temptation of literally leaving my mark, so to speak. 'Quick!' I shouted excitedly, 'Let's sort this prick Mullen out.' 'Are you sure about this, Weavy?' replied Auldy who was going through a rather morose period following the death of his granny. 'Aye, fuck him ... let's jist dae it!' shouted Jeg, who needed no more encouragement than the mere hint of a suggestion for mayhem. With great precision we began spray painting all sorts of abusive slogans in two-foot letters about Martin Mullen and his family on the freshly roughcast external gymnasium wall, overlooking the playground: 'MARTIN MULLEN'S WIFE IS A PURE COW.' I was undoubtedly the main instigator of these particular insults, having an inherited vocabulary of abuse at my fingertips and knowing through first hand experience how hurtful they could be. I consciously blocked out the niggling feelings of guilt. Martin Mullen thinks he's a hard man, I reminded myself, and he deserves everything he gets.

As I entered the school playground the next morning, I couldn't fail to notice the muted stillness as both pupils and teachers read, aghast, the vulgarities which scarred the playground walls; I could sense the moral outrage. To my horror I then read on one wall in giant black letters, 'MARTIN MULEN IS A WANKERR – JEG ROOLS.' Knowing Jeg as I did, I knew he would buckle under any pressure from Mullen and grass us in unless he was drunk, which although far from a star pupil, I didn't really expect of him first thing on a Wednesday morning. I resigned myself to my fate. The inevitable happened halfway through the first period of the morning as Martin Mullen came bursting through our classroom door like a raging bull with two other male teachers who proceeded to haul me out of class by the scruff of the neck.

'You've went too far this time Weaver!' he bawled, as he slapped me repeatedly along to his office. Sitting defiantly in his office, I denied every accusation put to me until Jeg was strategically hauled in by the hair a short time later, stuttering and stammering as he still tried to rub the dry black paint from his hands. 'There's nae point denyin it, Weavy … they know it wis us,' sobbed Jeg. Following several further well aimed slaps, Mullen sat behind his desk with a smug expression on his face as if he had just rounded up a gang of ruthless villains, rather than a group of schoolchildren who had the audacity to retaliate directly to his bullying and victimisation. Jeg and Auldy were suspended from school immediately whereas I, for some unknown reason, was taken to the main assembly hall and made to sit at a solitary desk and table in the middle of the large hall under the direct supervision of a teacher. If it was a deliberate ploy to humiliate me before my pending suspension, it certainly worked. I felt like a freak in a Victorian circus show as the rest of the pupils and teachers walked past the assembly hall staring in at me, which kind of set the tone for the remainder of the school year.

CHAPTER 5

Fearful to Feared: Violence Equals Respect

From an early age I liked the feeling of being drunk as it helped me to overcome any social inhibitions and this enhanced level of confidence proved helpful on two important fronts: it meant that I could talk away to lassies without my face going bright red with embarrassment, which was neither an irrelevant nor inconsequential development in itself at the age of 14 and, perhaps more successfully, I found that I could fight anyone without fear or apprehension.

My introduction to drink coincided, perhaps inadvertently, perhaps not, with the increasing publicity surrounding the convicted murderer, Jimmy 'Baby Face' Boyle. Following his much publicised conviction for a gang related murder, subsequent prison riots and increasing assaults on prison staff, he was being touted and even glamorised by the media as Scotland's most dangerous man. Inevitably, he became my first male role model; Jimmy Boyle was my hero and I wanted to be like him. I was acquiring the reputation as a good fighter through my involvement in numerous playground fights and I took increasing pride in this—the way that better adjusted adolescents would exult in getting a football trial with a professional team, or gaining some prestigious academic award. I also discovered that the more gory and bloodied the fight, the more people took notice, giving me an overwhelming sense of achievement as I revelled in this new found, somewhat envied status. As a result therefore, the fights became more frequent, progressing from the occasional playtime scrap to more overt acts of violence.

During the summer months following my second full year at secondary school, I was standing with the guys at the waltzers one night, drunk, and trying to look mean and moody when a solitary voice screamed in our direction, 'There's a big battle up the toon wae Glesga guys!' Fights with Glasgow guys during such times were almost as traditional as the summer holidays themselves and reputations tended to live or die by such confrontations. People still recall with pride the night old Deeds McKenzie battered four Glasgow guys single-handedly with a dog chain in 1959. Instinctively answering the call to arms, we ran to the aid of other guys from the town (or rather hurled ourselves with complete abandon into the fray) and quickly became involved in this particular scrap.

Following a mass stand up fist fight in the middle of the street and now outnumbered, the Glasgow guys began to disperse, eventually fleeing for safety. With the adrenalin pumping throughout my body, I was not going to be denied my memorable moment of glory as I began to chase one of the remaining guys, for what seemed an almost purpose-defeating length of time, until I eventually cornered him back at the fairground, right between the fairground caravans. Turning to face me directly his face turned a deathly grey colour in front of me as he noticed the empty wine bottle in my hand, which I had picked up during the chase. In my drunken and hyped-up state, I gave no thought to the potential consequences for either of us, as I walked slowly towards him. Quickly lunging at him, I crashed the bottle down over his head with a sickening thud; blood spurted up and out from his skull like a fountain as he screamed in terror, his hands shooting up to his head as he backed away, until cornered between two adjoining caravans, where he cowered, trying desperately to protect himself as I grabbed his head upright by the hair and stabbed the broken bottle hard into his face tearing his cheek open. With no further thought or mercy, I launched into a frenzied attack as I rained a flurry of kicks and punches into his head and body. As he tried to crawl under one of the caravans for sanctuary, I picked up what was left of the bottle and began stabbing and slashing at his exposed lower legs, although any further significant damage was mercifully prevented by his knee length Doc Martin boots.

As he lay whimpering under one of the caravans, I steadied myself against the same caravan with both hands and, due to a mix of physical exertion, drink, and my repulsion as I felt the wetness of the guy's blood sinking into my skin. I started to throw up uncontrollably. Trying to compose myself I began to walk away from the scene with a sobering realisation of what I had done. What would the guy's poor mother say when she saw her son with his face hanging open? Would he be okay? How would my maw be if it was me? Stained with the guy's blood, I soon met with the others and we all made our way home through the back streets to avoid the police. As we walked, the others each flippantly recounted in minute detail their respective battle exploits and the damage they had inflicted as a result of their *minor* skirmishes as I just walked alongside them silently, still troubled. However, we began drinking heavily later that evening and as the night wore on, with my initial angst alleviated, I began to re-enact the scene for the rest of the guys, recounting every gory detail; now completely abstracted from the guilt and self-loathing I had experienced earlier. I then convinced myself that I should have torn the guy's other cheek, just as Jimmy Boyle would have done.

In the small town that Saltcoats was, the story of my particular encounter with the Glasgow guys spread like wildfire and was grossly exaggerated to Deeds McKenzie proportions as I apparently stabbed and slashed my way through ten of them. Revelling in the attention, of course, I did nothing to discourage the story and having just recently discovered the hitherto unrecognised benefits of violence, I sought rapidly to make up for lost time by establishing myself as an uncompromising and aggressive individual who would fight at every opportunity, be it the playground, the street, or in the town; the context and environment were unimportant.

When we were not catapulting ourselves full pelt into offending behaviour, playing football in the Street was our favourite past-time and we would just as easily return to more customary childhood activities by spending many a happy hour chasing a ball about, mimicking our football heroes. Street football was something of a national obsession in working class areas the length and breadth of Scotland up until perhaps the late 1970s. Historically, Scotland had produced a number of world class players over the years who started their love of the game running about the streets playing football with their arses hanging out of their trousers. Such was the passion for the game that any guy who did not play football was normally viewed with great suspicion and talked about quietly with pointed fingers, as if marked by some terrible disability. I don't think it is a coincidence that the demise of Scottish football in recent years has coincided with the decline of street football. Football was indeed our great equaliser as we were all decent enough players and, unlike in most other social situations, we didn't feel inferior to anyone. In most cases however, we would only play football until it got dark, at which stage our attention would turn to more illicit activities.

On one such night, happily exhausted from a marathon three-hour football session, Eddie, Malky, Jeg, Auldy and I mischievously went on the prowl, initially more to alleviate the threatening boredom than anything else. As we walked about the town aimlessly, Eddie began reflexively pushing and pulling at the handles of various shop doors. Eddie Nisbet was the same age as me but went to the nearby Protestant school. A relatively quiet guy, Eddie was slightly bigger than me, lived with his mother and brothers in Anderson Drive and as with most of us then, there was little money in the household. Eddie was left to his own devices in many respects, his da having left the family home when Eddie was a toddler. He looked rather psychotic with his mop of curly black hair, deep brown eyes and thick bushy eyebrows which met scarily, like a warning, in the middle. Although staying mainly with his mother, he would also spend time living with two uncles nearby, who gave him a hard time and would beat him for the slightest thing. Many a day he would come up to the street bruised and grazed, but either brushed it off or just refused to talk about it. He had already spent a brief period in a children's home for housebreaking when he was 12 and like me, with no particular controls over his behaviour, was getting involved in more and more trouble.

Boring quickly from the lack of any apparent action taking place that we could get ourselves involved in just following our return to school, we once again decided to make our own mischief. We took a turn down a back lane in the town and pulled ourselves awkwardly up onto the roof of one building where we began almost intuitively to poke and scratch around the skylights of the nearby pubs and shops like hungry vermin, seeking a way into the hidden stores.

I can't remember who saw it first but we came to a stop at one particular skylight above a pub, and crouching down onto our heels, we began pulling away together at the rusty frame that encased it, until suddenly and happily it creaked—only to give way with an enormous crash that made the five of us jump to our feet. 'Holy fuck!' screamed Eddy excitedly, the first to recover and throw himself over the newly formed hole in the roof, through which he poked his head. 'We've just won the pools,' he continued, jumping back up and dancing around like some mad folk devil, rubbing his hands with glee. Looking through the hole we could all see immediately that this storeroom was stacked from floor to ceiling with case after case of drink.

'We need to think this through,' I said quietly to the others as they stood nearby wide eyed with excitement, 'how the hell do we get the drink up and then doon to the street fae here?' As Malky had recently worked as a milk boy and had been shown how to drive the milk truck in the factory yard, he suggested the idea of going to the local dairy and stealing one of their trucks to transport it. 'But am tellin you ... ah can drive that big baby, nae bother man,' he said indignantly. 'You sure?' I asked still totally unconvinced, but seeing no other alternative. 'Aye ... and ah know where the keys are kept,' he stammered in his excitement, at the prospect of playing a prominent role in this particular heist. No sooner had we made a collective agreement, than the five of us were crammed into the front cab of a massive milk truck heading towards the Crown pub, laughing hysterically and hollering away like a miniature cast out of the film, *One Flew Over The Cuckoo's Nest.* Jeg, with the restraint and discretion of an utterly out of control, lawless adolescent, then pulled down his trousers and underpants and began flashing his bare arse to everyone we passed. Barely able to see over the steering wheel, Malky, lost in his own special moment, blared the horn and waved at every possible passer-by on route with great pride.

Despite the anarchy of our journey, we reached the Crown without hindrance, and immediately, on arrival, a certain gravity infected the atmosphere as we instructed Malky to just quickly drive the truck straight into the back lane. 'No way, ahm gonnae reverse this thing right,' said Malky defiantly. 'Just drive it in front ways, Malky, before the polis come!' shouted Auldy now beginning to panic. With the gears crunching noisily, Malky, still clearly uninhibited in his own moment, insisted on continuing and with great precision undertook a seven point reverse manoeuvre into the narrow, secluded lane behind the pub. 'You've jist clipped the kerb there, Malky, dae ye want to pull it oot and try again ya wee arsehole ye,' said Jeg in his usual supportive manner as he refastened the last of his trouser buttons. 'Come on, let's jist get started,' I said as we all scrambled from the truck.

It was late in the evening when, after a successful mission, not-all-that expertly accomplished, we finished loading up. Tired and with the adrenaline completely dissipated, we decided just to park the lorry at the garages at the back of the Street and return to it the following morning. As Auldy, Jeg and I were still suspended from school, it was agreed that we would begin selling the stuff around the street the following day.

CHAPTER 6

Sent Down—So Much for Jimmy Boyle!

As I was leaving the house the following morning, ready for an enterprising day, I was wrenched out of my reverie and contented planning as I was immediately grabbed right on the door step and huckled by two clearly astute CID officers. 'Aye, you'll just be comin wae us son,' one of them said as his strong fingers gripped my arm painfully and dragged me from the doorstep, the panic rapidly escalating within me. I knew one of the officers from past encounters as he had hassled us several times previously; he was a tall skinny guy with light coloured frizzy hair, whom we affectionately nicknamed 'Flossy', because he looked like a big anaemic candy floss, with his skinny frame and bushy hair. Marching me promptly to the police car he quipped gleefully, 'Aye, ye'll no be seein your auld maw for a while noo sonny.'

Apparently, both me and Malky had been recognised in or around the truck the night before and reported to the police; astonishingly, Jeg's bare arse was never even mentioned, which on reflection, was something of a pity as the identification parade would have been interesting. As I was being led through the maze of corridors at the police station I tried not to grimace in pain as Flossy's fingers remained clamped tightly around my arm. Being dragged past a door I caught a glimpse of Malky sitting in one of the other offices, hunched over and looking suddenly young, no longer living his moment. When he saw me he quickly pulled himself upright and gave me a rather strained, nonchalant look and winked at me with a pathetic attempt at unconcern, through tear-stained eyes. 'How's it gaun, Weavy?' he choked as I was shoved into an adjoining room.

The initial stages of arrest, that endless hanging around and worrying, were always the worst parts and reminded me of how I felt lying, waiting on my da to start trouble in the house; the anticipation of a belting from the police would evoke a dull sickening feeling in my stomach and tightness in my throat that would have overridden any concerns of what might follow, even if I had known what the possibilities were. It must be said however, that my experiences at the hands of the police during this stage of my life were rooted firmly in the cultural norms of the period. In the mid-1970s for example, police practices were a lot less regulated, and professionalism and accountability were seemingly as yet, alien concepts; differing levels of brutality were to a large extent an accepted police method of deterrence by some officers within the force (not all, it must be said), irrespective of the age of the accused.

As the same two officers entered the room and sat down opposite me, I could only brace myself for the inevitable. One officer leaned right across the dividing desk, his eyes boring menacingly into mine for long enough to make me involuntarily jump when he shouted in my face, 'So who were your pals?'. 'Come on, Allan son, let's jist get this mess cleared up, eh,' his partner said in a far softer tone, which was wasted on me in my heightened state of vigilance against the oppressor, whose spit lingered on my face. 'Whit pals,' I answered, as casually as I could muster, in a tone far higher than I intended, as the knot in my stomach tightened, clearly affecting my vocal chords. Not to disappoint, the arm of the growler moved like lightening as he slapped me hard across the side of the head, knocking me from my chair. Shaken, I bit my lip tightly, determined not to let him see me cry, as I stood up and scrambled behind the chair for an element of protection. 'Sit ya wee bastard!' he shouted. 'Ah don't know what you're talking aboot! I cried back, bracing myself for another blow. As he made to lunge for me again, his colleague quickly got between us. 'It's okay, John … it's okay … let's just lock him up and get on with it,' said the quieter of the 'good cop, bad cop' duo, as he brought the well rehearsed, if not tired, scenario to a conclusion. It was a small triumph for us, as they never did find out who the others were and grudgingly accepted that they would have to settle for me and Malky—and the return of the drink of course.

Given the seriousness of the offence, we were not charged and released as on previous occasions; rather, an emergency Children's Panel had been specifically arranged for us both for later that day. The Children's Hearing system, or Panel, as it is more commonly known, is unique to Scotland, consisting of three lay people who have a legal responsibility for making decisions in the 'best interests' of any child who comes before them for offending or any range of welfare issues. This has been held as a preferable model of youth justice in comparison to countries like England, for example, that have specific youth courts and a youth justice system in operation, which in many respects mirror the adult criminal justice system.

Some hours later, I was taken from the police station in the back of a police car along with Malky, to the panel. As we drew up, I noticed my maw standing, looking distressed, with Malky's maw. With the weight of the world seemingly on her shoulders, 'auld' Jean, as she was known to us, stood with her jaws clapped around her toothless face, with a headscarf wrapped tightly over her greying hair. 'Wait till ah get you in the hoose ya wee bastart!' she shouted at Malky as he was frogmarched past her by the accompanying officer. 'You better hope they put ye away, ya thievin wee swine, because I'll kill ye when ah get ye!' she screamed as she swung her bag at him, before the other officer was forced, for the sake of appearances, to intervene and quieten her down. I, on the other hand, didn't need to dodge a torrent of abuse as my maw stood looking at me quietly, with a sad look of disappointment on her face, which was a far worse indictment of my behaviour and far harder to deal with.

Led into the panel room with my maw, I looked around nervously, unsure of what lay ahead of me. Three panel members, two women and one man, sat behind a large formal desk, with a fourth adult sitting aside them, known as the Reporter, who was assigned to guide all panel members on points of law. One of the women in particular looked a bit of a toff and I couldn't help but wonder what frame of reference she could possibly apply in any attempt, if at all she intended to make one, to understand my situation. As soon as the Reporter finished talking about some legal matter the woman immediately began to talk about the seriousness of the offence, to humphs and nods of agreement from her fellow panel members, utterly bypassing even a superficial stab at trying to elicit an explanation.

As I tried to avoid her piercing stare by examining every other facial peculiarity she exhibited, thus simultaneously securing an attentive expression on my face, I couldn't help but notice that she had facial hair under her nose like a wee moustache, which she tried unsuccessfully to cover with heavy make up. This perked me up slightly as I could see that she was not without her own imperfections and although my maw wasn't as well to do, at least she didn't have a moustache. The ensuing discussion pretty much passed me by as I sat silently awaiting my fate, all disguise of interest on my part disintegrating with the passing minutes, until I registered their concluding verdict. 'We have no alternative on this occasion but to seek a four week Residential Assessment with a view perhaps to a Residential Supervision Order,' said the spokeswoman, more to the adults present than to the sole subject of the discussion. My heart sank utterly at the prospect of going into care but was momentarily lifted some ten minutes later when I learned that Malky was subject to the same outcome.

As Malky and I were being marched purposefully back out of the building with the same accompanying police officers, we heard a commotion behind us in the foyer as Malky's maw began to shout at the panel members. 'Ya heartless swines … that's ma wee boy you've just sent away ... how cun you sleep at night?' I never even got a chance to speak to my maw before I went, as she departed the office immediately on learning the outcome, too upset to comprehend and accept what had just happened. Whilst we were being escorted to the waiting police car to take us to Darvel, me and Malky began firing off jokes along the lines that so hurried and urgent was our panel, some of the members didn't even get time to shave properly. This, of course, was all bravado, a way of diverting our concerns and mounting dread at the unknown prospect of Darvel. For me, it was also a way to try and block out the upset I had caused my maw and suppress the mental picture, which kept rising up in my mind, of her fleeing from the building in complete distress. This was the first time I had ever been away from my maw and my family. Being like Jimmy Boyle didn't hold the same attraction for me just then for some reason; I just wanted to hug my maw and go home with her.

Darvel, or Kirkland Park, as it was officially known, was an assessment centre set in the sleepy East Ayrshire town of Darvel, birthplace of Sir Alexander Fleming, the renowned scientist who discovered penicillin. I always considered it rather ironic that this backwater village and in particular, Kirkland Park, was a source of distress to countless children over the years yet it was once home to a pioneering doctor who discovered a medicine responsible for saving millions of lives throughout the world.

The centre usually accommodated around 25 boys at any one time, who were deemed to be unruly and beyond parental control, for short term periods, mainly for the purposes of assessment, as opposed to punishment, to help panel members decide on the most suitable outcome for each individual boy. The fact that the assessment was divorced from consideration of the lived realities of people's lives and their environments did not appear to concern anyone as most boys were in for offending and truanting and, like me and Malky, were being assessed for suitability for approved school as opposed to anything more fundamentally constructive.

To all intents and purposes, this was the Ayrshire equivalent of Glasgow's infamous Larchgrove Assessment Centre, which in later years became the subject of a massive physical and sexual abuse enquiry. The guys and I were well aware of Darvel as the certainty of this had been flung at us periodically over the last year or two by teachers and police officers as a dark, sinister threat—so often, in fact, that over the last year any fear it had initially evoked had long since disappeared. Until now that is. As we made our way up the long drive in the police car, I was struck by how much Darvel looked like a stately aristocratic mansion, set as it was in tranquil, idyllic grounds; but, having heard enough about it from other boys over the years, however, we were not fooled by its appearance. Malky and I sat quietly, undistracted by its material presence, in absolute dread of what lay within.

We were led directly into the reception area by the two Darvel staff members who had met us on the forecourt, where we had been abruptly delivered and deserted by the accompanying police officers. The rest of the boys suddenly appeared from every direction to gather round us both, seemingly scrutinising us against some institutionally developed criteria, implying an alternative assessment process that clearly took less time than that of the professionals to conclude. 'Haw, wee man!' barked one of the bigger guys towards Malky as he tried to cower unnoticed behind me, 'Huv ye got any nude photos o yer maw?' 'Naw, ah've no,' replied Malky in indignation at this gross insult of his maw, as I shuddered quietly to myself beside him, thinking momentarily of auld Jean in any such a pose. 'Well dae ye want to buy some?' he quipped to the great delight of the crowd as they stood around us laughing. I immediately braced myself for a stand off, knowing full well that if he made a similar crack about my maw I would rip his fucking head off.

'Come on, break it up lads ... give the newcomers time to settle,' shouted one of the staff members, making a timely intervention by handing us our standard issue, dull grey, Darvel garb with matching plastic sandals. Obviously an anti-absconding ploy, I thought to myself, as I accepted my bundle from the staff member, as there was no way you could be seen in the street with these clothes on: not even in the East of Ayrshire. We were then led to the shower area for the second stage in the admission process: delousing.

There was a strong stench in the place that hung in the back of your throat, which we were soon to discover was a head lotion to prevent lice, known affectionately as 'jungle juice'. As we showered quietly, lost in our own thoughts in the communal shower room, the staff member leaned across us and began lashing the jungle juice onto our hair. 'There's nothing I haven't seen before, lads!' he shouted over the noise of the water as, mortified, me and Malky tried to hurriedly cover our private parts and maintain a bit of dignity, a rare privilege in places like Darvel, as we were soon to discover.

After our shower, we were taken immediately into a room and given a full verbal account of the centre rules, including the need for personal hygiene; obviously there was little emphasis on pro-social role modelling, I thought, given that the staff member engaging with us had a distracting level of dandruff atop his head and shoulders, and his bad breath, which was wafting nauseatingly in our direction, might indeed have benefited from a swig of jungle juice. To our momentary relief, we were then led away to separate secure rooms, located on the first floor of the building. These rooms were totally bare with the exception of a single mattress in the middle of the floor and had barred windows. They were generally kept aside for troublemakers or new arrivals at the centre.

Alone in the secure room, I returned to my isolated thoughts and began to cry quietly, suffocating my sorrow into my pillow, for fear of Malky hearing me in the next room. My fears were unfounded and unnecessary, however, as Malky's wailing and choking sobs drowned out my own almost immediately. I just wanted to go home; I was worried about my maw and wondered who would be there for her if my da started his trouble? I cried myself to sleep that night.

For the most part, Darvel was a hellish experience, given my age and time of life. I missed my maw and my family terribly and seemed to worry about them constantly even though my maw, who got a run up from Malky's maw and da, auld Jimmy, visited me weekly. I both longed for and fretted about her visits which, whilst they were a comfort to me, also brought with them pain in their inevitable conclusion when, at the end of the visit, I stood with my heart in my hands, watching my mother get into the car which would drive her away again, without ever looking back. My da never visited and I'm not sure that I really expected him to. As I sat talking to my maw I would try to sneakily scan her face for signs of bruising, without appearing too obvious. However, as if sensing my concern she would instinctively reassure me: 'That's your faither aff the drink again, son, and he starts work again on Monday.' 'Aye, that's good maw,' I would reply in an equally unconvincing manner, as we accommodated each other's participation in this fantasy existence, for the sake of the other.

From the visiting room window I would see Malky's da sitting in the car, never actually to come in; on one occasion he was drinking a can of lager. Not exactly father of the year material either, but at least he made the effort, I thought to myself. I casually wondered what Malky made of this; whether he thought his da's presence in the grounds was enough.

The only time I could really escape the loneliness, isolation and everything that, for me, Darvel represented, was when I was playing football in the centre. As a child I was good at two things: fighting and football, although my real passion was football. With or without my pals, I devoured and idolised every aspect of the game and even sometimes as a younger child, I could happily stand alone for hours kicking a ball against a wall, totally absorbed and lost in the 'skelp, skelp, skelp' of the hard plastic ball as I kicked and headed it against a wall, any wall, fantasising about scoring a goal for my favourite team, Celtic. I heard the tribal roar of the fans, the team, and the manager, as they rushed towards me in my moment of glory; the commentator screaming my name, verbally replaying the details of the goal for the benefit of those who didn't get to see it but wished they had.

I was never encouraged to pursue this passion in any way and despite being a decent enough player, I was never allowed to play for any of the school teams for any length of time due to the trouble I was causing. Following my first game of football in the centre, a staff member seemed to take something of a shine to me and after overcoming the initial awkwardness and distrust on my part, we got on well during the remainder of my stay there. Ironically, he was an old famous footballer called Sammy, who played in the 1950s for Celtic's bitter rivals, Rangers.

From an early age I remembered my da ranting and raving about Rangers, who were traditionally a Protestant team. 'Rangers scum … don't trust thae dirty Orange bastarts!' He would scream this drunken cliché in reference to all things Protestant. Of course, as part of the socialising process in our part of the world, I naturally grew up half-hating, half-thinking I hated, Rangers and all things Protestant, as if they were all relatives of the devil and all things deviant. As I aged, however, this didn't extend to any of my own guys who were Protestant and avid Rangers fans; nor to my maw, of course, who was Protestant; nor to any of my Protestant relatives, some of whom were actually members of the Masonic Lodge and then, of course, there were people like old Sammy ... Sometimes this Protestant thing was hard to work out, I realised as I got older, but God knows I tried.

Malky wasn't long in the centre before handing himself over to the pack and ingratiating himself by enacting the laddish behaviour you would expect within such institutions, including banal pranks, the odd skirmish and mild forms of bullying; he would hold court, recounting his driving exploits to the great delight of the rest of the guys. Conversely, I had no interest in seeking this sort of acceptance; I chose to keep myself distanced and generally just went about my own business. Hoping for anonymity, I sought to make myself as inconspicuous as possible, which meant that I increasingly sat alone at the big bay window in the centre, particularly during the last couple of weeks, waiting on Sammy starting his shift.

As part of the activity structure within the centre, we were taken on long walks into the Darvel countryside escorted by staff members; on several occasions Sammy and I would walk along together. 'So tell me about your family, Allan ... what about your teachers ... tell me about these daft pals of yours,' he would casually drop into the conversation. Although it was all part of the assessment process and Sammy had a job to do, there always appeared to be a genuine interest and sincerity in his questions and, real or not, a mutual attachment. As such, I began to increasingly trust his genuineness enough to respond to his enquiries. On the first such occasion, when he asked about my da, I stopped in my tracks and said to him, 'I'll answer your questions on one condition, Sammy.' 'Aye ... and what would that be?' he enquired. 'That you tell me about the time Celtic hammered you when you wir playing fir Rangers,' I laughed. It seemed like a fair trade to me.

CHAPTER 7

Rage to Ritalin—Who is the System For?

Several days prior to my return to the panel, I was summoned unexpectedly to the office of Mr Millar (the centre's headmaster). Although I had not previously been called for like this during my stay, such a summons was generally regarded as a bad sign as it usually served the end of meting out some form of punishment. As I was ushered into the office by a staff member, I noticed with some surprise that in addition to Mr Millar, a social worker from Saltcoats, Margaret Clark, was sitting there. I had seen Margaret on a voluntary basis back and forth for a short while before arriving at the centre. If reincarnation was to be believed and there is such a thing as a previous life, then Margaret had obviously committed some hellishly major sins and for her penance me and the guys had been mercilessly imposed on her, as part of her caseload. I always liked Margaret; she was a warm and caring individual who genuinely tried to help those she worked with over the years and who actually seemed to have some understanding that, fortunately, wasn't dependent on an explanation, which for me and the guys was something of an irregularity.

'And how are you, Allan?' she asked as I tentatively sat down beside her. 'Aye, okay,' I said in my normal monosyllabic manner, still unsure as to why I had been summoned, and whose side who was on. Looking like a stereotypical comic-book character of a mad scientist, Mr Millar was a tall, balding man, who wore thick glasses which looked as if they were made from the bottom of two milk bottles, distorting his eyes into bulging saucers. I had seldom seen him during my time at the centre and it was this elusiveness and thus unpredictability that secured his authority over the boys, which in turn ensured that he was held in almost mythical esteem by the staff group due to his apparent knowledge and application of child psychology, despite his limited interaction with any of the boys directly.

'So, Mr Brown (Sammy) tells me you have progressed really well over the last three weeks, young man,' he said as his big eyes bore into mine and unsure if this was a question or a statement, I stuttered nervously, if not ridiculously, in my efforts to fill the uncomfortable silence, 'Eh, well .. eh, well I've tried my best, sir.' Mr Millar then proceeded to talk at length about my emotional and behavioural triggers, which I didn't understand, and then concluded, 'and that is why we think that a further residential placement is not required at this stage and will strongly recommend to the hearing that you return home under a home supervision order.' 'Does my maw know?' was all I could blurt out in my excitement at the prospect of going home as I sat before them awash with both relief and elation. As I left the room, Sammy was sitting in the recreation room quietly looking at me with a beaming smile on his face.

Retrospectively, I had no real awareness of what was said to me in that room or why and I was really only concerned with the fact that I was going home. How thoroughly my assessment had been undertaken within the strict confines of the centre could perhaps be questioned. I discovered later that no one had spoken to my maw as part of this assessment process and certainly not to my da; my troubles at home and at school were going to be no different and I don't know how an awareness of my 'emotional and behavioural triggers'—had I ever managed to acquire such insight—would have made any difference the next time my da was kicking my maw's head like a burst leather football or the next time the guys and I were roaming the streets bored with no-one knowing or worrying about where we were or what we did. Or indeed, the next time someone wanted a square go and I had no alternative but to oblige. But what the hell; I was going home.

Following a brief appearance back at the children's hearing, and with no further thought of the tears or sleepless nights, Malky and I swaggered out of the panel like mini-cardboard gangsters, subject to statutory home supervision orders. Jeg and Eddie were milling around and both hollered loudly as we made our way out of the building. 'Hey, Malky, can ah get your autograph, ya wee mad mental jailbird,' laughed Jeg as he bounced up towards us. In an instant however, Malky's maw bundled through us and grabbed Malky's ear before he had the opportunity to bask in the attention, 'Mental. I'll show you who's bloody mental when I get you up that road, ya wee swine!' she roared. 'But maw ... but maw,' was all that could be heard of Malky as he was dragged along the road kicking and screaming, by his maw.

My reception home was, thankfully, far less of an eye-catching spectacle; I left the guys and walked home with my maw. 'Well, son, I hope that this is the end of the trouble because you won't get another chance,' she said to me quietly. 'Ah know, maw,' I said, reflecting seriously on what she had said, as I relished the peace and tranquillity of the moment we had together as we made our way home. On my return, the house was fairly quiet with my da sitting in the living room, sober, reading a paper. I was unsure how to react to the silence between us, and so I shuffled about the room aimlessly, waiting to see if he would say anything; eventually he turned to look in my direction and, before returning to his paper, mumbled, 'And don't you huv the polis back near this door.'

Going back to school was expectedly difficult; I was unsure, at first, how I would be received but it was rapidly made clear to me that my return was slightly more difficult and far less welcomed by some teachers than it ever was going to be for me. A couple of them felt the need to make reference to the fact that I had just been 'released' and that I was lucky to be back in the community at all and when I came across Mullen through a chance encounter in a corridor, he turned to me and, in front of other pupils, merely said, 'Weaver, you don't belong here.' He could have had a point I thought quietly to myself at the time, as I certainly didn't feel as if I belonged, but that said, I didn't really know where I *did* belong. Not only had nothing changed through my admission to the centre but things appeared to have got worse: I felt increasingly isolated and excluded at school, my da was still causing the same mayhem at home and the guys and the Street seemed to be the only stability and source of acceptance in my life at the time.

Within weeks of my return home from Darvel, it was approaching the school holidays, the end of my third term, and there was a lot going on in terms of the traditional extra-curricular activities; not all of them lawful. Every couple of years an incident or an exchange of verbal abuse would occur between St Andrews pupils and those of the nearby Ardrossan Academy, resulting in mass gang fights in the local playing fields as both sets of pupils taunted each other in a testosterone-fuelled frenzy.

The source of such conflict was generally sectarian in nature, with territorial undercurrents. This ritualistic behaviour was usually nurtured in the early years of our primary schooling, reinforcing the pious wisdom of certain religious institutions that were, and remain, actively against non-denominational schools to allow us to preserve our religious identity. I do not believe any significant purpose to this has ever really been articulated. In our efforts to embrace our cultural and religious heritage, however, we worked hard to soak up the 'four Rs' which characterised our primary school education: reading, (w)riting, (a)rithmetic and rioting with the weans from the Protestant school as we conveniently passed them on our way back and forth to school every day.

There I was at the age of six, school satchel slapping against my back, 'knee length' shorts scratching the backs of my calves and once-white ankle socks, now grey from age and with all the elastic gone, gathered uncomfortably around my heel and bunching up under the sole of my foot in my slightly over-sized shoes, as I skipped merrily past the Protestant school. I would then change direction and skip up playfully to the weans, obliviously playing away in the playground. 'Big stinkin Proddie bastarts!' I would shout at them as I hurled stones in their direction. The predictable response would result in them running towards the perimeter fence *en masse*, screaming, 'Ya wee smelly Fenian dick!', as I bolted hell for leather to the safety of my own school, with my satchel flapping away behind me in the wind, easily, forgivably mistakable for an enthusiastic young student upon whom older generations would gaze and smile wistfully at my eagerness to get to school.

St Andrews and our Protestant counterpart, Ardrossan Academy, were perhaps 200 yards apart, almost within stone throwing distance of each other and with only several weeks of the centre behind me I was forwarded by others in our school for a 'square go' with one of the Ardrossan Academy guys at dinner break. Not particularly wanting or seeking this, at the same time I felt I had no real option as the momentum gathered with some enthusiasm within the school. If nothing else, it gave me a much needed sense of significance and, in a round-about way, I viewed it as a direct acknowledgement of my increasing reputation as a fighter and, Christ knows, I had little else to be known by.

With the scene set and my heart pounding in nervous anticipation, I made my way over to the guy in the middle of the park as the crowd followed excitedly. Before I could formulate a plan of action, there we were, squaring up to each other, circling around in the middle of the park when he started goading me for the benefit of the onlookers: 'You're no so hard noo, Weaver ya bam.' I don't think he actually realised how right he really was. With the baiting concluded, we flew for each other and in my panic, and given his size, I could only grapple with him and cling on for dear life. My main motivation was to avoid losing face in front of the swelling crowd: a fate worse than death. With brute strength, he broke free from my grasp and threw me through the air making me land square on my arse.

More embarrassed by the indignity of the spectacle of my landing than hurt, I could scarcely believe my eyes when I saw this guy pull a knife out from his inside jacket pocket. If he too had passed something of a misspent youth, his was definitely spent in front of the television set at home as he crouched before me and began passing the knife from hand to hand like a demented Cherokee Indian in a John Wayne film. Where was Martin Mullin when I needed him, I thought to myself, as I backed away slowly, still unsure if this guy intended to use the knife or merely wave it about to impress everyone. Sensing the seriousness of the situation, the crowd fell into an anxious, tense silence as this guy worked the spectators and milked every second of attention. As I continued to back away unsteadily, someone from my side of the crowd, with either a stake in the proceedings or a sense of justice and understanding of what the term 'square go' meant, threw part of a small fencing post at my feet.

Now, with things evened up slightly, this guy didn't look so self-assured and I guessed then by the look on his face that his knife was just for show. Having seemingly gained control of this situation and seizing the moment, I quickly jumped towards him and battered the lump of wood into the side of his head, with which he fell to the ground half-conscious. With a mixture of fear, relief and rage swirling around inside me, I began kicking instinctively at his head and body as he lay on the ground in a mute, protective ball. As the school bell rang in the background, the crowd quickly dispersed, myself especially, as we rapidly made our way back across the park with my reputation consolidated and enhanced and, of course, our religious identities firmly intact.

Being subject to statutory supervision meant that I was required to see Margaret on a regular basis, although in effect, the reality of her 'workload' meant that priority was given to those deemed to be more in need of her attention. Nevertheless, I would make my way down to see her after school most weeks, as I quite liked the solitude of just sitting alone waiting for her, which offered momentary respite from the everyday hassles of life at the time.

On reflection, I was always difficult to engage and despite liking Margaret, I generally didn't participate openly in conversation and would respond to her questions in my usual, minimalist, monosyllabic manner. As a child, I was never really comfortable around most adults, particularly those in authority whom I had learned, through direct experience over the years, were untrustworthy and unpredictable and as such I would avoid any interaction with them where possible. I would sit in the social work waiting room, patiently waiting for Margaret to see me, which despite my own difficulties in life, I generally found to be a humbling experience as I sat quietly, watching the different people coming and going.

The social work building at this time was effectively a large wooden hut partitioned off into separate offices, each occupied by a strange array of professionals conforming rigidly to the social work stereotype with their corduroy trousers or polyester flared slacks and standard issue patterned tank tops. As I became increasingly acquainted with social workers, I couldn't help but observe that, perhaps more so than any other profession, they were guilty of committing some hellish crimes of fashion. Reflecting perhaps the sense of hopelessness and universal insignificance of the client group, the waiting room itself, was a small, darkened space at the far end of the building, the size of a police cell, with eight or nine dented plastic chairs placed strategically around three of the walls. This area was generally dirty, with litter, chewing gum and cigarette ends discarded about the floor, and graffiti and gang slogans daubed over the walls as ageing, outdated posters about various support groups hung, torn and tired, from the walls. I wondered if anyone ever actually contacted these organizations or if they were just kind of standard social work waiting room wallpaper.

I would always come across the most interesting characters in the waiting room and would be intrigued by their conversations as I sat listening to them or else I just sat quietly observing them, their mannerisms and expressions, their studious disinterest, as we waited for our respective social workers to summon us. Weary looking mothers would come in with their wee dishevelled looking grubby weans, who would then proceed to play quite happily among the chewing gum and cigarette ends as their maw tried to negotiate the price of a dinner for them.

One mother in particular would come in with her wean on a regular basis and, openly psyching herself up in the waiting room, would always haggle loudly for money. Looking like a throwback to the 1960s with her beehive hairstyle and hot pants three sizes too small, which seemed to affect her ability to walk upright properly, she looked a hardy soul with a big grumpy face under an inch of crude make up and a nose which had obviously seen its fair share of breaks. She would make her unavoidable and exasperated entrance into the waiting room with a deliberate stride, impatiently hauling her weans through the door by their forearms as they trailed and tripped behind her, their tangled legs in constant overdrive trying to keep up with her. 'Sit there and don't move your arse till a see if a get us money!' she would bark to the vacant looking children. However, when the office door was dramatically thrown open after several minutes, it was always a clear indication that she had been unable to negotiate money from her social worker. 'Miserable bastart!' she would shout back at him over her shoulder as she stomped back into the waiting room for her sprog, the beehive now tilted to one side. 'Come on, fucken move it!' she hollered at the wean.

On the other hand, on the odd occasion when negotiations for money obviously met with far more success, she would skip out of the office and say with more transparent maternal concern and attentiveness, 'Come on, son, put doon that fag doubt … whit have a warned you about eatin' other peoples' chewin' gum, Eric.'

I remember vividly sitting in the waiting room, late one particular afternoon, with several other people who had long since ceased to interest me, when we were joined by a young waif of a mother and her scruffy looking son who must have been aged around six. No sooner had she taken the only spare seat when, like a persuasive argument for force feeding young weans Ritalin, he began running around mad, arms outstretched, bumping into us all as he loudly and extremely annoyingly imitated a crashing plane; as the spittle and slevers peppered us all I could only sit and wish that he was actually in one.

Not content with merely treating us all to his human aeronautical display, he stopped abruptly in mid-flight and, pointing to the graffiti on the wall, asked loudly, 'Mum, whit's a scrotum?' Amid the embarrassed and pronounced silence, simultaneously, we all seemed to find the group support posters extremely interesting reading after all, as we each scanned them painstakingly, pretending that we didn't hear his question. Sneaking a sideways glance at his mother, however, I could see that her face was bursting in sheer mortification. Still standing before the graffiti with his arms outstretched, trying to make sense of the message before him, he began to read out loudly, emphasising every word torturously slowly, 'Mum, it says—'"big Danny fae Adrossin is a pure scrotum".' He then looked with a puzzled expression on his face towards his pained mother, who by now was furiously writing down the phone number of one of the support groups, such was her recent interest. 'Mum … is that ma Uncle Danny that's a scrotum … whit *is* a scrotum, anyway?' he asked her again.

Denying any involvement with him, she ignored him totally as I sat sniggering away to myself and thought, you'll know soon enough what a scrotum is, son, when your mother puts the boot into yours on the way out of this office.

CHAPTER 8

A Sad Twist to the Beautiful Game

Obviously more innovative than anyone gave her credit for and tapping directly into what few positive interests her wayward client group had, it was around this time that Margaret Clark came up with the idea of organizing us into a football team. With great excitement, we were all right behind this idea and I was unanimously appointed captain by Margaret and the rest of the guys. 'Remember you can lead by example, Allan,' she said to me—more out of hope, I thought, than expectation. Nevertheless, I accepted and embraced the position proudly, creatively naming ourselves the Probation Team. As we were short of several players we collectively decided, after weeks of deliberation, that to be eligible for selection a person had to be on some form of social work supervision. However, still finding that we could not attract the proper calibre of player, we sportingly decided to relax the entrance criteria to include those individuals who had previously been charged by the police at least six times, and, of course, had not grassed anyone up; a covering letter from their lawyer verifying outstanding charges, it was agreed, would be sufficient.

As word of the team spread, there was great demand locally, within the delinquent fraternity, to get into the team. Unlike conventional football trials however and with the stringent eligibility criteria by then completely abandoned, we arranged for Malky's wee brother, Graham, to prove his bottle for team membership by stealing something from the local Co-op shop, which of course we had to witness.

Before long, five of us found ourselves huddled in the shop ready to execute our well rehearsed plan and, as instructed, Graham, then only 13, nervously made his way up to the counter and stood before the big crabit looking shopkeeper, 'Eh ... 20 Widbine fags, mate.' As the shopkeeper put the cigarettes on the counter, Graham grabbed them and bolted at great speed towards the exit, pulling frantically at the closed door, a look of sheer panic coming over his face as he was unable to budge it. Unknown to Graham, Jeg had walked over to the door when Graham was at the counter and pulled the bolt over at the top of the door, locking it firmly. As we all fell about laughing, an utterly defeated Graham turned sheepishly and walked back towards the incredulous, speechless shopkeeper at the other end of the counter with a handful of loose change saying meekly, 'Could ah just huv ten, Mister, an I'll gie you the rest o' the money later.' We had another player.

We were preoccupied with the football team for a while and played a number of games against certain approved schools, children's homes and teams who had in turn followed Margaret's innovation and were organized by social work departments in nearby areas. One night we had arranged an early evening game against one of the local rival teams, Redheugh Children's Home, and before our game started we had to sit on the sidelines waiting for an earlier game to finish, which happened to be our year group at St. Andrew's School playing against a Glasgow team, in a well attended and apparently exciting Scottish cup tie. I sat alone quietly on the sidelines, looking at them in their new strips, completely lost in the intensity of the game, longing to have been part of it all.

Sitting glancing at my own team, I thought that we had far better individual football players, but the contrast in organization, context and even football strips was inescapable as our kit, the outcome of our direct lack of alternatives, merely consisted of something white, be it t-shirts, jerseys or just shirts. The contrast in general professionalism was equally stark and somewhat representative of our rather rag-tag approach. I noticed Jeg beginning to do some kind of bizarre warm up jump in preparation for the game. 'Fur fuck sake sit doon, Jeg! 'I shouted before anyone could see him. 'Nah, you've goat to get the muscles worked up, man,' he replied, conscientiously jumping away as if practising some revolutionary star jumping therapy for weans with learning difficulties — complete with a fag in his mouth, ridiculously tight shorts and a sparkling white shirt which scarily resembled his wee sister's blouse.

Thankfully, his antics were soon interrupted when Malky suddenly shouted, 'Quick, there's wee Margaret!' Our social worker and coach *extraordinaire* was making her way up the park towards us, laden down with two plastic bags full of sweets and drinks; our normal after-game treat. We did not need a tactical post-match discussion as positive reward and reinforcement was flavour of the day within social work interventions at the time, and who were we to criticise? In an unconscious, overtly childish manner, instinctively we sprinted *en masse* down towards her and as if suddenly aware of the crowd at the other game looking at this gang of misfits pegging it across the field, we kind of clicked at the same time, stopped running and swaggered slowly the rest of the way in a manner more in keeping with our status as the town's Probation Team.

The team lasted for about three months, played maybe seven or eight games in total and then disbanded because of the increasing trouble surrounding the players on and off the park. Almost every game ended in a fight and on one occasion a full scale battle erupted during the game when we were denied what I *still* maintain was a stonewall penalty, with Eddie chasing the referee the full length of the park with a wooden mallet. In the last ever game, the police were called to a fiercely contested match against Kerelaw Approved School and on arrival, were met with a blinding scatter of white t-shirts and, of course, some young delinquent wearing a wee lassie's blouse.

Watty Wilson, our kleptomaniac in waiting, came to the fore among us during this footballing campaign and remained one of our inner circle for years to come. With his rusty hair and slight frame, Watty was a relatively inconspicuous guy from the top end of Saltcoats who went to the same school as us. Although he had been quiet and unassuming at primary school, by the time he hit secondary school, he had become increasingly involved in offending, which in many respects resulted in a natural gravitation towards me and the rest of the guys. Unlike the rest of us however, he appeared to have a fairly stable home environment from what I could tell and his da was the only ever adult, apart from Margaret that is, to attend our football games. Understandably, his da, a small meek and mild mannered man, tried his utmost to keep Watty away from us and on the straight and narrow. 'Take it fae me, son, if you fly wae the craws, as sure as God is ma judge, you'll be shot wae them,' he would often say to Watty within earshot of us, as Watty looked over at us and squirmed visibly in embarrassment. Maybe it was just as well that he never knew what lay ahead for his son.

Having recently turned 15, some form of magnetic force appeared to draw me towards the street and the guys at every possible opportunity and I began to spend less and less time at home. Weekends were the exception, however, when I would still make a point of being home to ensure that my maw was okay, as my da was due in. Although there wasn't *always* violence in the household, the anticipation and threat of it seemed to be constant throughout this time of my life and my presence in the house was as much to reassure myself as anyone else.

Capitalising on our early successes, and with my experience of Darvel now seemingly well in the distant past, the guys and I were now breaking into more and more shops, and within a short period of time we were becoming more innovative in our efforts. Iron bars covering shop windows were sawn through slowly over the course of a week and the full window frames removed. With muffled chisel head and hammer we would dig our way through the brick walls of some premises over the course of several nights. We would sometimes hide in certain shops until after closing time and then help ourselves to the most saleable and moveable goods at our leisure. On several occasions we broke into upstairs premises and then got into the shop below through the floorboards. With a list of buyers locally we would often break into shops to order and then offload the cigarettes or drink the same night with minimum fuss. Like young captains of commerce, we were showing ambition, innovation, drive and hard graft, although admittedly this wasn't recognised by everyone. We were not making a fortune, but we had enough for drink, clothes or just to splash about in front of the lassies and in turn, therefore, it brought us a social kudos in and around the Street, which at this point was all that mattered.

This way of life seemed to be the only source of anything that meant something to me at this point. It was the same for all of us, I suppose, we never really felt accepted elsewhere and of course, to a large extent, we all experienced the same social and familial problems, albeit in slightly different forms; the exception was Watty whose family situation seemed relatively stable at this point. In and through each other we found at least some form of predictability and security, which was further bolstered by our shared interests and values which brought with them a sense of understanding and recognition.

That said, however, our primary diversionary activity—breaking into houses—was never my particular thing. Instinctively, I never felt comfortable invading someone's own private space and rifling through their personal belongings, preferring instead to break into shops, where goods could be turned more readily into hard cash and, I could persuade myself, people of our own backgrounds were less directly affected. Irrespective of the complexities of the various moral arguments about what we were doing, which we left to other people to thrash out, we were nevertheless criticised by a range of police officers, teachers and other self-righteous do-gooders for such offences although these very same people actively excluded us from almost every other opportunity to participate in their closely guarded wee worlds. Although a couple of the guys and I never really did it in any serious way, breaking into houses nevertheless became an art form for some of them and, put to other uses, such skills and ingenuity would have seen them excel in any given trade or profession under different circumstances. From our beginnings, several of the guys did indeed develop into hard core housebreakers and this was how they earned their money well into adulthood; resulting in lengthy custodial sentences along the way, which they seemed to accept as an occupational hazard.

Before my housebreaking career petered out, I would join or, more accurately, lead the guys in such excursions with a clear parallel agenda of my own. As they set about rifling through the houses in search of items of value that could be appropriated and peddled, I would often head directly to the kitchens and pantries and begin bagging food to take home to my maw, particularly if we were struggling at home to make ends meet. Some of the bigger private houses, I was soon to discover, had big industrial sized freezers in their garages containing enough food to feed a small army. This had the effect of diminishing my sympathy for them, or perhaps my own sense of guilt and niggling conscience, as I began the process of bagging away like some latter-day supermarket checkout trainee. So, the guys would be in the houses turning them over and I would be outside with a crow bar trying to force open the garage door. Although we were never actually caught red handed, I dread to think what any social work report or psychiatric assessment would have teased out of this scenario should one have occurred.

Even though I was already subject to statutory supervision, during this period I was summoned to attend more than my fair share of children's hearings by virtue of my persistent offending. Due to our frequent arrests for relatively minor offences we gradually became well versed in the ensuing police processes and proficient in negotiating our way through many of them. In general, following arrest, you could usually expect to be subjected to a few slaps by the arresting officer, which would be quickly followed by the semi-scripted threats from him, derived from years of worn-out experience, that you would be processed through the adult court system as a juvenile (under the age of 16) if you did not 'clear the books' for him. This, we all entirely understood, could lead to any number of worrying possibilities, not least a spell of remand in the notorious Young Offenders Remand Centre, Longriggend.

'Clearing the books' meant that you admitted to a number of local unsolved crimes still on the police books, all generally minor offences. 'Come on, ya wee bastard, ye were seen takin the bike,' said the arresting officer, as he moved down the list before him. As a result, you were merely charged with the offence(s) in question and let out after several hours in the police station to await a citation for the children's hearing, which had no real teeth as a deterrent and had long since lost its capacity to invoke fear in any of us. It wasn't an admission of *real* guilt, nor was it a public spirited gesture on our part; rather, it was a means of getting us back out onto The Street at the earliest possible point to resume our usual activities.

When I was eventually called to attend the panel following occasions such as these, my statutory supervision was generally just continued, with no particular fuss, or questions asked. Offenders then, even legally defined persistent offenders like myself, were given little priority by the generic local authority social work departments, resulting in additional attention being devoted to more pressing matters such as child protection, at the expense of other social concerns.

Despite being on statutory supervision, however, *still* no one seemed overly interested in the issues underpinning my offending behaviour, or in the extent and nature of the aggression, abuse and violence to which I was being routinely exposed. There were no family-orientated methods of intervention and the only quasi-family contact we had was initiated by my maw when she accompanied me to the social work office to ask for money as my da had drunk the housekeeping money again.

In addition to this, there were *still* no real efforts to address my increasing difficulties at school, or the obvious escalation of my offending behaviour in the community for that matter; the universal expectation appeared to be that, somehow, I would naturally, somehow, outgrow my criminal exploits. The domestic pressures faced by my maw in many respects rendered her unable to achieve any positive change in my behaviour and this, coupled with my practical invisibility within the social work department, meant that my delinquent behaviour was continuing unchecked and, indeed, becoming more entrenched, driving me ever further from normal adolescent life.

CHAPTER 9

Does Anyone Have Boundaries?

The night that the guys and I ended up at a party hosted by Big Johnny Parker was typical of the madness and mayhem we too often found ourselves in and which characterised this period of our lives. As he was a friend of a friend we kind of ended up there by default. Big Parker was 15 years old and his parents, who were on holiday, clearly considered him to exhibit all the necessary characteristics of adult responsibility such that they could entrust him to remain in the house himself for the weekend.

However, with responsibility still a word whose spelling escaped him and whose application to himself was yet a tenuous hope for the future, like most adolescents faced with such a rare opportunity, he decided to go ahead and organize a massive party. With the night in full swing we stood in a corner in our normal cliquish manner, drinking by the barrel load and ogling the lassies as they danced away oblivious to our presence. Predictably, two or three fights broke out over the course of the night which, reflecting the organizational skills of the host perhaps, were low key affairs and, rather conveniently, if not strategically, spread out over the course of the night, and were generally contained in one room of the house to minimise damage and disruption. Uncharacteristically, we remained merely enthusiastic observers.

With most of the crowd dispersing at the approach of midnight, we maintained our corner position, still drinking, albeit tempered with a degree of reservation. The early signs of panic had set in on our realisation that the drink was running precariously low, particularly given that we still had hours to go—although, to be fair, Big Parker had not yet been informed of this. 'Six cans o' lager left and nae wine,' muttered Jeg into his half-empty can. As if coming to life and by way of a contingency plan, the ever suggestive Watty added, 'Aye, we need tae dae a turn, man.'

Following a heated discussion, it was collectively decided that someone should at least *try* and break into an off-licence, to stock up our alcohol supply, naturally. Always ready for a 'turn', and conscious that in this isolated moment of our lives we had nothing to lose and absolutely everything to gain, Clicker and I agreed to go on a reconnaissance mission; we'd be waiting for a drink all night otherwise, I thought. 'Aye let's go, Weavy ... cause we'll need to keep the burds tanked up before the last o them disappear,' said the suddenly worried Clicker Casanova as he headed towards the door, pulling on someone else's jacket, and searching the pockets thoroughly as he went.

Clicker was from Stevenston and we were in the same year at school. He was a good pal of mine and had been hanging about with us on and off since he had been drafted latterly into the Probation Team as a goal scoring centre forward. From the occasional thing said here and there, it was evident that Clicker had a difficult home life with his family, although such matters were never really admitted or discussed openly. He too failed to build a rapport with most teachers at school, to say the least, and due to his academic limitations, was in remedial classes for most subjects. It was obvious to me even then, in mid-adolescence, that this was a terrible stigma for schoolchildren and Clicker was no exception as any mention of the subject would embarrass him greatly, only adding to his insecurity and feelings of low self-worth. This aside, however, after a good drink he was always up for a turn, a bit of a smooth talker and with a definite eye for the lassies; any lassies. On this particular mission, me and the Click soon found ourselves staggering down the road singing Irish rebel songs as we basically struggled to hold each other upright, obviously taking our reconnaissance duties seriously. Within a fairly short period of time we were both standing in the doorway of a Tesco supermarket, peeing away.

'Listen, Weavy, see first thing in the mornin', me an' you are headin' for Belfast to join the IRA, man,' he said, looking at me as he pissed down his leg. 'Ur there any boats during the night that we can get?' I asked, choked with his undying commitment to the cause. 'If no, we could maybe just go next week, eh?' I continued as I began pissing down my *own* leg. 'Aye fair enough, next week then,' he replied.

Peeing finished and our futures firmly sorted, I happened to glance up and notice that the main supermarket doors had little individual slat windows above them, which, on further investigation, I discovered could be easily removed. 'Here, Click, gie's a lift up here,' I said pulling him over towards the door. 'Nae offence, but ma back widnae take the strain, Weavy,' he said to me, rubbing the bottom of his back for unnecessary emphasis. Being the smooth talker that he was, it was agreed that he would stand on my clasped hands and remove the slat windows from the door. With great care and precision, with the windows that is and not my hands, he impressively removed the four slats with minimum fuss. Then, with the grace of two drunken hippos, we somehow managed to manoeuvre ourselves up and over the door, falling in a heap on top of one another inside the supermarket. 'How's the back?' I asked sarcastically as I dusted myself down. 'Just aboot haudin' up,' he replied as we began staggering about the shop looking for the drinks aisle. Stumbling into the alcohol section we opened a can of beer each and sat on the floor to finalise next week's plans for Belfast; like me, Clicker was also force-fed a rich diet of Republicanism and felt morally obliged to further the cause.

Whilst innocuously sitting and sipping away sedately at our cans, we heard a commotion as the front doors were flung open, and suddenly the shop became awash with noise and bright lights. 'Stay where you are, we've got the place surrounded!' roared a gruff voice from the front door area. Easing himself up, Clicker half-staggered, half-bolted towards the toiletries aisle with three uniformed police officers in hot pursuit. Fortunately, his back still seemed to be holding up okay, I noticed. Always conscious of his appearance and being a bit of a lady's man, I wound him up for years afterwards by saying that I knew he consciously headed for the toiletries section to Brylcream his hair and freshen up before he got lifted.

'You'll never take me alive, ya bastarts!' Clicker screamed. His almost endearing warning was wasted on the police who, unmoved by his threat still ringing through the supermarket, huckled him away, very much alive, to the waiting police van outside. With little time to think, and as true to form as Clicker's beeline for the toiletries, I subconsciously headed for the sanctuary of the bread and pastries section, where I lay under the shelves and watched through a drunken haze as the shiny, seemingly, disembodied boots stomped towards me. Before I knew it, I was getting hauled out from under the shelf by my hair and then kicked as I was dragged along the floor to the entrance. 'It's no even sore anyway!' I shouted in drunken defiance, which only seemed to encourage further and harder blows and had slightly less of the drama than Clicker's rebellious protest. As I was thrown head first into the van, Clicker, lying restrained under two police officers, started laughing and shouted, 'Get in here, ya wee scallywag ye!' Solidarity and sympathy were a definite strong point between the guys at times. The next morning, bruising had come out all the way down my back and across my right shoulder and Clicker sustained cracked ribs, which along with the clearing of several unsolved items on the 'book,' ensured that we were both flung out of the station sober the following morning with a number of fresh charges pending.

Clicker and I remained really good pals over the years and although ultimately going our separate ways in later life, we kept in contact with each other and often made a point of meeting up and having a drink together. Clicker developed mental health problems as an adult and latterly suffered from depression, going off on tangents relating to his increasing sense of worthlessness. Due to our upbringing and the kind of culture within which we existed, both as children and as adults, personal feelings of this nature were never discussed between us in any meaningful way. At the age of 38, Clicker finally succumbed to depression and life's pressures and threw himself in front of a train. I don't know the exact trigger for this and I guess that no one ever will, but I miss him at times and still feel guilty periodically that I wasn't there for him in his time of need.

As life trundled on beyond my 15 birthday, I was by now pretty much living by my own rules and my relationship with my maw was becoming more and more of an anomaly. Historically, responsibility for delinquency in children was, and still is in many quarters, laid squarely at the feet of the parents. However, in my maw's case she had so many complex and demanding needs of her own. Despite this, she tried frequently to dissuade me from getting into trouble and would be openly critical of my behaviour and the impact it was having on both me and the rest of the family, but like me, she could only operate within the oppressive confines of her own world. This said, she would *also* be fiercely protective of me should anyone else dare criticise me and particularly in her dealings with the police when they came looking for me at the house for one thing or another. 'Can you not just leave the boy alone for two minutes and stop picking on him?' she would say to them sternly as they stood shuffling on the doorstep. As a mother, I guess her maternal instinct was to safeguard me and she probably felt the need to believe that I wasn't this uncontrollable wee monster who was causing so much trouble in the community.

Likewise, I felt compelled to protect *her*: from worrying about me; from my da's abusive behaviour; and from financial hardship where possible. When I had money from a turn, I always made a point of giving her some, telling her that I got it from Jeg's granny for painting her garden shed, or that I had found a purse, or some other tall tale. Again, whenever I took a couple of bags of food home from a turn, I would tell her that Margaret Clark had dropped them off earlier, or the like. I strongly suspect that she knew where the money and/or the food came from, but fabricating the source and the subsequent unspoken words between us during such moments, ensured that both our roles were protected I suppose.

Admittedly, I was perhaps less successful than I hoped in protecting her from the general worry I was causing her, as her face seemed to be permanently etched with that tired, worried expression only a mother can wear. I would sometimes sit silently at home with her on the couch, late at night, ridden with guilt at the trouble I was causing her but feeling powerless to change this, or indeed comfort her in any significant way.

Adding to her seemingly unending woes around this period, my brothers, Jerry and Billy, also began getting into trouble, which on reflection, I suppose had a degree of inevitability given the environment they also were subject to. When aged around nine, Billy, by then already no stranger to trouble, got involved in a playground fight at school and apparently tried to stab someone. It materialised that, for reasons still unknown to everyone else except himself, he had slipped my maw's potato knife into his school bag one day and had taken to carrying it to school on a regular basis.

The subsequent fight and Billy's attempted use of this knife on the other pupil, as you can imagine, proved a fairly significant incident locally, particularly given his age and the eventual repercussions. A school outing which had been arranged for the following week and which had been planned for months beforehand, was immediately cancelled and the playground was heavily and stringently monitored by staff for months afterwards like a junior penitentiary. In addition to this, the incident reached a national newspaper which publicly condemned the decision to punish the whole school because of one tiny knife wielding thug, rendering our Billy the most unpopular pupil *ever* to grace St. Brendan's Primary school in Saltcoats.

Similarly, 13-year-old Jerry and his pals were starting to get involved in trouble, manifesting more as nuisance or disruptive behaviour than anything more serious, but occasionally including breaking into garden huts and suchlike. Although I was very much pre-occupied with my own brand of deviance, I loved Jerry and Billy dearly and worried constantly about them. I could still remember how I had felt when I was lifted and put in the cells for the first time, and when I was taken to the centre, and all the subsequent hassles I had experienced at the hands of the police and my teachers and I did not want any of this for them. I was also acutely conscious of the distress that I was already causing my maw and I did not want them adding to it.

Although I was only two years older than Jerry, I was far more mature in many ways and was generally overprotective of him to the point of being suffocatingly paternalistic, and Jerry unquestionably accepted this assumed authority, if not expected it. I suppose, looking back, it not only afforded him a measure of protection, but gave him some kind of boundaries that were not otherwise forthcoming from other sources. If anyone was giving him hassle I would just steam right into them with my boots and fists and whenever I saw him hanging around the shops, venturing into the Street, or associating with certain individuals who were known for trouble, I would chase him home. Despite my own experiences of getting into trouble, I would administer my own form of 'tough love'—a kick in the arse—to Jerry and Billy without fully acknowledging at the time, I suppose, that this type of punitive approach had failed miserably and consistently in providing an incentive for *me* to stop offending. As an older brother with a 'reputation' I was afforded some sway and influence over them and sought to take full advantage of it whenever I could.

Around this period, an explosion of hormones and escalating sexual awareness was strongly challenging notions of getting into trouble, football and policing my wee brothers, as my main leisure pursuit. I briefly became involved with a lassie from the 'shorefront', an affluent residential area of Ardrossan where the large detached houses overlooked the beach, creating a picturesque and exclusive setting.

Phyllis Porter was a rather portly 15-year old girl with a tight bonnet of black hair, a rounded face and almond shaped eyes, whose clothing, although tastefully plain, was of good quality, which in my book translated as expensive. She knew of my reputation from school, despite her attending a neighbouring school, and I think I intrigued her a bit and symbolised in many respects, her brief adolescent rebelliousness. As per our prior arrangements, I went down to her house to meet her one evening, as she had strenuously assured me that her parents were not going to be in; I would never have contemplated going near her house otherwise. 'Come in, come in, you big scaredy', she teased as she opened the front door to me and dragged me in by the hand. 'Are you sure that your maw and da urny in?' I asked nervously, as I nimbly entered the house, only ever used to entering such domiciles through the back window. 'They had a blazing row last night and probably won't both be home till late,' she said softly trying to reassure me.

Standing in the entrance hall surveying the plush surroundings, I sarcastically, if not needlessly defensively, blurted out in Tourettes-like fashion, 'Your da's no a brickie then, eh?' 'No, I'm an accountant actually,' boomed a man's voice behind me unexpectedly. Startled, I turned to see a plump, suited man behind me shaking the rain from a long black pointed umbrella, his jowls vibrating in unison, with a velocity reflecting his enthusiasm for the act. My initial feeling was one of dread and regret and I was instantly unsettled standing before this man of such seeming authority and social standing.

'Pour dad a drink, darling,' he said to Phyllis as he struggled to get out of his jacket. 'Don't be ignorant, dad, this is Allan,' she said to him before setting off to fix his drink, thus hopelessly abandoning me instead of spearheading my rescue as I had hoped she might. I was painfully self-conscious, standing there in front of him as he stared quietly at me in a hostile manner. 'What's your name, lad?' he asked abruptly, less out of interest than for the purposes of assessment and evaluation. 'Weaver, Allan Weaver,' I replied, quite unsure how to deal with this situation. 'Where do you live?' he continued. 'Up the scheme.' What scheme?' The top end of Saltcoats. 'What school do you go to?' The interrogation continued, as my discomfort soon turned to resentment towards this fat man before me. I stood staring silently into his piercing eyes; the atmosphere tangibly charged as he stood momentary motionless, speechless, holding my stare. Just at that moment, Phyllis glided back into the hallway and with one swooping movement put his drink into his hand and grabbed mine, pulling me right out of the open door. 'See you later!' she shouted over her shoulder. 'Nice meetin' you, Mr Porter,' I added smugly over mine as I skipped down the driveway with his beloved daughter in tow.

Thinking that I would get a serious bit of winching done as my house was supposedly empty, I suggested to Phyllis that we went up to my place, which was definitely to prove one of my more ill-conceived ideas. As we approached the house, I noticed that it was in complete darkness. My heart lurched into a painful, almost fatal thump and my throat tightened in anticipation with the intuitive knowledge that something untoward had happened. From years of experience, I had learned that my gut instinct was never far wrong, the product of its own aching tuition since early childhood.

The front door was ajar. I swung it open, warily, while rooted to the doorstep; with no reaction forthcoming, I crept tentatively into the darkened house, entirely forgetting that Phyllis was with me. On reaching the living room, I again stood still as I quietly and slowly swung the door open, not knowing what to expect. I could feel an unexpected draught chilling my face and as I turned the light on, I saw immediately that the place had been wrecked. The wall unit had been pulled to the ground and its contents lay strewn across the floor, smashed; the television had been hurled against the far wall and lay in pieces; the suite had been upended, thrown across the room and slashed with a knife or something. I could see items of furniture and ornaments lying in the garden, obviously thrown right through the windows and the draught that I could feel was coming from the front windows; every pane of glass had been smashed and I watched, stunned, as the curtains flapped, dancing eerily with a life of their own, emphasising the menacing stillness.

All the pictures on the living room walls had been smashed or torn down with the exception of one. This remained untouched, offering an unnecessary clue as to who was responsible for this chaos. It was a photograph of my da's younger brother, James, leaning out of a hospital window as a young boy some months before he died from leukaemia. The same scene of destruction was evident in the kitchen. Every piece of crockery had been smashed, drawers upturned and scattered on the floor. What little food there was had been emptied in a pile in the middle of the kitchen and seemingly ground into the floor. Items of kitchen furniture had been thrown through the kitchen window and lay in the back garden. A tugging on my hand brought me back to my senses as I felt Phyllis's fingers tighten fearfully around mine. Looking shocked and terrified she whispered, 'Do you think the burglar might still be in the house?' Aye, I thought to myself, he'll be in the house alright, lying in his bed drunk. 'Naw they'll be long gone,' I replied making her none the wiser.

Having ushered Phyllis quietly outside, I quickly checked the rest of the house to make sure that my maw and wee brothers weren't in. They had obviously performed the normal drill and sought sanctuary in someone else's house, most likely Margaret's. Nevertheless, I quietly searched the house and, having satisfied myself that they were not at home, I crept up to my maw and da's room and held my breath as I slowly pushed the door open with my fingertips. From the light of a lamppost immediately outside the bedroom window, I could see my da's unperturbed figure lying sleeping, alone, on top of the bed, fully dressed. Standing staring at him from the darkened doorway, I felt a seething hatred for him and wanted to knife him as he lay defenceless and indifferent on the bed. I could even set fire to the house and leave him lying in his drunken stupor, I thought, as I visualised the complete devastation downstairs.

Perhaps fortunately, my train of thought was broken by Phyllis's voice as she shouted to me from outside the house, worrying that something had happened to me. Before leaving, I took the photograph of his dead brother from the living room wall and, knowing how precious it was to him, I tore it to shreds, went back up to his room and threw the pieces of the picture all over him. This minor act at least afforded me some form of revenge, some way of inflicting a measure of pain. As usual, the house was patched up and returned to what we considered to be relative normality within several days. Nothing was said of the incident that I recall and nothing was ever mentioned about the picture of his brother. Just after this incident, Phyllis dumped me and, when I tried to phone her at home, her father answered the phone and told me in no uncertain terms never to contact his daughter again.

CHAPTER 10

A Night at the Theatre (the Hospital Variety)

Despite the fact that I disliked school increasingly and was engaging in ever more disruptive behaviour, resulting in a 'belting' every other day and/or brief periods of suspensions, I did, nevertheless, begin to enjoy my English class when I was actually in attendance. This was, initially, due to the personality, and perhaps perseverance, of my English teacher, Mrs Robertson, whose constructive approach and teaching style stood out in direct contrast to anything I had earlier experienced.

Mrs Robertson treated her pupils equally as individuals worthy of respect; she appeared to have no preconceptions about any one person and this non-judgemental approach enabled her to focus on actively encouraging and involving her students in the class work; it is perhaps no coincidence that I grew quickly to enjoy this particular class and in turn developed a liking for the subject matter. I liked the form of escape I was afforded through creative essay writing, albeit fleetingly, as it allowed me to be whoever I wanted to be, within a setting of my own choice, overcoming the ordinary, everyday restrictions which confined me to an ever decreasing sphere of experience.

Initially I would write dark, sombre stories inhabited by cruel characters and gory endings. Rather than chide me, however, Mrs Robertson checked my work and then quietly set me a 'challenge,' that I had to include a 'laughing' character and 'bright summer sunshine' in every other essay I wrote. The thought of the 'laughing' man hacking away at his terrified victim with a machete in the bright 'summer sunshine,' did not quite have the same effect, so acknowledging her point somewhat, I was subsequently forced to change my plots and characters to a less disturbing framework. As my interest in the subject flourished, I would lose myself totally in essay writing in particular, whenever I attended school.

One day, ensuring that I was first to arrive for this particular lesson and thus alone in the classroom before the rest of the pupils meandered in, I sheepishly raised my hand. 'These stories that we're writing Mrs Robertson, dis anybody else read them?' Perhaps acknowledging my anxiety, she smiled and replied gently, 'Only if you want them to.' 'Naw ... naw, ah'd rather they didnae,' I replied all too quickly, no doubt confirming her suspicions. I was mortified at the thought of anyone else reading what I had written, as I had progressively developed a narrative style and plot formation reminiscent of Enid Blyton with the laughing characters running barefoot through the sun-baked cornfields in the sleepy English counties, in their efforts to solve a range of perplexing local mysteries.

Around this period of my life, I stumbled upon another path of self-discovery and route into escapism: the local museum. One day I was truanting alone and in order to avoid a sudden downpour I went into the Saltcoats Museum, as most of the shop owners were, by now, wise to my antics and were unlikely to be persuaded that my unwelcome presence, whilst not for the purpose of shopping, was for anything as innocuous as shelter. Lurking in the porch, at the doorway, I happened to look in the building and was immediately distracted by some mannequins dressed in Victorian clothing. After a few minutes of nervous hesitation, my curiosity got the better of me; I quietly entered the building and began examining the models more attentively. I was equally struck by the short written notices accompanying each one which briefly described life in Saltcoats in the previous century. With an unprecedented, insatiable curiosity, I proceeded to examine the other exhibits in great detail and, before I knew it, I had spent several hours there. I developed there a fascination for the town's history that has never left me, about how people lived their lives then and how the town subsequently developed. As I became a regular visitor I would scrutinise the exhibits repeatedly and pore tirelessly over the multiple books of old photographs of the town and its people. I would even sometimes engineer my own exploratory excursions, or field trips as I conceived of them, outside the museum to locate the original, historic sites of old buildings. I was mesmerised.

The museum was staffed by an elderly, somewhat disinterested, male attendant and, as very few people ever visited the place, this seemed to afford it even more value and importance to me—a trouble free environment within which to immerse myself. Getting used to my regular visits, presumably, he would just wave over to me on my arrival with a welcome smile and make some random comment about the weather. Not befitting of my reputation, I never told anyone of my museum visits, particularly not the guys, and would sometimes create fictitious situations to allow for my museum visits when we were all together. On approach, and employing the skills I had acquired from numerous break-ins, I would scan the area carefully to ensure that I was never seen entering or leaving the building.

Naturally, there were times when I was unable to escape into my own world, and, whenever I dragged myself along, the mundane existence of school persisted as a mandatory requirement that I intermittently chose to comply with. However, timetabled into my schedule were the more sinister practices of a certain temporary supply teacher, Mr McCaig. During his short stint at the school, he was both the bane of my educational life and my art teacher; he told us that he had been a rugby hopeful before embarking on a career in education. To his perpetual disappointment and my eternal delight, having barely even played for the reserve team for a brief period, he was subsequently invited to leave the club, as he had fallen short of the required standard.

I had many spats with him during my time at school and I had disliked the man from the outset as he was a bully of a man who seemed to take out his resentment at life on a certain calibre of pupil; myself predictably included, despite my artistic endeavours. As I was unable to meet him head on at any level, I took a quiet satisfaction and pleasure from the knowledge that he now, less enviably, taught brushstrokes for a living from school to school as an alternative to the glamour and fame of the rugby circuit as the hero of his and every other boy's dreams.

It was within weeks of my da devastating the house, that I found myself sitting in McCaig's class, one wet winter afternoon, as he bleated on and on in his relentless monotone about some modern artist that the curriculum had dictated as being crucial to our future functioning in society. As I was both bored and tired, I nodded off momentarily whilst sitting at the back of the class only to be awakened by a sharp, searing pain inflicted by McCaig who had crept up the aisles between the desks and snapped a wooden ruler over my exposed hand. Embarrassed more by the laughter of the other pupils, I quickly pulled myself upright on the chair as I rubbed the painful welt on my hand. 'Were the police cells busy at the weekend, then?' he asked presumptuously, as he played brazenly to his juvenile audience. Encouraged by several stifled titters he continued as he stood over me, 'Well come on ... what do you have to say for yourself?' Mortified and resenting this public ridicule, I retorted, 'Don't take it oot on me because you're a poxy music teacher.' The class fell deathly silent and McCaig's sneer contorted his face as it darkened with a menacing rage.

Dismissing the rest of the class quickly, he turned and wordlessly signalled to me to remain seated, with a crudely pointed finger. McCaig was a tall, athletic looking man, perhaps even six foot two, which served to enhance his intimidating demeanour. As he closed the door behind the last of the hastily departing pupils, he turned to me and said quietly, in a measured, threatening tone: 'Come on, delinquent, you haven't got much to say for yourself now,' as he walked towards me, with a degree of restrained purposefulness. I stood fidgeting, alone at the back of the classroom as my heart pounded loudly in my chest. 'Not so fucken' smart now,' he hissed, as he towered over me and without warning, punched me hard in the stomach. As I doubled over, he grabbed the back of my hair and yanked me upwards until I was straining on tiptoes to try and lessen the searing pain in the back of my head. 'Is there something you want to say now, lad?' he spat through a perverted grin. 'Aye' I spluttered unable to speak properly through pain and rage, 'You're jist an arsehole.' He then punched me again in the stomach, this time letting me slump to the floor. 'Get up and leave my classroom' he said in a different tone of voice as if trying to introduce some form of moral justification into the situation, just like the countless other professionals who seemed to devote their careers to battering and condemning the likes of me for failing to adhere to *their* so-called codes of decent behaviour. I knew by his demeanour that there would be no more violence and, with not another word spoken, I held myself together, quietly gathered up my belongings and left his classroom.

Some 20 years after this incident, I was astonished to read in a newspaper article that McCaig had been suspended from another school around three years earlier after being arrested for shoplifting. With the help of his union, however, he was reinstated and for reasons that were not fully explained further criminal proceedings were not pursued. Rather, he took the subsequent liberty of filing a lawsuit against the store detective and one Sunday broadsheet in particular followed the entire process with great interest and reported that, following a protracted civil court case, McCaig's claim was successful and he was awarded damages. It would have been more appropriate if some of his pupils had sued him.

The school holidays just prior to my fourth year at school brought a fairly predictable pattern of behaviour and with no real structure to our day and, left pretty much to our own devices, we continued to create our own entertainment in several different ways. I had more money at my disposal, than I had ever known, acquired through various turns, which I would generally just splash around, surrendering myself to the self-gratification of the moment. Like most boys my age, I was becoming more aware of my own identity and in turn I was increasingly conscious of my image; my more generous financial circumstances meant that I was now able to buy the clothes that reflected the image I wanted to portray. This was a vastly improved state of affairs as I saw it, compared to my earlier fashion crimes when, desperate for the latest trends and with no means of procuring them, the guys and I would creep around peoples' back gardens under the cover of darkness scouring for decent clothes on the washing lines. It certainly gave 'off the peg' a whole new meaning.

The return of the fairground during the summer months always signalled a return to the fighting season and with cheap wine aplenty, in our pristine new togs, we generally embraced this with an enthusiasm usually reserved for the gentry attending Ascot. It was during one such time that we ended up in a fight with guys from Maxwell Road. Maxwell Road was another deprived area in Saltcoats categorised by its *own* distinct subculture in the area. It had its own close knit community, in which the majority of residents were Protestant with clear Loyalist leanings, and where the local Orange Walks would assemble before marching amid a sea of red, white and blue bunting, which of course made them our natural enemies. Rarely deviating from their own patch, this gang had a fearsome reputation borne from their tendency to inflict brute violence upon anyone who strayed into their territory, inadvertently or otherwise. That said, they lacked both panache and character!

This particular clash occurred after a rather uneventful night at the fairground; somewhat disappointedly and definitely the worse for wear, Jeg, Watty, Jimmy Newell and I left to head back to the Street. As we staggered along the road, oblivious to our surroundings, we suddenly became aware of the Maxwell Road mob lurking in a doorway some way up. 'Whit are you looking at, ya drunken bastarts!' shouted Big Johnny Johnstone at us. Not the brightest of the gang, Johnstone was a burly guy who liked to throw his weight around whenever the opportunity arose. Undeterred by the difference in numbers, we stood our ground and considerately obliged the mob by trading insults as per expectations, culminating in Jeg drunkenly trying to focus out of one eye as he shouted, 'Here, JJ, get ower here and gies aw a big kiss!' Naturally, this apparent assault upon his masculinity had the predictable effect of provoking Johnstone to lead the gang to retaliate by launching empty milk bottles in our direction, which smashed noisily all around us. 'Dirty bastarts!' I shouted, and as Jeg grabbed me, we bobbed and weaved away together to avoid the missiles in our very own version of *Last Tango in Paris*. Meanwhile, Jimmy's contribution was to throw a half-empty beer can at them and run in the opposite direction; we did not see him again for six months. Jimmy was at school with us and was a decent enough guy, but he was not heavily involved in trouble like the rest of us and as such I never held his panicked departure against him. He was from a big family, and because his maw and da worked full time, and provided well for them all, they lived in a more desirable area of the town than the rest of us. Mind you, his maw worked as a ticket collector on the buses and several years previously when my maw was talking about looking for a part time job, my da said it was only whores who worked on the buses. As I first got to know Jimmy, I always wondered to myself how he felt about his maw being a whore.

Jimmy was gone and Watty was hot on his heels as the Maxwell Road guys descended on me and Jeg, leaving us with considerably fewer options when it came to the fight-or-flight gamble. Jeg was blatantly drunker than me and seemingly oblivious to the fact that there were only two of us left, which might explain why he took a wild swing at one of them, missed his target completely and landed on the ground with a clatter. Before we knew it they were on top of us kicking and punching any part of us that moved. In an attempt to protect the by now defenceless Jeg, I scrambled to my feet and stood over him, swinging a plastic bag with four beer cans in it like a crazed dipsomaniac, momentarily succeeding in keeping them at arm's length. 'Come on, ya bastarts!' I shouted as I swung the bag like a man demented. However, with my arms tiring rapidly, I could not hold onto the bag any longer and let it go mid-swing; the bag fired off on its own loyal course hitting one of them square in the face with a clunk. As the struggle, continued, unbeknown to me, one of them managed to manoeuvre behind me; he gave me little time to rejoice in my brief moment of victory before he crashed an empty wine bottle full force over the back of my head and, as I began to fall under the increasingly swirling sky, he stabbed the jagged edge of it hard into my neck. With the blood spurting uncontrollably, I immediately felt sick and began falling into darkness as a woman's voice screamed loudly for someone to get an ambulance, the boots still battering into me. I then lost consciousnesses.

As I came to, I realised that I was being wheeled along to a hospital theatre; every clatter of the trolley felt like a further stabbing as waves of pain and nausea engulfed me, the overhead corridor lights jarring me back to a painful consciousness at ten-yard intervals. As I tried to sit up, two hospital attendants kept me firmly pinned down on the trolley and tried to calm me down as I launched into a tirade of abuse about them, about Johnstone, about everyone. I hated the world. I awoke the next morning on a hospital bed with my blood soaked into the pillow case and covers and, as I discovered immediately to my cost, I was unable to move my upper body at all due to the searing and crippling pain in my neck and the throbbing ache in my head. I had required over 30 stitches to patch the wounds in my head and neck. With the effects of the anaesthetic still muddying my brain, I lay there willing myself to think of vengeance. I could not be seen to let this go; I could not lose face. Despite my best efforts, however, and my need to lie in a rigid corpse-like position, I could not really move beyond the incredible sense of loneliness I felt.

For the first week after the assault I moped about the house in pain, feeling vulnerable both emotionally and physically, and I consciously avoided the guys for this reason. My maw was worried sick, making a terrible fuss over me and for the whole week I don't think she ever let me leave her side. 'You'll need to get yourself back to school, son, and stop getting into so much trouble,' she chided gently as she swabbed delicately at my wounds to keep them clean. My da made no reference to what had happened as I sat at home grimacing in pain and unable to move properly for fear of bursting the stitches. With my mobility all but returned the following week, I could not suffer my self-imposed exile any longer and alternatively ventured out to the sanctuary of Margaret's office on several occasions.

For several months, I seemed to have the same appointment schedule as Jeanette McGoogan, who would be routinely sitting in the social work waiting room when I arrived to see a different social worker. Big Jeanette lived near the Street with her husband and five weans and was always in the social work office looking for money or handouts of some sort; although she was probably not much younger than my maw, she looked permanently harried and significantly older. The McGoogan family were worse off than most of us, and lived in what can only be described as abject poverty; my maw would sometimes discreetly give them some of our old clothes for her weans and warned us all within an inch of our lives never to mention this, for fear of embarrassing the McGoogan weans. I always suspected that Jeanette's weans only had one pair of shoes between them to wear, which they shared on a rota basis, as you never ever saw two of them out together.

Big Jeanette was a large heavy woman, who was not renowned for her personal hygiene and who always reminded me of the comedian, Les Dawson's toothless housewife character, as she sat opposite me supporting her massive bosoms with her meaty folded arms, her lips clapped in around her toothless mouth. Sitting in the waiting room just staring straight ahead, she would suck away on a roll up cigarette and then begin moving it around her lips without ever touching it with her hand. When she was finished, she would just sit and gob it across the floor. With something of a shudder, I could not help but wonder if wee Eric, the doubt and discarded chewing gum eater, was going to chew on that particular one the next time he was in at the office with his mother. Her chair would then creak away painfully under her weight as she manoeuvred her heavy frame on the awkwardly designed seats, post-cigarette, in search of a more comfortable position.

'Ah heard you git stabbed last week,' she said without looking at me as we sat alone in the waiting room. Unsure whether to treat this as a statement or a question and deciding quickly on the latter, I replied, 'Aye, it wis jist a daft fight, Mrs McGoogan.' Assumingly in reference to her husband Robert, she returned immediately as if oblivious to what I had just said, 'Ah mind when ma Boaby wis stabbed.' Scanning her expressionless face, I was again unsure if this was an upsetting memory on big Jeanette's part, or indeed an admission, as I sat looking at her pensively, waiting on the details. However, she just continued to sit staring ahead, silently. Margaret appeared a short time later to interrupt this stimulating social interaction and as I was leaving the waiting room, Jeanette said in her normal trance like manner without moving a muscle, 'You'll put that mither of yours in an early grave.'

The guy who stabbed me became heavily involved in glue sniffing and following a sniffing session some months later, hung himself from a tree. I am ashamed to say that, at the time, I was glad to hear of this in many ways as I was no longer required to execute my half-planned act of vengeance. The crude physical scar that I still carry and the periodic pain in my neck ensures that the memories of this particular encounter remain with me.

CHAPTER 11

On the Rampage — Living Up to 'Type'

Having started my fourth and final year at school and with the summer assault well behind me, the drinking and impromptu parties continued like an alternative subcultural education of sorts. At 15, like most other adolescents of this age craving a kind of quasi adult status, parties were becoming more frequent social events for us. These were normally hastily arranged affairs in the absence of unsuspecting parents and, given our reputation for trouble, naturally, personal invites for me and the guys were never forthcoming, but we always got to hear of the events anyway.

One cold bleak October's night, with nowhere else to go, we all gatecrashed Alice Peter's party in Ardrossan. Because Alice went to our school, we all knew that she lived in Kirkhall Drive in Ardrossan. Kirkhall Drive was built before World War II and consisted of a medley of houses and tenement flats; it had historically been a slum area in which were housed Ardrossan's poorest and most troublesome families. Even then, I used to wonder how specific areas and streets like New England Road, Maxwell Street or Kirkhall Drive came to be so disadvantaged. Was it a kind of chicken and egg syndrome — did the person create the area, or the area the person — or was it rather more of a destructive symbiotic relationship? Did anyone care?

Either way, Alice was born and bred in Kirkhall Drive, and had grown into a painfully thin lassie with a pinched face, which housed decaying teeth and something of a haunted expression. Alice appeared to blend like a chameleon into her surroundings; a human manifestation of her physical environment. She lived with her chronically alcoholic mother and two elder brothers in a two-bedroom flat, her da having left the family when Alice was a toddler. As we were initially unsure *exactly* where Alice lived, Jeg, Clicker, Eddie, Auldy, Watty, wee Shuggie and I staggered up and down the street with our carry out in hand, listening intently for signs of a party. Hugh McIvor — wee Shuggie — originated from Glasgow somewhere and his family had moved to Saltcoats when he was aged around 12, thinking ironically that it would provide a better environment for Shuggie and his older brother. Although they were a fairly stable family, this became increasingly unlikely as he became more and more mixed up in our company.

On this night in particular, we were marauding up and down different garden paths in Kirkhall Drive with wee Shuggie cupping his ear with his hand, listening through the letterboxes for signs of a party. As the drunken banter increased, one guy opened his front door quickly, to be confronted by Shuggie bent over with his ear pressed against his open letter box, Jeg and Watty peeing on his flower bed and the rest of us standing there swigging from wine bottles. As quick as a flash, wee Shuggie straightened up and half-shook his beer can at the man in an inspired improvisation of a collecting tin. 'Eh …. Spastic weans …. we're collectin' for spastic weans, mate.' 'Whit the fuck?' the guy murmured in disbelief at the sight in front of him. 'Spastic weans? av already got a gairden full of spastic weans, so get to fuck the lot of you before a phone the polis!' he hollered. 'Ah take it that's a naw then, ya miserable auld prick!' wee Shuggie shouted back as we all bolted from the garden.

Several tenement buildings later, we finally located the party as the strains of Candi Staton's 'Young Hearts Run Free' echoed through one particular close. 'Alice … you're the best lookin burd in ma remedial English class, ya wee stouter!' shouted our smooth talking Clicker as Alice opened the door to us with a look of sheer horror on her face. This look rapidly turned to one of embarrassment as we piled in and followed her into her living room.

A motley crew of her friends and neighbours sat in a dingy, sparsely furnished living room drinking out of stained mugs. The carpet was matted with stale drink and cigarette burns; the curtains hung off, rather than from, the window frame; and large patches of wallpaper had turned a kind of nicotine-coloured yellow through dampness. The place was completely dilapidated yet, pathetically, in pride of place in the living room was her cheap, plastic record player belting out the music. 'Grab a cup,' Alice suggested meekly with no eye contact as Jeg and Clicker tripped over themselves to grab one before she finished the sentence. Scanning the cracked and dirty cups, I declined the offer and decided to swig from my own bottle.

Poor Alice's party passed in something of a blur. Her friends, wary of our presence, had long since left, along with Candi Staton who had since been replaced by raucous rebel songs. We all sat drinking ourselves senseless as, characteristically, Auldy struggled to unravel the meaning of life, Watty was starting to poke around the living room for anything of value and Eddie sat brooding on the neck of his bottle. Sensing an opportunity, Clicker catapulted himself towards it like a dog in heat as he and Alice left the room together only to return a short time later, flushed and breathless to announce their engagement.

After Clicker and Alice had come back, Watty, with similar opportunism slinked out of the room and after an even briefer period returned with his hands and pockets full of 50 pence pieces. 'We're loaded man … the meter was full to the brim!' he shouted excitedly as he sat down to count the money. Realising that he had broken into Alice's meter, rage welled up inside me. 'For Christ's sake, Watty … that's bang out of order,' I said struggling to prise myself from the couch. I was still pissed off with him for doing a runner and leaving me and Jeg to face the Maxwell Street guys ourselves; however as he was not a fighter, I did not really pursue the matter with him. Nevertheless, tonight he had broken one rule too many. Steadying myself on my feet, I swung a kick at the pile of money on the floor in front of Watty's hunched figure, sending it scattering noisily all over the living room. 'You're bang out of order!' I shouted at Watty, as he sat quiet and shamefaced on the floor. While everyone fell into a guilt infused silence, Alice appeared totally unconcerned as she whispered absorbedly to Clicker, 'Just think, Click, we could buy a ring wi' aw that money'—more lost in her dreams than in the reality of the situation. Poor bastard, I thought, as I sat back down shaking my head in silent drunken bewilderment, not much chance of Phyllis Porter relying on her meter money for her engagement ring. By way of a compromise and as a means of squaring things up between us, we agreed to leave Alice money for fags, albeit with a degree of reluctance on Watty's part, before leaving the house in the early hours of the morning.

We were quieter than normal as we walked through the cold, deserted streets towards Saltcoats until we found ourselves walking past our school, which appeared to impel Watty to reflexively suggest breaking into it. 'For fuck's sake, Watty,' said Clicker, 'I think you like thievin' better than shaggin', man.' As Watty and Clicker launched into a philosophical debate on the relative merits of thieving and sex we gravitated, unthinkingly, towards the school yard. On reaching it, we collectively stood, steadying ourselves with one hand each, as we concentrated on peeing against the wall, only to be startlingly thrown off course by an almighty crash—which for some had fairly damp consequences. Wee Shuggie had lifted a dustbin and launched it through a ground floor classroom window. 'No way, man. Ahm off hame', exited Auldy in a suddenly sober panic, immediately followed by Clicker. 'Of course it's better than shaggin!' Watty shouted after them excitedly as he upturned another dustbin and prepared to enter the school.

The utility of the dustbins would provide some weight to arguments for situational crime prevention but as far as we were concerned, we were just being resourceful as, laughing, we climbed up after Watty, each manoeuvring comically and clumsily through the broken window. Totally oblivious to the shards of glass still hanging menacingly in the frame and to our shoes grating on the broken glass, we noisily entered the school through the history classroom. Triumphantly, we walked around the room looking in cupboards, drawers, desks, more inquisitive than malicious. 'Right listen up, imbeciles!' boomed Jeg in an exaggerated, hackneyed impression of a teacher as he sat at the front desk, peering at us through what must have been the teacher's spare reading glasses which were eccentrically cocked on the tip of his nose with the black teaching cape thrown over his shoulders. We appreciatively began pelting him with sticks of chalk, getting into character ourselves, as he dived under the desk, admirably maintaining his role with a little too squeaky, 'Leave my class immediately, you riff raff!'

Wanting a piece of this ourselves, we swept into the neighbouring classrooms with the decorum of a herd of running wildebeest, switching lights on as we went, emptying cupboards, desks and drawers until we each had a teaching cape. The five of us stormed through the corridors on the ground floor like a pomposity of mad professors lighting up the building, shouting, swearing, laughing and singing as we went, capes flapping behind us like anti-heroes. Ignoring the locked classrooms we continued to move through the corridors as if on a pre-programmed collision course, utterly unstoppable.

When we reached Martin Mullen's office on the first floor, I knew that this was too good an opportunity to pass by; a locked door here was not now going to be an obstacle. 'Come on, guys, we need to get in here,' I said as we all gathered round the door. 'Come on lets get the fucken' door kicked in, man!' shouted Eddie as he began kicking away at the door like a man possessed, every kick met by a loud, encouraging cheer from the rest of us. 'Go on, Big Eddie ... go on big man ... jist wan mare,' we shouted supportively. After six or seven kicks, the door frame creaked and groaned under the strain, then finally crashed open. We danced around excitedly like some demented liberating army, capes still flapping away ridiculously as Mullen's office door lay battered and conquered before us. As we all knew from our frequent visits to the office, a small table stood in the middle of the floor with low cushioned seats surrounding it, obviously designed and constantly prepared for some kind of staff meeting with Mullen's big oak desk sitting at the top of the office, symbolising his authority. After the initial storm, and at a loss really to know what to do next, we threw ourselves onto the seats, exhausted and still drunk.

As we all sat about catching our breath, wee Shuggie and Jeg got up and began to rifle through Mullen's desk. We sat and watched as wee Shuggie slyly took Mullen's belt from his desk drawer, proceeded to sneak round behind Jeg, who was rifling through the other set of desk drawers and cracked him right over the backside with the belt. 'McCleary, you useless, ugly bastard!' he screamed with two or three other hearty slaps in quick succession before chasing the fleeing and screeching Jeg around the office. Getting back into the spirit of things, we all hollered and laughed loudly. Amid the fracas, Eddie got up and began looking through the drawers of a filing cabinet nearby. Steel filing cabinets lined two walls of the office, all of which had keys in them. Very security conscious, I thought, as Eddie nosed through them intently. 'Christ' sake, Watty, here's your file,' said Eddie as he began flicking through it.

With this, the rest of the guys catapulted themselves at the filing cabinets and began scouring them for any files of interest. 'Here!' shouted Shuggie, scanning a particular file with great interest. 'Listen tae this wan.' Demonstrating that we could indeed be quite attentive at school under the right conditions, we fell into silence as Shuggie, summarising the contents of one particularly interesting section of the file, sensitively informed us: 'Big Shona Turbet got caught in a state of some undress in the guys' toilets at last year's Christmas party.' 'You're a dirty liar!' shouted Jeg defensively as he rushed over and grabbed the file from Shuggie. We all knew that he had a soft spot for big Shona and he had actually gone out with her for a few weeks some months earlier. 'The dirty big cow!' he shouted incredulously, as he read through the report with a look of disbelief, 'Ah never even got to feel her tits', he protested loudly to himself. Unable to maintain straight faces for more than several seconds, we all doubled up in loud hysterical laughter. Given the mayhem of the moment, of course, no-one really gave a thought to this poor unsuspecting lassie.

Silence soon fell as we all became engrossed in our reading. 'Here, read this wan, Weavy ... should be a laugh,' said Shuggie throwing a thick file down beside me as I was mulling over the personal information of yet another classmate. It was my own file, which unlike the other files I had read had a small photo booth type picture of me clipped to the inside cover—where that particular gem of a portrait originated from still remains a mystery to me.

I experienced a surge of anger and resentment as I began to read through the reports. McCaig, the child beater, had written, 'Refuses to engage and shows no interest whatsoever …. disrupts the class at every opportunity …. tends to lead other boys astray.' My guidance teacher had written, 'No input from the home and Weaver obviously gets to do what he likes.' Another one highlighted, 'Not long out of assessment centre and mainstream education is perhaps not best suited to his needs.' These people barely knew me, I thought, though being the experts, both they and everyone else *thought* they did; they did not actually need to, I supposed, they knew my type. They rarely even acknowledged me and they did not know what went on in other parts of my life, nor were there ever any attempts to find out. 'So you think you know me!' I shouted bitterly as I stood up and threw the file violently against the wall, papers scattering everywhere. 'Wis it no' a very good report then?' Shuggie asked me sarcastically, yet with a somewhat startled look on his face.

Rightly or wrongly, I felt unjustly treated and without thinking I picked up one of the low cushioned chairs and, holding it above my head, ran towards the wall of windows at the far end of the office and threw it as hard as I could. There was a deafening crash as the chair careered right through the large window pane, bringing a momentary release for me and instilling a shocked silence amongst us all. Still not spent and desperate to anaesthetise the confusing turmoil within me, I shattered the tense silence by picking up another chair and throwing it through another large window pane.

As if on cue, the guys quickly joined in. Chairs were hurtling through the windows, along with every other piece of moveable furniture. Filing cabinets were pulled over, their remaining contents torn from the drawers and scattered all over the office. Remnants of reports, gathered up in the chaos, were swept up and hurled through the smashed windows. School photographs of former pupils were grabbed from the walls and thrown to the floor. 'No' even a photo o' us!' shouted Watty as he picked them up and sciffed them out of the broken windows one by one, like flying saucers sent into orbit. 'Naw oor photos ur in oor files like mugshots!' I shouted, manoeuvring past Watty to lob Mullen's coat stand after the exiting flying saucers. I then threw the last chair through a window; refusing to be ignored or excluded, I was going to make my presence felt. 'Big two-timing bastard!' I heard Jeg screaming out his own pained rejection, as he gouged the leg of a chair repeatedly into Mullen's desk top like a man possessed. Every pane of glass in the office was broken and no piece of furniture or equipment remained undamaged.

Teaching capes long since discarded, we staggered, physically and emotionally spent and still drunk, from Mullen's office. Still, I was hell bent on revenge and the guys in some sense were really just caught up in the momentum of this. We returned to the locked classrooms and proceeded to kick the doors open, leaving a trail of utter destruction as we went. We rarely spoke as we worked our way systematically through the school floors. Despite the bedlam we had created, we left the school undetected several hours later.

CHAPTER 12

Juvenile Chain Gang to Barlinnie Prison

'Allan … Allan …Allan,' my maw was saying with a note of agitation in her voice as she shook me from my drunken sleep. 'Waken up … come on … waken up … where the hell were you last night?' As my maw stood over me I lay in bed, disorientated, trying to prise my pickled eyes open and make sense of what was happening. 'Whit is it?' I asked, my head thumping and throat burning through dehydration. As I started to come to, I was conscious of the sharp pains I had all over my hands and arms, like hundreds of gnawing little paper cuts; I quickly pulled the bedcovers around me tightly to hide them from my maw. 'What time did you get in last night?' she continued, unable to mask her anger. 'Ah was jist roon at Jegs … nuthin happened … ahm awright'. Quietly and more in resignation than anger, she kind of shuffled from the room.

With little time or capacity to dwell on how my maw was feeling, I dragged myself out of bed; now that I had the chance to give myself a proper inspection, I was alarmed by the number of tell-tale cuts and scratches to my arms and hands and the several deeper gashes on my lower legs, obviously from shards of glass. As I fingered the cuts thoughtfully, the realisation that last night wasn't some kind of surreal dream gradually dawned on me, and instantaneously, the enormity of the events came flooding back to me like a tsunami. 'Shit,' I thought to myself as every act, every movement, every word of the previous night began racing through my conscious mind, until on reaching the conclusions of my rapid, final, unsettling analysis, I came to a halt in the sickening awareness that—no matter what angle anyone cared to look at this from—we were in serious trouble. Feeling beside myself, quite literally, and with a desperate need to extinguish the growing panic, I needed the camaraderie of the guys to reassure me that things weren't that bad. I quickly got dressed, made my way into the toilet and gulped down cup after cup of water from the tap before I slipped out of the house without a word to my oblivious maw.

Jeg, Watty and Eddie, were already in the street when I arrived, each looking uncharacteristically subdued and morose. On seeing me, Watty rushed up and blurted out, in an outward expression of nerves as opposed to an attempt to obtain any form of therapeutic recognition, 'Ma da gave me a right kickin when ah got in last night cause it wis three in the morning and ....' 'Don't mention grief to me,' Jeg said sharply, cutting Watty off, 'ma maw went pure ballistic.' Eddie sat quietly lost in his own thoughts, perhaps wishing that someone had noticed to give him grief; or even a kicking for that matter, as Jeg and Watty argued over who was more harshly treated. Acknowledging my inquisitive look as he hobbled around in his emphatic assertion of suffering, Jeg stammered, 'A lost the heel o' ma shoe last night as well'. Returning to the reality of our situation, I was beginning to realise that the police would find our blood and fingerprints all over the school and, of course, half of Jeg's shoe.

As if the mere thought had been sufficient to secure our fate, a police van and an unmarked police car screeched round the corner and came hurtling down the street towards us catching us all unaware and giving us no real time to react. 'Polis ... it's the fucken polis,' said Jeg in obvious distress, discarding his roll up fag in panic as if at worst he would be reprimanded for smoking, as the vehicles braked to a violent halt in front of us.

It was like a scene from the TV detective drama, *The Sweeney*, when the police exited the vehicles, slamming the doors loudly, and painstakingly avoiding eye contact we moved around the vehicles with somewhat over-rehearsed swaggers befitting the moment. Wullie Steel, one of the CID officers, had taken slightly longer to get out of the car due to his size, which had exerted an unfortunate impact on his every movement, but regaining his composure, he headed towards us, undeterred, with a leering grin on his face, swinging a small clear polythene bag in our direction. On closer inspection, I could see that it contained what looked like the heel of a shoe. Thanks, Jeg.

Wullie Steel had lifted us on a number of occasions in the past and hated us all with a passion; we were the bane of his largely unsuccessful and frustrated career. Although he was not routinely violent towards us, we still knew that he had the capacity to be unpredictable, as had been evident in the past from the odd unprovoked, violent outburst. He was a big dour looking man with a giant beer belly which hung grotesquely over his trousers like a dead weight, and which wobbled repulsively when he over-exerted himself carrying out even the most minor actions. He had a big puffed-up moon face which was unflatteringly exaggerated by his tightly cropped greying hair and tightly fastened collar.

'Good morning, gentlemen,' he said smugly, avoiding any attempt at wit and sarcasm, which he had learnt previously, was liable to backfire. Instead, he settled for taunting us by swinging the bag with part of Jeg's shoe in it slowly in front of us in an irritating, pendulum like fashion, savouring his part, which he had obviously rehearsed in his mind all the way over. 'Have any of you young chaps lost part of your shoe by any chance?' he asked, walking around us slowly, scanning our feet. Realising his fate was by now sealed and before Steel could examine his feet, Jeg held his hands aloft and said in a mock defeated tone, 'Okay, Wullie, it's mine ... it's mine ... I know you found it under your bed along wi' my underpants ...... but tell your missus she can keep them.' Without uttering another word, Steel pounced, grabbed Jeg by the jacket collar and ran him bodily towards the back of the police van. 'Watch the shoes ya fat dick ... watch the shoes,' Jeg struggled to shout as his collar tightened around his neck. Similarly, we were all dragged and bundled forcibly into the back of the van behind him.

When we arrived, the police station was a hub of activity as they were still dealing with the regular aftermath of the havoc created by the weekend's drunks, misfits and vagabonds. We were immediately separated and led to different 'holding' rooms within the CID part of the station and left to await our questioning, with no form of responsible adult present to advocate for us or protect our rights, despite our age and the seriousness of the situation. The endless waiting to be dealt with, or charged and processed was always the worst part of getting lifted and whether or not it was a deliberate psychological ploy, the silence and isolation would unfailingly throw up the worst case scenarios in my tormented mind. *I'll get five years*, I thought as I paced the small room, agitated, like a caged animal, rubbing the betraying cuts in my hands and arms. *What will happen to my maw when I'm away ...? Who'll make sure that my wee brothers are keeping out of trouble ...? When will I get to see the museum again...?* My mind raced through snapshots of a childhood which I knew barely belonged to me anyway. Seeking respite from my anguished thoughts, I pressed my mouth against the gap between the door and the frame and hoarsely straining my voice in cupped hands in an attempt to stifle my shouts, I called: 'Jeg ... are you there .... Jeg?' 'Eddie? Watty?' Startled, I jumped back in fright as the door vibrated fiercely under a hard kick, followed by a booming voice instructing, 'Shut the fuck up in there.'

Through the barred skylight, I could see that darkness had fallen, which could only mean that I had been in the room for at least five hours before the door was suddenly opened up and I was led out again, without explanation or comment. To my surprise I was taken straight through to the charge bar, the final part of the arrest process where the accused is formally charged and placed in the cells. This was a bad sign because it usually indicated that the police had a clear cut, confident case. As I stood at the bar, waiting to be charged, fidgeting and dwarfed beside Steel and several other flanking, uniformed officers, a tall, thin elderly man walked into the area. In an indication of his rank, the officers present turned to him and each greeted him with a respectful, 'Sir.' With an unusually kind face, like someone's benevolent grandfather, he looked at me intently and then sighed. 'Well, Weaver … what are we going to do with you, son?' he said, ignoring the welcomes from his subordinates. 'Whit do you mean?' I asked craning my neck to look up at his face. 'You're in here every week for one thing or another and that poor mother of yours ....' Standing before him silently, I was caught off guard by his personalisation of the situation which resulted in a hasty attempt to deny the pain any thoughts about my maw conjured up. He then turned and walked away briskly. With no opportunity to clear the books this time, Jeg, Watty Eddie and I were charged with theft and malicious damage totalling thousands of pounds; we were to be held in custody under an Unruly Certificate and scheduled to appear on Solemn Procedures at Kilmarnock Sheriff court the following morning.

Saltcoats police station, already well familiar to us, boasted ten cells, five on each side of a small darkened corridor, which was located at the back of the station with a heavy door isolating it from the main building. Each cell was about eight feet square with a barred window on the high ceiling, containing a heavy wooden bench raised about one foot from the floor where prisoners would sleep and a small white lidless ceramic toilet bowl in one corner. There was never any toilet paper and the flush chain was outside the cell, reinforcing in many respects, that the police were even in charge of your very bodily functions; all your basic human rights and sources of self-respect were surrendered. At night each prisoner was given a thin plastic coated mattresses and a flimsy horse type blanket which was coarse and uncomfortable and stained by the constant use of other prisoners. The white marble type bricks in the cell compounded the cold, depressing, bareness of the place, giving it the appearance of a Victorian public toilet befitting the human waste who occupied it. The doors were thick and metallic, with a small serving hatch in the middle where food and the like could be passed through to the prisoners, although if negotiated carefully, you could actually fit your head right through it, as we had discovered some time ago.

As I was led through the back to the cells I could see Jeg, Eddie and Watty through their open hatches, sitting quietly in separate cells. I had already been stripped of my shoes and trouser belt as I was led in to my own cell; we could not be trusted to be responsible, after all our lives still had some worth where there was a conviction to be obtained, and thus protection from self-harm was in *everyone's* interests.

No sooner had I sat on the cell bench when I heard Eddie's desperate voice, 'Weavy, quick … quick come to the hatch.' Manoeuvring my head slowly out of the door hatch, into a position reminiscent of an execution scene from the French Revolution, I saw Eddie's head protruding from the next cell, 'I think we're done fur this time,' he offered insightfully. Joined by Jeg and Watty, we soon clucked away like battery hens as we discussed the legalities of our case and our pending court appearance, without any concrete idea of what could be facing us. With each of us putting on a brave face and ignoring the pain in our necks, we bantered for some time and at one point even broke into our own version of the American Southern Blues song, 'Working on the Chain Gang.' Anyone overhearing the jovialities could easily have mistaken it for a boisterous school outing.

As our laughter and voices reached a shrilling crescendo, the custody officer unlocked the corridor door and entered the cell area. 'Right, the hatches are getting shut …. this isnae a bloody comedy show!' he bellowed as our heads darted inside the cell doors for cover. 'Can you no keep them open?' asked Watty with a note of panic in his voice, no doubt at the prospect of returning to his isolation and thoughts, 'We'll be quieter … ah promise,' he pleaded. Ignoring Watty completely, the police officer walked along the corridor slamming our hatches shut. 'Ya big fat poof,' came Jeg's muffled tone behind his closed hatch as the officer walked up the corridor unruffled, with his keys jangling noisily at his side. 'Sleep well, lads, sleep well!' he shouted just before he banged the main corridor door shut. Without each other's company and camaraderie, we returned to the reality of our situations, emphasised by our cold, isolated cells. Lying alone thinking of what lay ahead, there was little sleep for any of us that night.

The following morning we were driven, handcuffed to each other in the back of a police van, to Kilmarnock Sheriff court some 13 miles away. The court cells, maybe six in total, were left unlocked although the main corridor was blocked off by a heavy metal grill. The place was filthy and littered with rubbish, cigarette ends and discarded paperwork of all sorts; graffiti covered every inch of the walls and ceiling, providing a form of diversion for the preoccupied and entertainment for the less concerned. There was no natural light, and so the dark, dingy cells were like caves, fitting enough for the Neanderthals of the underclass that were fed in and out of them. Fortunately, however, with the cells unlocked we were afforded more freedom than the police cells in Saltcoats which meant we could mingle with each other and the five or six other guys who were also due to appear at court for various offences. Being with each other was a source of strength as we walked together from cell to cell, almost playfully sliding about in our stocking soles to pass the time.

As our court appearance neared, understandably our thoughts turned to the prospect of bail. 'Do you think we'll get bail, mate?' Watty asked an older looking man, with a well worn face and a jaded expression, who gave the appearance of being sufficiently experienced in the system to remain utterly untroubled as he sat alone in one of the open cells rolling a cigarette from a battered tin, despite Jeg still absurdly sliding in and out of the cell behind us. 'Aye,' he replied abruptly without looking up at the owner of the young voice invading his solitude. 'This is our first time ever at court, whit dae ye think?' continued Watty, perhaps hoping that further information would be of assistance in his analysis of our case, oblivious to the man's obvious disinterest. Drawing deeply on his roll up, he ignored the increasingly agitated Watty in front of him. 'But do ye think we'll *aw* get it?' probed Watty further. 'Aye,' he replied again in an equally brusque manner, drawing out his monosyllabic reply, in a vain attempt to communicate that his limited patience had deserted him already. 'But dae you …' 'For fuck sake gie's a break, son!' he snapped as he proceeded to march through to the main door to ask if he could be locked into a cell away from us.

Prior to appearing in court, we were summoned to a small room, just outside the cell area, to speak to the duty lawyer, who, we were informed, would be representing us at our brief bail hearing. We were unfamiliar with court procedures and in the absence of any legal representation of our own, we had been appointed a duty lawyer, which gave us no say in who we wanted to represent us, not that we would have known who to select anyway. Our unfortunate lawyer, Mr Hart, stood before us and ran his worried eyes along this gang of stocking-soled misfits before him. Mr Hart was a tall thin man, of no significant character, with a long narrow, weak face, which exaggerated his anxious frown of inexperience. As he spoke, he continually smoothed his hair, with a tension that seemed unconsciously to transmit his nerves to the strung out Watty who immediately jumped in to ask, 'Dae ye think we'll get bail, Mister?' In a zealous display of fidgeting with his pen and staring at the papers that he was shuffling in his hands, Mr Hart rather conveniently ignored this question. Following a further brief discussion surrounding bail application, which was beyond our understanding, we were led back to the cells to await a call to court.

When we were summoned a short time later, the police came into the cells and handcuffed us together. With not a further word spoken between us as the heavy metal shackles were snapped around our skinny wrists, we were taken from the cells, chained together, to the court room. As we were hustled into court and into the dock, we each quietly scanned the room, absorbing the strange, formal, hostile surroundings in which our immediate future would be decided. Looking around, I felt intimidated by the stern, formal setting of the court. Flags with Latin script of some sort stood aloft on each side of the Sheriff's bench. Everything was in dark oak wood, enhancing the increasing sense of foreboding and the severity of the situation; not unlike a church, I thought ironically, though with none of the forgiveness forthcoming.

As I was observing the surroundings with awe, those present in court were loudly instructed to rise as the Sheriff entered the courtroom. Somewhat surprisingly, I was able to recall and apply fragments of my education as it occurred to me that he looked like the mad Russian monk, Rasputin, whom I had seen in pictures in my history class, as he strode slowly and deliberately to the bench, taking his seat as if no-one but him were there. Or at least no-one who mattered. He looked an overpowering man in his regalia of robes and wig, his big black tousled beard masking three-quarters of his face as he surveyed the papers that had been placed before him. After glancing up at the legal representatives and court employees, he turned his face towards us and glared menacingly at us through his piercing, unblinking eyes, over half-moon spectacles as if noticing our inconvenient presence for the first time. I felt Watty shaking with nerves as he stood beside me. Before addressing us, the Sheriff barked out various instructions at the court officials, who seemed visibly to cower at the sound of his voice. *What kind of place is this?* I asked myself. *What chance do we have with our lawyer?* I thought, as he sat before us fidgeting and stroking his hair manically, as intimidated and subservient as everyone else present.

In response to the charges read out, our lawyer made no plea or declaration on our behalf. Apparently, we could apply for bail today and if unsuccessful we would appear at court seven days later when we could make a final bail application. Failing that, we would be remanded in custody, although our trial date would have to be set within 110 days, which of course felt like a life sentence; it was longer than the summer holidays, for God's sake. Despite the fact that I was now developing a vague knowledge of the legal process, I was still unsure why we were making no plea as we were obviously guilty.

There was a brief exchange between our lawyer and the Procurator Fiscal regarding some legal issue. It was again beyond our understanding, and obviously our own lawyer's too judging by the way he sat down quickly mumbling away to himself. Like irrelevant extras who had no speaking part, we were ordered to rise as Rasputin addressed our lawyer with undisguised disinterest. 'Mr Hart,' he boomed, 'don't waste your breath asking for bail, remanded for seven days for further enquiries ... take them away', he concluded quickly with a dismissive movement of his hand, not once addressing us directly. Confused and shocked, we were dragged back to the cells in the same hurried, intimidating dog like fashion as the next case was brought before him.

We sat in a cell quietly troubled by our own thoughts knowing we were finally bound for Longriggend, the Young Offenders Remand centre on the Lanarkshire moors. We had heard so much about Longriggend and its brutal regime over the years and the horrible, unavoidable reality of going to this place was now beginning to sink in.

My concentration was soon broken by the sound of my maw's muffled voice shouting to me from outside the cell window. Excitedly, I clambered up to the window, which I could only reach by jumping up and holding on to the bars. As the windows were heavily barred, I could not see her but could hear her clearly as she stood in the court car park at the other side of the window. Straining with the effort of holding onto the bars I shouted desperately, 'Maw ... maw, is that you?' 'They won't let me in to see you, so take care of yourself in there, son' she replied in an equally desperate voice. 'Don't worry about me, I'll be okay ... the lawyer said I'll definitely get bail next week,' I said, starting to choke on my lies and tears. 'Get down fae that fuckin window!' barked a policeman from the cell doorway before I even had a chance to say cheerio to her.

A short time later, the police entered the cells and began handcuffing us together for our journey to prison. Feeling dispirited after talking to my maw in such a manner, I thought it better that I did not make eye contact with any of the guys. As if sharing my dilemma, none of them looked in my direction or spoke to me or each other for a while. As we were being led out to the waiting police van like an infant chain gang, we were told that we would spend a night in Barlinnie Prison before being taken to Longriggend the following morning. Because we were only 15 we would be segregated from the main population in Longriggend and placed in the schoolboys' section for our own protection when we arrived.

Barlinnie Prison had the reputation of being one of the toughest prisons in Britain. As we approached it, the sight of the imposing

Victorian institution sent a shiver down my spine. It was a wet, dreary day; grey clouds gathered menacingly as the chilling bleakness of a late November afternoon was slowly turning towards its premature darkness. On nearing the entrance, I felt a strong sense of uneasiness, shared doubtless by the many who had gone before me. Built by French prisoners of war in the nineteenth century, the pained faces, the broken bodies, the blood, sweat and tears of the slave labourers and the sinister secrets that the prison had subsequently hidden seemed to be soaked into every brick of the walled, grey building.

As the van drove through the gates, we forced nervous smiles as we silently exchanged worried glances. Watty was looking increasingly grey, Jeg looked quietly stunned and Eddie chewed frantically on what was left of his fingernails. Once inside the gates the van drove the short distance to the main reception block and came to a jolting halt, almost flinging us from the hard wooden benches in the van. Just as suddenly, the doors were flung open with a clatter and, still handcuffed together, we were half-dragged from the van into the reception area, struggling to remain upright as we slid about in our stocking soles, no longer gaining any joy from the experience.

The intense light and the sudden noise of the place was immediately unnerving. Everyone seemed to be barking different orders simultaneously—'Come on, you bastards, we don't have all day, move it, come on quickly, quickly!' screamed a prison officer. He was a big beefy man with a grey complexion, who appeared eyeless as the peak of his prison cap was pulled down to the bridge of his nose. Sneaking a nervous glance at him as he stood before us, I could see that over the duration of his service, he had acquired the ability to morph chameleon like into the background of the grey prison walls as he stood directing the human cattle.

We were herded into a bare corridor area to join a large queue of other prisoners who had arrived just before us from various courts across the central belt of Scotland; we stood, overwhelmed and shackled, amongst the adult prisoners in the corridor, quietly apprehensive in anticipation of what would come next. Everything, particularly in relation to younger prisoners, was done at double quick time; handcuffs quickly snapped off our wrists, and rounds of instructions were fired off. 'Over to that queue!' barked the eyeless officer. 'Report to that officer … quickly, come on, come on!' yelled another in my ear, as I darted over as instructed.

I struggled to answer as the questions were fired off rapidly. 'Name, address, age, religion?' 'Have you ever had a venereal disease?' 'Eh, … ah don't …' 'Come on, you must know if you've ever had syphilis or gonorrhoea, ya fucking imbecile … go to that officer over there, come on fucken move it.' 'Drop your pants,' spat the other. Hesitant, in front of the other prisoners, I began to undo my trousers. 'Come on, turn around, quickly, bend over and part your cheeks. Have you had crabs recently?' he continued, now talking to my arse as he scanned my exposed testicles from behind with a flash light. 'Trousers up and report to that officer … come on, fuckin move it!' he shouted.

Feeling degraded and humiliated, I shuffled quickly along to the next officer in the conveyor belt of shame, trying clumsily to fasten my trousers as I went. 'Box 13!' the next one roared as he pushed me roughly towards another officer who stood further up the corridor aside an open door. 'Move your arse,' he scowled, as I half-ran, half-shuffled towards him, trying to keep my balance in my stocking soles. Without looking in my direction, he shoved me into a small cupboard sized room, slammed the door and drew the heavy bolt behind me.

These rooms were known as dog boxes, presumably because of their size; they were no more than three foot square and each contained a fixed bench which could seat only two people. Prisoners were held in these boxes until everyone was ready to be taken over to the main halls and could sometimes be held in them for hours at a time. There were three adults already in this box, two of whom were seated. I stood awkwardly trying to catch sight of the guys through the cracks in the door. With no room to turn or move, I could feel someone's tobacco stained breath on the back of my neck. I had no idea how long I would be kept in here or when I would see the guys again. The cold inhumanity of my reception into the prison system filled me with bitter horror as I tried to imagine what would inevitably follow in the coming days. As if sensing my shock, an old prisoner behind me said quietly, 'Welcome to Barlinnie, son, welcome to Barlinnie'.

CHAPTER 13

Dark Days, Rainy Nights: More Living Hell

With the shirt sticking to my back and beads of sweat running down my face, I gulped for air at the cracks in the dog box door as feelings of panic and claustrophobia began to engulf me. I have not been able to tolerate enclosed, confined spaces since. On this occasion, we must have been in there for several hours before I heard the doors being unlocked noisily. As we were taken out and led back down to the main reception gate in preparation for the main halls, I looked behind me and noticed Jeg determinedly, if not frantically, weaving in and out of the other prisoners as he made his way towards me. I was never so glad to see his big ugly face and felt like hugging him. 'Ah cannae go back in they dog boxes, Weavy,' he said in a panic, his clothes like mine, drenched in sweat. Although sharing his alarm, I tried to comfort him by changing the subject casually.

We were allowed to keep our own clothes on as we were going to Longriggend the following day. This was something of a comfort in a place deliberately designed to dehumanise and strip away the layers that comprise an individual's identity. D Hall was for short term prisoners, generally older alcoholics, hence the unappealing description, the 'Jakey Hall' was for prisoners waiting to be transferred to other institutions, like Longriggend, or other convicted young offenders awaiting transfer to borstal.

As we entered the hall, I was struck again by the relentless, persistent noise of the place; booming voices shouting and swearing aimlessly; loud banging sounds made by the heavy metal doors being slammed shut; old deranged and screaming alcoholic prisoners hammering desperately on their doors. There were four 'landings' in the hall, each joined by a metal staircase. Each landing comprised symmetrical rows of cells on either side, with a toilet recess at the end of the landings, where prisoners 'slopped out' their pots full of piss and shit. prisoners slopped out three times a day, to order, and would make their way to the recess to empty their human waste in one small toilet bowl per landing; the smell was overbearing. Perhaps more degrading, however, was having to actually piss or shit in the confines of a closed cell in front of strangers as they lay on their beds and conformed to the unwritten rule of lying facing the wall while the other person squatted and defecated into a small plastic bowl.

Once we had been issued with bed sheets, Jeg and I were led up to a cell on the first floor landing. We were ecstatic when we found out that we would share the same cell and ran childlike ahead of the other prisoners to find our cell number. As we stepped into our allocated cell, the door was immediately slammed shut behind us. We both stood in the middle of this damp, darkened cell, quietly taking in our surroundings and subconsciously drawing our bedding closer to us as if seeking some kind of comfort—wondering at our haste.

There were two beds, separated by an old set of wooden drawers, positioned at the far wall. The heavily barred window was set high up in the wall, so that looking up towards it, all that could be seen was the sky; the only indicator that another world was going on its way without us. The light was fixed into the middle of the ceiling and although it was switched on, it gave out a kind of eerie darkened yellow light, giving us both a jaundiced look. Because we were children, the cell light would be kept on all night for observation purposes. We certainly weren't complaining; the strange light was far more desirable than being plunged into a brooding darkness, which could only serve to emphasize the unfamiliar and frightening sounds of the prison at night. Unfortunately, however, the light also served to illuminate the mattresses which were heavily stained with piss, blood, fag burns and food stains. Well, I hoped they were food stains. Tiny roll up doubts littered the floor and discarded pieces of stale bread lay about the place; graffiti and gang slogans were spread right across the cell. Inquisitively, I picked up a piss pot and slowly lifted the lid off not quite knowing what to expect. The smell of stale urine almost made me sick as the stench hit my nostrils with a violent collision. Although it was empty, it had a crust of dried layers of urine around the whole pot and I prayed that I did not need to use it during the night.

Whilst we were still absorbing our surroundings, the door was opened by a prison officer and we were handed a bowl of minced meat of some description and a mug of cold tea by another prisoner, in total silence, broken only by the slamming of the door as they moved along to the next cell. Seeing food of any kind reminded me how famished I was; I had not eaten since the police cells that morning. Despite my hunger however, I could not get the smell of the piss pot from my nostrils and I could not have eaten in this rancid place had my life depended on it; even the plates and cups were filthy and covered with gang slogans.

Having devoured his own bowl of meat in record time, Jeg noticed mine sitting on top of the drawers, untouched. 'Are you goin' to eat that?' he asked, poking about my bowl, his hunger obviously outstripping his earlier anxiety. 'Naw, ah'm no' that hungry dae you want it?' 'Awright then …. save it goin' to waste, eh?' he said, oblivious to the irony of his comment as he wolfed my food down hungrily. That night, we curled up in our own beds, fully clothed, with our single, soiled sheets wrapped around us in an attempt to fend off the bitter cold. Lost in our own cyclical thoughts, we never really spoke much at all. Instead, we lay awake for hours, fretting, wide eyed, and listening to the withdrawal screams of the old alcoholic prisoners on the ground floor, who sounded equally traumatised.

Early the following morning, we were taken, hollow-eyed, back to the reception area to begin our journey to Longriggend. This was the first time we had seen Eddie and Watty since we were lined up in the Barlinnie reception area the previous day. Thankfully, the four of us were put in the same dog box, which was far less claustrophobic this time round, due to our somewhat lesser frames, and we soon forgot our surroundings and managed to have a laugh while we were together. Conveniently ignoring the trauma of the previous night, we exchanged stories of our first experiences of Barlinnie, Eddie and Watty having been held on the second floor landing directly above us. 'Slept like logs, we did,' said Watty masking an exhausted yawn. 'Aye, we were the same,' I replied, ignoring their gaunt, tired looking faces, which I knew mirrored my own exactly. Trying desperately to deny the fearful reality of our situation, we indulged each other like unshakeable auld timers until it was time to head out for Longriggend.

The bus taking us to Longriggend was furnished with two rows of cold metallic seats either side of a narrow walkway, and was painted dark green inside and out, giving it something of a military feel. The windows were made of reinforced glass covered by a heavy sheet of mesh, which meant you could barely look outside, and which added to the claustrophobia of the human cattle wagon. Two prison officers sat at the back of the bus, two in the seats around the middle and four sat down the front next to the only door. The rest of the young offenders on the bus were all older-looking than us. Shackled in pairs, the four of us were placed near the front directly behind the prison officers. I was sitting next to the window handcuffed to Jeg and because we had remained shoeless, our cold and dirty toes were by now sticking through newly formed holes in our socks.

As the bus made its way through the wet Glasgow streets, I peered through the mesh at the blurred passing scenes and envied so much the people on the streets going about their ordinary everyday business, oblivious to our plight. I quietly wondered what my maw and wee brothers were doing. Trying to escape these thoughts, I turned to Watty and Eddie behind us and asked, 'Do you think the bus driver would drop me aff at the hoose if ah asked him nicely?' only to be met by half-hearted smiles.

With little concept of time, the journey to Longriggend seemed to us to have taken an age. We had a rough idea that we were approaching the place, however, when the bus began to swerve nauseatingly round the small winding roads of the Lanarkshire countryside The prison officers, in response and preparation, began stamping out their cigarettes and pulling on their long black raincoats. Straining to look through the mesh, I could see that the rain had now turned to grey sleet; dark, moody clouds were hovering above the dull, lifeless fields, seemingly intensifying as we approached Longriggend. As we turned the final bend in the road, a prison officer, stretching his arms upward as he yawned, said loudly and with undisguised pleasure, for the benefit of us first timers: 'There she is, the place that sorts oot the tough guys'.

We could see Longriggend anchored menacingly and remotely in the distance. A former tuberculosis hospital, it sat fortified on top of a nearby hill, surrounded by a large grey double fence, crowned with heavy coils of razor wire. As we neared the main gate, I noticed a prison officer marching around the perimeter fence with a large Alsatian dog straining at the leash wearing the same scowling face; I wondered if they were perhaps related.

Unlike Barlinnie, Longriggend dog boxes were limited to three people. Any initial considerations as to whether this was a conscious humanitarian gesture on their part were soon decided as we were dragged out of the dog boxes one by one to begin the whole, by now increasingly familiar, admission process again. Put through the full degrading procedure, we were forced to endure the same humiliating questions bawled at us by aggressive, eyeless officers in the same violating fashion. There wasn't much chance of contracting syphilis or gonorrhoea on the bus between Barlinnie and Longriggend, I thought, as I bent over to present my bare arse to this adult stranger for inspection. I was soon to discover, however, that a further and far more disturbing admission practice was in operation in Longriggened.

Following the battery of degrading bodily inspections, those people entering the institution were forced to line up naked while an officer moved down the line with a big electric flashlight checking pubic and head hair for lice. Anyone found to have lice was taken immediately into a separate room to have their heads shaved bald. This public symbol of uncleanliness was the ultimate in human degradation and erasure of one's identity and the only other people I knew at this stage to engage in such a practice were the Nazis in the death camps. Although we had spoken of this briefly the day before, we were very much in our own individual denial that this kind of thing still happened.

Standing naked in the line, blinded by the searing light, my heart pounded loudly as the officer crouched over me, with what looked like a distorted sneer. It felt like a form of molestation, as his cold, long, bony, fingers disturbingly slithered through my hair, slowly and deliberately scanning for lice. Struck with fear, I stood deathly still, unable to breathe properly; the light then slithered, intrusively down my naked body, to my bare genitals, where he continued to probe. I felt utterly violated and almost cried out in relief as he moved sloth-like, to the naked Eddie beside me and began the whole grotesque process again. Fortunately, we were all in the clear, although several other guys were led, head down in resigned silence, into the side room to have their heads shaved.

The reception block, I noticed, did not have the stale musty smell of Barlinnie; it was replaced instead with an antiseptic odour, perhaps indicative of a more modern, but no less clinical institution. On our arrival, Longriggend contained around 16 'schoolboy' inmates who were on remand for trial, or who had been recently convicted but were awaiting sentence; all inmates were subject to 'unruly certificates' and therefore classified as serious offenders.

The schoolboy section was located on the first floor of one of the four main halls in the institution, segregating us from the older young offender population as much as possible. We would be routinely taken to the main dining hall only when the rest of the young offenders had been taken there and seated, and for the sake of expedience and convenience, would be forced to eat hurriedly and leave the dining area before the rest. We had no association with the older population at any time; even their visits were at different times. I wasn't sure whether this rigid segregation was to avoid our young minds being corrupted by the older more experienced criminal population, or to prevent something more sinister happening to us, which inevitably then meant it was a back-covering exercise as opposed to something reminiscent of care or concern. Either way, being a 'schoolboy' meant that you were rooted firmly on the bottom rung of the penal pecking order in Longriggend, and everyone seemed at pains to remind us of that fact.

In theory, provisions were in place for the continued delivery of education for the schoolboys. The school was a small separate building within the grounds of the institution; razor wire ran along the edge of the roof, up each corner of the building and covered the length of the drainpipes and all of the windows were heavily barred. It was not exactly a warm educational environment, conducive to learning. In reality however, we never even saw the inside of the 'school'; instead, like the rest of the young offenders, we were locked in our cells for 23 hours a day. To my knowledge no-one ever received schooling as such within Longriggend; perhaps the continued education of these children was considered immaterial, their futures prematurely written off.

Having been processed through the reception block and presented with our standard issue, ill-fitting uniforms, we were assembled and led over to the schoolboy section. The prison clothes we wore were stained and dirty, physical testament to the existence of the last four or five unfortunate wearers. The collection included dreary grey-coloured trousers, finished off with a dull red and white striped shirt and shoes which came to an unnaturally sharp point, demonstrating that even in prison, the fashion howlers of the 1960s still retained a foothold.

Unsurprisingly, my clothes were too big for me and so I had to resort to tying the waistband of my trousers in a crude knot to keep them from falling down. The shirts were also ridiculously oversized, bizarrely sporting one button each. With something of a wry chuckle, I thought I was at least fortunate that my one button was on the middle of my shirt, unlike Jeg's, whose sole button was on the neck of his shirt. 'Ah feel like fucken' batman,' he moaned, his shirt flapping about in the wind, as we walked across the cold empty exercise yard towards the schoolboys' section. Mind you, the last time I had seen him sporting a cape, he was striding ahead of me through our school corridor, waving two broken chair legs like a demented professor. The whopping great shoes restricted our walk and made us flump along like circus clowns; we looked entirely ridiculous and would doubtless have found it all funny had we been less frightened and more sure as to what to expect. Instead, we inadvertently clutched our bedding closer to our chests as we neared the building.

The actual schoolboy area was relatively small and set around a darkened corridor; with no access to natural light, it relied on a dull yellowish electric strip light. The corridor was approximately two metres wide and around 30 metres in length, with ten cells on each side, reflecting once more the institutional obsession with architectural symmetry.

We were marched down in single file to the far end of the corridor, where a prison officer sat at a desk inside a small recess, awaiting us. He was a tall thick set guy with a big square chin. Studying him from the corner of my eye as I stood before him, I could not help but wonder if heavy square chins were listed as 'essential' in the entrance criteria for the prison service; it was fast becoming an oddly familiar facial feature amongst the officers we had come into contact with. Then again, perhaps the shared facial features of prison officers suggested an equal predisposition to their fate as the nineteenth-century influential Italian criminologist, Cesare Lombroso, would have us believe about the criminal population and their physical predisposition to criminality, when he argued that all criminals had large protruding foreheads and eyes which were too far apart. Without once looking at us, Desperate Dan scanned a sheet of paper in front of him, distractedly scratching his big square jaw and obviously stretched at the task of identifying which cells were empty. As I squinted at the sheet, I could see that cells five, ten, 11 and 12 were empty, however, with uncharacteristic restraint, I did not consider it appropriate to assist him at this stage by pointing this out.

Some minutes later, without sharing the sense of triumph he can only have felt at resolving this conundrum, he casually drawled, 'Weaver and Wilson cell five, Nisbet and McCleary in ten, Cavani and Smith in eleven.' 'Now listen up,' he growled sweetly, as he put his sheet of paper down slowly and glared along the line of youthful scoundrels before him, boring his eyes into each of us individually, with well rehearsed emphasis, obviously better suited to this aspect of his role than the more mentally taxing administrative tasks, 'Any trouble from any one of you scumbags and I'll personally take you into an empty cell and give you the battering of your life.' What a prospect, I thought. We would have to stand in tortured anticipation for 20 minutes while he scanned his sheet trying to work out which cell was empty, before battering us. Rising sullenly from his chair in one languid movement, pressing his hands down onto the desk with the effort whilst pushing his chair back with his legs, he led us along the corridor and locked us into our cells, thoroughly inconvenienced by the whole process.

The cells in Longriggend were, like their Barlinnie counterparts, bare and sparsely furnished with two single beds fixed hard against the two side walls, divided by a battered set of wooden drawers, two matching chairs placed at the end of each bed and, of course, the obligatory piss pots hidden under the beds. There was a small barred window high on the wall which, we discovered, could only be accessed by standing on the set of drawers.

Thankfully the cells were relatively clean; I wasn't going to starve to death. Still, Watty and I never really spoke much that night; certainly, I wasn't in the mood, I was still trying to make sense of the madness around me and, likewise, Watty did not seem too keen to talk, lost in his own thoughts. He struggled more than the rest of us in coming to terms with what was happening and was therefore prone to lapsing into longer periods of silence, just staring into space as if unable to reconcile himself at all to our situation. A main light was located right outside our cell window, lighting our cell throughout the night, which, again, I was oddly grateful for; I still can't bear to be awake surrounded by darkness. Glancing over, I could see Watty lying with his eyes open, staring quietly at the ceiling.

The week in Longriggend almost crushed us, particularly when we were told that we had no right to visits, given that we were only in for seven days initially. If the regime was brutal, the routine was soul destroying; we were briefly let out of our cells three times a day for meals and, weather permitting, allowed into the exercise yard for a 30-minute walk. The time spent together in the exercise yard was the highlight of our day, as we walked around the yard, forcing ourselves to banter in an effort to raise each others' spirits. Sensing our inexperience, further underlined by the constant flap of Jeg's shirt and the collective flumping caused by the ridiculous shoes, the rest of the schoolboys increasingly ostracised us.

As we were forced to spend around 23 hours a day in our cell, passing the time was difficult. Although Watty was often reluctant to take part, on the occasions that I had successfully worn him down following a barrage of well-intended cajoling by myself, we would occasionally pass time playing football in the cell, using our prison issue socks which we rolled into a small cotton football. We would also play I-Spy, which inevitably resulted in numerous petty arguments, particularly when I was drawing on all my literacy skills, arguing that it was 'c' for chamber pot and not 'p' for piss pot. Being unable to concentrate for more than two minutes and with virtually little choice at our disposal, reading was out of the question. So, for most of the time we would just lie on our beds quietly staring at the ceiling, wondering what would happen to us when we returned to court, unable to consider the prospect of coming back.

As if to compound Watty's distress, he contracted a bad bout of diahorrea which lasted for several days, during which time he had limited access to the toilet or indeed toilet paper. Trying to lessen his humiliation, I would stand on the set of drawers and talk away to him loudly whilst looking out of the window, as if unaware that he was squatting over his piss pot, squelching and defecating noisily. The eye-watering stench hung in the air like a sinister, grey cloud as he filled his own pot and then waddled over, trousers and underpants around his ankles, to empty the remainder of his uncontrollable bowels in mine, already containing my piss. With tears in his eyes and the shit running down his bare leg, he tugged gently on my trouser leg. 'You'll no tell anybody, Weavy, will you?' he whimpered, as he looked up at me. 'Tell them whit, Watty … whit have a got to tell them,' I replied, returning quickly to the window, unable to look at my pal.

Longriggend seemed to come alive at night with the din of those confined. With the onset of darkness, people would start shouting from their cell windows to others they knew in different halls, with some taking advantage of their anonymity to hurl venomous abuse at other inmates, or their mothers, for hours on end, employing the only form of retaliation at their disposal. As if awakened from their slumber, the psychotic inmates would then join in, wailing and howling, merged with regular disappearances back into their cells to batter desperately on their cell doors. Cutting through this mayhem would be the incessant banging on the pipes, with a constant, dull clink, clink, clink, clink, causing everyone to live permanently on their nerves. We had a long sleepless last night before our return to court; if we did not get bail we would spend the next four months in Longriggend schoolboys' section awaiting trial.

CHAPTER 14

High Maintenance Lifestyle and Reputation

With slightly more purpose than on the outward journey, the prison van returning us to court sped through the early morning traffic in the outskirts of Lanarkshire and headed straight towards Kilmarnock; our mood fluctuated rapidly between elation at the prospect of going home and panic, at the thought of a return trip. Other than the heavy metal handcuffs, it felt, at times, like a school outing as we gibbered away in nervous anticipation in the back of the van, consciously trying to put the horrors of Longriggend behind us.

Watty was almost neurotic in his perpetual questioning of the police escorts and the other prisoners. 'But we've no' been in serious bother before … so do you think we'll get bail?' 'Any chance ay a draw on that fag, pal?' Jeg bleated in unison at regular intervals. Intently concentrating on their own dilemmas, the other prisoners sat focusing quietly on their shoes, ignoring our excitement and hope. We, on the other hand, consciously chose not to give any attention to our shoes. No doubt to avoid the embarrassment of transporting children to court barefooted, as our socks were by now frayed beyond use, we were made to wear our Longriggend shoes to court.

On reaching Kilmarnock Sheriff Court we were held in the same cells that only a week ago had been the scene of so much angst; it was hard to believe that we had experienced so much in seven days. There were now around 15 prisoners, including ourselves, held in the cell area awaiting their afternoon court appearances. Perhaps more in denial of the shit and tears than anything else, we recounted our Longriggend tales to anyone who would listen, not sensing the absence of interest or surprise on the faces of our enforced company. By mid-morning we noticed that four of the older guys were now sitting in a cell, the door and hatch jammed shut from the inside. 'Ignorant bastards!' shouted Watty through the spy hole before we managed to drag him away.

As if avoiding the place when possible, our solicitor, Mr Hart, again appeared in the cell area immediately before our court appearance; scanning the surroundings he struggled to mask his look of disgust. He seemed to look even more appalled when he noticed we were still attired in our Longriggend footwear. The additional week's legal experience had obviously empowered him though, I thought, as he stood before us, not stroking his head as incessantly and definitely looking more dapper and authoritative in a striking pin-striped suit. He indicated a successful bail application whilst clapping his hands together briskly with the confidence of a veteran lawyer on the cusp of concluding business, betrayed only slightly by a solitary smoothing of the fringe. 'You're the best lawyer in here, Mr Hart … your really ur,' said Watty, over our gibbering excitement, extending his hand proudly to the lawyer with tears of joy in his eyes, as if struggling to restrain himself from giving him an admiring hug. Looking somewhat flustered, Mr Hart hurried out of the cell area with a backward glance, still unsure if Watty was taking the piss. He most definitely was not.

Before long, we were again led from the cell area into the dock; reflecting our recent experiences, we now cut a more drawn and dishevelled appearance. Unlike the previous week, the court was open to members of the public. Looking over at the public gallery, I could see, amongst what must have been other prisoners' families, my maw, Jeg and Watty's parents and Eddie's mother and brother. Lifted by this sight, we sat and cackled in the dock, the handcuffs clanking as we individually and uncoordinatedly tried to lift our shackled hands to give our families the thumbs up. The solemnity of everyone else in the face of this absurd sight was almost laudable.

Entering the court with his customary pomp, Rasputin quietly made his way to the bench, as we once again fell into a fearful silence. All hopes of release soon deserted me as the Procurator Fiscal opened the proceedings by laying bare the details of the offence which included: over £10,000 worth of damage; the school closing completely for three days to repair the damage; and a sum of money allegedly stolen along with a seemingly endless list of other items, including a teacher's watch strap. Whilst I was contemplating the absurdity of the latter item, Watty, as if on cue, whispered under his breath, 'Well … it was fucken' broke anyway.' Ignoring Watty's warped justification, I just wanted the Fiscal to stop his seemingly never-ending attack on us through which he seemed to gain ever more confidence, ensuring that Mr Hart could not possibly counter this endless indictment against us, when it came to a bail application.

In contrast, Mr Hart spoke with less assurance and authority, accompanied by a rapid return to incessant hair stroking, as he twittered lamely on about our age and this being our first court appearance. To the horror and seeming betrayal of me, Watty and Eddie, he then proceeded to emphasise the fact that unlike the rest of us, Jeg had fewer Children's

Hearing appearances and fewer previous convictions than his more 'hardened peers'. An argument then ensued between Mr Hart and the Fiscal who, to our naïve shock, vehemently opposed our bail application without further ado.

The Fiscal, although appearing to look a small insignificant man who would not have warranted a second glance in any other walk of life, worryingly altered his demeanour as the proceedings continued. His gown hung awkwardly from his slight shoulders giving it a cloak like appearance and with his chalky complexion and large hooked nose, coupled with his apparent growing hatred of us, he reminded me in many respects of the child snatcher from the film *Chitty Chitty Bang Bang*, as he tried through every means possible to secure our return to the hell of Longriggend. With all arguments exhausted, Rasputin sat looking down at the papers in front of him before characteristically instructing us to stand without glancing in our direction. 'You can all think yourselves extremely fortunate that I have chosen to disregard the warning forwarded by the Procurator Fiscal,' said the Sheriff as if noticing us for the first time. 'McCleary, you will be released on the bail of one pound. Weaver, Nisbet and Wilson, you three will be released on the bail of £50', he concluded, bringing down his gavel sharply.

With no time to acknowledge our families, or little thought of where my maw would get the money, we were hastily returned to the cells to be processed for release. Hollering with unrestrained delight, we jumped and danced around the cells. Unsure whether they were pleased for us, or themselves, the guys in the closed cell hollered with equal delight. With new found bravado, we defiantly pulled the Longriggend shoes from our feet and threw them down the toilet bowl. 'They can stick their daft shoes up their arse,' Eddie shouted with glee, as we playfully pushed each other round the bowl in our efforts to piss all over them. Turning to Jeg, we supportively told him to keep his spirits up as it wouldn't take too long for his maw and da to raise his bail money.

Seeing Mr Hart enter the cell area we quickly made our way towards him in our eagerness to thank him for his skill and efforts. Slightly, behind us, Watty was attempting to give the resilient shoes a further final flush. Amid the hysteria, my heart sank as I immediately noticed that Mr Hart was standing quietly and unsmiling, stroking his hair more intently than the occasion should have warranted and avoiding all eye contact with us. 'Eh … bad news, lads, … apart from you, McCleary, the Procurator Fiscal has appealed against your bail and you three have been remanded in custody again.' I felt sick to the pit of my stomach. 'Wit dae ye mean!' screamed Watty at Mr Hart as he made towards him in unrestrained desperation and with disbelief manifested all over his face. 'Does ma maw know?' was all I could shout to the hastily departing Mr Hart, who did not stop to reply.

Heads in hands, we sat quietly in one of the cells for the remainder of the day, all pretence of bonhomie shattered. Jeg had been released sometime earlier and although we were devastated at our own plights, we were still glad for him; even Watty was, in his own depressed way. As if things weren't bad enough for us, we were getting ready to leave for the journey back to Barlinnie when Watty screamed in panic, 'Oh fuck … whit aboot the shoes?' The dreadfulness of what would happen to us if we returned empty footed, hit us simultaneously. Speeding through to the toilet we began fishing the shoes out one by one. Utterly demoralised and bound together once more, we squelched our way out to the waiting bus. Unsure as to whether forewarned was forearmed, at least this time we knew what was awaiting us, but the uncertainty as to how long for chilled us.

Following a night in Barlinnie and one more night in Longriggend, we were summonsed early the following morning to the admission block and informed that we were being released on High Court bail. This was due to a last minute bail application by our lawyer to a higher court. In a state of some shock and in fear of someone reversing the decision yet again, we dressed quietly and hurriedly. Looking back at the closing gate in nervous disbelief, we tiptoed gingerly over a thin coating of snow in our stockinged feet towards a car where one of Eddie's relatives was waiting for us. We sped away in a haze of exhaust fumes, leaving Longriggend behind us, ugly and misshapen.

Although I had only been away for over a week, initially it felt rather strange being back in my own house and the experience, albeit fleeting, had changed me in a way that I did not really know how to articulate. When my da arrived home from work that night, he did not really say anything to me and shuffled about uncomfortably in my presence. Although causing his own kind of chaos at home and despite the odd skirmish when he had battered my maw, which as said, was never really considered an offence as such, he had never been in trouble with the police. Although ironically not in those days approving of criminality *per se*, I think there was part of him that admired the image of the whole hard man culture which he in some way identified with and saw in himself.

Reinforcing this point to an extent, several days later when he was drunk, he became confrontational towards me. 'Fuckin' big man, eh?' he sneered in my face as I walked past him on my way to my bedroom to avoid inflaming the situation. Following me up the stairs he continued into my face, 'Come on ... me and you outside for a square go ... and we'll see how hard you ur.' With my adrenalin pumping, I stood on the stairs nervously and unsure how to respond; I did not want this—I did not have the heart for it and I was still recovering from my recent unsettling experiences without feeling under siege when I got home. As if sensing my distress, my maw rushed up and wrestled herself between us, interjecting defensively, 'Leave him alone, you, he's trying his best to keep out of bother.' As I braced myself for the worst, he turned aggressively towards my maw and shouted in her face before staggering downstairs, 'Aye, well if you had bought him up right, we widnae huv this fucken' embarrassment.' Trying to diffuse the situation she pushed me gently up the stairs.

For the first few days I did not leave the house at all and spent most of my time moping about my bedroom, feeling increasingly despondent. I hadn't seen any of the guys since court. Eddie returned to his school the following week, and Watty and Jeg were granted permission to return to St Andrews. When hearing of this, my maw contacted Margaret Clark to see if I too might return, only to be informed that, following a recent meeting at the school regarding our situation, where no doubt Jeg and Watty's return had been negotiated, they had steadfastly refused to take me back. Irrespective of the yet to-be-decided conclusions of the criminal justice system, they had not only determined my guilt but also the relative extent of my involvement. Ominously, Margaret added that she had further information she wished to discuss with me and my maw in person.

The following morning, as arranged, I went down to see Margaret Clark along with my maw. As it was first thing in the morning, the waiting room was relatively quiet, it being a bit early in the day for Big Jeanette, unfortunately, I thought to myself, as I was in need of a stimulating conversation. After a brief period, Margaret appeared, inviting me and my maw into her office. 'Look, Allan', said Margaret, directly getting down to business, and looking more intense than I had ever before seen her, as if trying to subliminally prepare me for the inevitable, 'we had an emergency meeting in your absence last week. You have a Children's Hearing arranged for three weeks' time and the school are definitely not having you back,' she confirmed. 'We had no choice but to ask for a residential placement, Ellen,' she said quietly turning from me to my maw. As my maw started to cry, I stood upright and shouted angrily, 'How come Jeg and Watty get back to school an' ah get sent to approved school!' Ignoring my maw's pleas to calm down, I stormed from the office, unable and unwilling to accept what had been said.

Aimlessly, I walked about the town for some time and then made my way up to the school to see if I could catch sight of any of the guys. No one was around as I walked along the perimeter fence of the school where once I had been a pupil, albeit not a particularly enthusiastic one, scanning the building for a friendly face. I hovered about watching the other weans in their classes, wishing it was me and yearning for another chance. Feeling excluded, dejected, isolated and lonely, I made my way down to the museum my mood lifting a little when it occurred to me that I had not been for some weeks and by now, perhaps, they would have some additional exhibits. When I arrived, however, I was met at the door by a different attendant who told me sharply that schoolchildren were no longer allowed in unescorted. Suddenly, everything appeared to be closed off to me and my entire world seemed to be shifting out of all recognition and beyond my control.

In the countdown to approved school, it was becoming increasingly evident that Watty and Jeg's return to school was not the rehabilitative success that many had hoped for, as they stopped attending after a very short period. 'Life wisnae worth living and aw they went on aboot was smashin' the school up,' Jeg said later in an intoxicated analysis of the situation. 'Fuck that,' he said in a somewhat profound summation. Eddie had lasted even less time at his school and like me was now awaiting a residential placement.

With the immediate Londgriggend dust settled and now feeling even more isolated and excluded beyond our own immediate circle, we soon re-established our old patterns of behaviour. On schooldays, we spent most of our time drinking at the home of a lassie who lived in the Street, whilst her mother was at work. Mary Feeney was a wee overweight lassie who had only recently left school and any attention she received was generally unwelcome and largely derogatory in nature, usually surrounding her weight and unfortunate nose.

Hearing of our alternative timetable, the other guys started to float back on to the scene one by one. Clicker's arrival ensured that Mary continued to tolerate our overbearing presence during this brief time span. 'Well, you're definitely no' the wurst burd ah've seen, Mary,' he said to her sensitively, when introduced, as that knowing sparkle returned to his eyes. Predictably, Watty began to disappear from the living room where we sat drinking to rummage around the other rooms. Following him into the kitchen one day, I cornered him and cautioned quietly, 'Remember if anything goes missin', Watty, we're talking aboot the polis cummin' … getting lifted … and then before you know it, we're aw talkin' aboot how some people shite aw over the cells when they get to Longriggend.' 'Aye, its no' worth the hassle, eh,' he replied scrutinising my face quizzically and then sauntering from the room with his hands fixed firmly in his pockets

Shuggie soon turned up and, foregoing the more traditional hospitality gifts, thought it better in his wisdom to bring a slug gun and full box of pellets. With Clicker and wee Mary in one room, it wasn't long before we commandeered the other upstairs bedroom with the window raised several inches and the closed curtains parted just enough to accommodate the barrel of the gun. One after another, the passing strangers would let out a startled yelp and bolt down the street holding their arses as the heavy lead slugs pinged painfully into their fleshy buttocks with frightening accuracy. With seemingly not a care in the world, we all rolled about the bedroom floor in uproarious laughter and only stopped when the police arrived and started searching the nearby gardens for the mad gunman.

With everyone together again and our offending profile worsening, it was clear that our status amongst our peers had been elevated yet further due to our time in Longriggend and I was becoming increasingly seen as the ringleader. Naturally, I did nothing to dispel the myths, untruths and misconceptions. Why the fuck should I, I thought in my drunken sense of reason, I had paid a heavy enough price after all. However, as with *all* reputations, I was to find later that this would require maintenance and inevitably make the type of demands on me I would have wished to have avoided. But such was the way my life was already shaping at this particular period, this reputation was all that I seemed to have and, with nothing left to lose, I wasn't going to let it go readily.

CHAPTER 15

Out of Control or Just Plain Indifferent?

The panel building in which my dreaded, and as it turned out, final, Children's Hearing was to take place, was located on the shore front, in a leafy residential area of Saltcoats. It was a large two storey detached sandstone building which had patently been someone's exclusive residence in the distant past. Its main function was now to serve as a Registrar's Office with one of the downstairs rooms serving as a venue for Children's Hearings and other public functions. If you wanted to register the death of a loved one, arrange a wedding and put your child into care, you could conveniently and efficiently do so in one quick and easy visit.

Walking into the building with my maw, I noticed Jeg and Watty sitting on a wall nearby. Jeg was wearing a fireman's helmet, a trophy from the previous night, which, by way of a memorable send-off, had descended into a spontaneous riot with the fire brigade in the Street. 'Right, whit smart bastart reported the fire!' he shouted as he waved over. Although nervous and uptight, I stifled my laugh as I waved back to them. I knew that my maw was trying to remain composed and she chose to ignore the all too obvious indications that we had again caused mayhem the night before. I had noticed that my maw had been more subdued in the run up to my hearing and I knew that she was worried sick at the prospect of me being taken into care. I, myself, had been unable to sleep the night before, and on one of my unsettled excursions to the toilet in the early hours of the morning, I caught a glimpse of her through a crack in the door of the living room, just sitting there, alone.

As we sat together in the waiting room, barely talking, two staff members from Darvel, whom I recognised from my previous time in the centre, came in and sat opposite us. It was normal procedure for weans to go to Darvel for a night before being taken to approved school the following day, so I knew they were there to collect me—*fait accompli*, then. A horrible realisation that I was being sent away soon engulfed me; once more, I did not know when I would be allowed to return home, I did not know what I was going into, what approved school would be like. I was afraid that my own wee world was again disappearing and the two men sitting opposite me represented an uncertain and frightening future that might displace and replace all that I had come to know. With a lump in my throat, I nodded dryly in their direction.

'Allan Weaver!' came a voice from the corner of the waiting room as one of the panel members, an older bespectacled man, shouted over in my direction. My maw squeezed my arm as we both made our way into the room in silence to face three hearing members seated at a large desk. Welcoming the momentary distraction from my brooding, introspective thoughts, I smirked inwardly to myself as the desk reminded me of Mullen's office and Jeg battering it insanely with a chair leg over big Shona's infidelity. As well as the elderly man who summoned me, there was a middle-aged man with a big bushy black beard sitting in the middle of the three. Shit, I thought, I hope he's not related to Sheriff Rasputin in any way; to his right sat an elderly woman, who looked fairly well to do. What could these people, whom I had never seen before, possibly understand about me or my situation, I thought, or maybe my behaviour had already forfeited any entitlement to understanding that I might in different circumstances have been awarded.

Margaret Clark was already sitting in the room and she smiled at me as I awkwardly took my seat in front of the hearing members. My chair seemed to be lower than everyone else's, which immediately made me feel smaller and less significant than all the other people in the room, particularly the hearing members. 'Do you know why you're here today, Allan?' the chairman addressed me directly. 'Aye … so that you can send me to approved school,' I said defiantly, in an attempt to assume more control than I actually felt. 'Well, that's not really the way to look at it, Allan,' he replied indignantly. 'Oh right … so ah'm no' goin' to approved school then.' 'Well yes you are, but … ' 'Exactly … that's why I'm here … to be sent to approved school,' I said enjoying his growing discomfort which served to temporarily ease my own. 'You are obviously outwith your father's control, young man.'

I was seething and resented the way he was dismissing my maw's presence, influence and the pain and worry that she had suffered over the years. I was also conscious of publicly taking sole responsibility for my own behaviour; even though I was aware that I could probably have given them a number of mitigating reasons to absolve *some* of that responsibility, I was trying to defend my maw and ease the embarrassment and guilt she was experiencing in this situation as a parent. Acknowledging my mood and attempting to defuse the situation, Margaret quickly intervened and said, 'Allan's father has no input with him and yes he fully understands why he is here.'

With the exception of my maw, the adults in the room continued to talk over me for a short period about my 'best interests'. As it was a foregone conclusion, I consciously took no further part in the proceedings and sat back in the chair, trying to mask my fear and apprehension. 'Do you have anything to say in conclusion Allan?' asked the chairman in his efforts to bring the hearing to a close, to which I responded by disdainfully ignoring him. It was decided that I would be placed in St. Andrews Approved School in Shandon, near Helensburgh, for an unspecified period of time. With the hearing over, we made our way outside and before leaving the building my maw threw her arms around me. 'I'll be okay, maw,' I said uncomfortably, with my arms hanging limply by my sides, embarrassed at this public show of affection. Margaret merely stood silently with a look of genuine sadness on her face and touched my arm lightly.

Without looking back, I walked outside between the accompanying Darvel staff, when one of them suddenly stopped and shouted, 'Some swine's let the tyres down!' I noticed that the two nearside tyres were flat as the staff member kicked one of them furiously in disbelief. At that point, Jeg and Watty came swaggering innocently along the pavement towards us. 'Huv you got the time, please?' Jeg asked one of the staff members politely. He winked at me as the man naïvely checked his watch and replied accordingly; this was their deviant wee way of saying goodbye.

My overnight stay in Darvel was uneventful and so quick was the turnover of boys at the centre that I did not know anyone there. However, the boys had heard prior to my arrival that I was a Longriggend veteran and on my way to approved school. Accordingly, I was automatically given a level of kudos which meant that I got no hassle and so had no cause to defend this bestowed identity which before long would become inseparable from any genuine sense of self that I had previously known. I was relieved that old Sammy wasn't on shift when I arrived at the centre as I would have been too embarrassed seeing him, feeling that I had let him down by my return. I knew that my somewhat prestigious status amongst my peers would not have impressed him and whilst his indifference to this did not matter so much, it was his disappointment I could not bear. As a result, I was impatient to leave the following morning and was glad when the same two staff members appeared early to take me to approved school.

Sitting alone in the back of the car, I was jerked out of my gloomy reverie by the intriguing content of the conversation between Mr McVey and Mr Lamb. The former was talking about his father who had recently suffered a heart attack and was obviously concerned over his continued ailing health. I was struck by his sincere concern for his father whom he obviously loved very much and the bond they had between them. I was equally captivated by this genuine openness, the expression of such close feelings as I had never before witnessed it to this extent, particularly between two men. Mr McVey proceeded unreservedly to tell an attentive Mr Lamb about his relationship with his father, their closeness and the experiences they had shared over the years. Engrossed in the stories, I fidgeted in the back of the car trying to lean forward, unnoticed, to listen to the stories more closely.

Instinctively, I began to think about my relationship with my own father and to my surprise I started to feel quite sad and empty that I had never experienced the same relationship with him as Mr McVey had with his father. I certainly hated the way he abused my mother, but thinking about it seriously, I wasn't really sure if I hated *him*. I hated his misplaced need to be a hard man, yet I could identify vulnerability in him. I hated the way he would smash up our house and our belongings, but did not really think that he did it to deliberately *hurt* us. I hated the way he seemed to be indifferent to, or even resentful of, my very existence, but acknowledged the distance I maintained. On reflection, I am unsure what role, either conscious or subconscious, I played in maintaining this distance between us. Where do the boundaries of responsibility and blame reside within such a complex and tormented relationship? On the other hand, he had always appeared closer to the rest of the family than he ever did to me, always seeming to have at least some semblance of a relationship with them, particularly Jerry, which to an extent was understandable but which also demonstrated a level of paternal interest, at least, which had otherwise by-passed me.

All of this got me thinking of a time when I was aged around nine; Jerry, I and some other weans were playing away in a neighbouring street one summer evening and as usual my sister, Ellen, was sent down to get us as it was getting late. Lost in the moment of play, however, I resented this and refused point blank to go home with her and as Ellen eventually chased and caught me, I turned to Jerry and shouted, 'Quick, Jerry, don't let her catch you!' At that, Jerry immediately bolted and, without looking, made to run across the road in his efforts to escape Ellen's clutches. He did not even notice the car coming and both Ellen and I stood watching helplessly as the speeding car hit him with a dull thud, throwing him into the air, before his head smashed onto the road surface with a sickening crack. We all stood motionless and, despite our ages, knew immediately that Jerry was seriously injured, maybe even dead, as he lay completely still on the road with the blood seeping from his head.

The silence was broken by the cries of the female driver as she clambered from the car and stood over him, screaming hysterically. He was not expected to live through the night and my maw and da were warned that there could be some form of brain damage in the event that he *did* survive. It was a traumatic time around the house as Jerry lay in hospital in a coma for days. No-one spoke to me directly but, despite being so young myself, I knew that it was generally felt that I was to blame for what happened and I subsequently carried that feeling of guilt for years afterwards, which only lessened in later years when more pressing and distressing issues came to the fore. Fortunately Jerry made a full recovery and was brought home amid great fuss after several weeks in hospital.

Did my role in Jerry's near death play an irreversible role in the relationship between me and my da? Perhaps it was the fact that he perceived me more to be a mummy's boy or was he merely mirroring my attitude towards him? Amidst my confusion, I sat in the back of the car in emotional crisis as the adults in the front blethered away; hitherto my whole familial identity seemed to have been formed around protecting my maw, providing for her where possible, and seemingly hating my da—it's what appeared to define me and without this I'd be nothing, I thought. Despite my further efforts and experiences over the course of my life, these conflicting emotions surrounding my da continue to create a conflict, an inner turmoil at times, to the present day. I remain perpetually torn between feelings of incomprehension and understanding, between anger and pity.

Due to my interest in the adult conversation the drive to Shandon passed incredibly quickly. 'Well, here we are, Allan', said Mr Lamb, as if thinking aloud. Turning to face me he said, 'If you stay out of trouble you'll be home with your family in no time, Allan, so good luck'. On entering the administration building between Mr McVey and Mr Lamb, I scanned my surroundings nervously; it reminded me of the Registrar's building in Saltcoats with its wall-lined seating arrangements and numerous dark wooden doors enclosing the waiting room. Without a word being spoken, Mr McVey handed over my file, as if passing on the service history documents of a second-hand car, to a plump middle-aged woman who sat behind the administration desk. I was now the official property of St. Andrews Residential School. Saying a brief goodbye to me, Mr McVey and Mr Lamb made towards the main doors of the administration block. 'Mr McVey!' I shouted over quickly. Turning inquisitively to face me, with a look of surprise on his face equalling my own at my sudden outburst, I said to him quietly and now embarrassed at the direct attention, 'Ah hope your da gets better.' Following a momentary silence, he walked back across the floor to where I was sitting and looked directly down at me, 'You take good care of yourself, young man,' he said gently. He then turned his back on me and made his way outside to join Mr Lamb.

CHAPTER 16

The Best Interests of the Child

St Andrew's was one of maybe five catholic residential schools for boys in or around Scotland's central belt in the mid-1970s; a number of other schools were run by the Church of Scotland. The term residential school was interchangeable with the term, 'List D', which categorised the pupils of such establishments as being 'problematic'; however, the old term of 'approved school' very much prevailed during this period. Approved schools were meant to be used as a last resort in the wider child welfare system theoretically to provide care, control and rehabilitation for youngsters who were deemed beyond control and who were generally involved in persistent offending. Although predominantly referred there by the Children's Hearing system, some youngsters, still under the age of 16, were on occasion sent to approved school as part of a court order, generally the last stop before borstal. As I was to experience some months later, a 16th birthday held great significance within both the Children's Hearing system and the adult criminal justice system. On reaching the age of 16 transition into adulthood was an overnight phenomenon and what until then were children were automatically processed through the adult system, regardless of maturation, mitigation or circumstance.

The average stay in approved schools during this period was approximately 12 months and people could only be discharged by a Children's Hearing or through the expiry of a court sentence. By the mid-1970s, the effectiveness of approved schools as a deterrent or a rehabilitative measure was being seriously questioned and slowly replaced with more cost-effective methods of intervention in the community supposedly more appropriate to the needs of these children. The full extent of the brutality and appalling child care practices of some of these schools would not be fully realised for some years to come. For example, one such school, Kerelaw, which was located in my neighbouring town of Stevenston, would several decades later, between 2006-7, become known for the biggest residential child abuse scandal in Britain with some staff members being prosecuted and sent to prison for the systematic physical and sexual abuse of children in their care, spanning a 30-year period. Thankfully very few such establishments remain today.

Like so many of the significant buildings of my early history, St Andrews was steeped in history and character; the main building was a large sandstone house with castellated turrets and had been owned by a tobacco baron at the end of last century. Located in a semi-rural area at the edge of a very affluent and picturesque village called Shandon, the building was surrounded on three sides by a heavily wooded area; the remaining side overlooked the Firth of Forth where the submarines could be seen leaving and returning to the nearby Faslane naval base. Just next to the main building were two separate modern two-storey buildings. A further way off was a large gym hall, a number of workshops, classrooms and around 20 residential houses for the staff who chose to live on site. The school accommodated about 60 boys aged between 14 and 17, who were housed in three separate units between the main building and the two separate purpose built structures, with a full compliment of care staff, teachers, cooks and maintenance workers.

'Ah, you must be Allan Weaver,' said a tall skinny man in his late thirties, as he entered the reception block briskly, his face just recently shaved but already blue in preparation for the never ending onset of stubble. His hair was unintentionally tousled and a thin frame made his clothes appear ill-fitting. 'I'm Mr Alexander and I'm the housemaster of Douglas Block, where you have been assigned,' he said in a normal matter-of-fact tone. Whilst not particularly warm or friendly, I was immediately struck by the contrast between my reception in Barlinnie and Longriggend, which had increasingly occupied my mind as I sat alone in the waiting area. He must have noticed my hesitation as I stood before him awkwardly, as he quickly added, 'Don't look so worried.' In continuation of what must have been a regular routine, I was led over to my assigned unit by Mr Alexander who proceeded to give me a brief introduction to the school and a more detailed one to the school rules and regulations, oblivious to, or at the very least unperturbed by, my complete lack of response.

The vast majority of Douglas block's 20 boys were from the Glasgow area, the nearest city to the school, who were all vaguely similar to me in age and background. The sleeping quarters were on the upper level of the building and consisted of six rooms, each of which held four beds. Downstairs were the recreational room, eating area, staff room and shower room. I was in my assigned dormitory changing from my own clothes into school issue, navy blue jeans, denim shirt, and navy sweatshirt with black plimsolls, as the rest of the boys arrived noisily in the eating area from workshops and classes for lunch.

As I made my way downstairs to the eating room, I felt intimidated, embarrassed and rather vulnerable being the new boy in the block; the automatic focus of unwanted attention. I was also conscious that I did not have a pre-existing reputation to protect me, which left me increasingly unsure as to how to conduct or portray myself in this potentially hostile environment. As a failsafe, I settled on moving anonymously about with my eyes focused predominantly on the floor as I queued and collected my first meal from the serving hatch at the top of the dining hall.

Being generally shy and withdrawn in the company of strangers and with no alcohol or the acquired acceptance of my own crew to give me confidence, I found the initial period of settling into the school a bit of a struggle. As a consequence of avoiding, for the most part, direct communication with anyone for the first month, I was feeling increasingly lonely, withdrawn and isolated, not to mention terribly homesick. Letters from my maw were the highlight of my day as she faithfully wrote to me several times a week updating me on everything that was happening at home, news I longed to hear to reassure and comfort me, providing confirmation of an existence beyond the one into which I had been thrust. I was initially left to my own devices by the other boys, who were unable to work me out, and I would generally find a quiet corner in the unit where I would be left in peace to read; disappearing into books afforded me a way of passing time and a much needed means of escape. Be it books, museums or other interests, I have always needed my solitary routes of escape from the limits of my mind and the confines of my world.

'Whits wi aw these books, man?' asked a young guy called Psycho one day as I sat in my room alone devouring John Buchan's *Thirty-nine Steps*. 'Ah just like to read, Psycho, ... its good fur ye,' I replied looking up at him as he stood over me with something of a concerned look on his face. 'Any shaggin' in them?' he retorted with a wry grin as if stumbling across my well kept secret.

Psycho was a dwarf-like character who had been born with foetal alcohol syndrome and his hyperactive demeanour gave him a pixie-like quality, which of course ensured that he was a regular target for bullies in the unit, although he worked hard on his wits to minimise this, often resorting to mimicking insanity which would afford him a degree of safety in the unit. Drawn to me by an impulsive yearning born from an appreciation of our status as outsiders, he intruded into my personal bubble with increasing regularity and as he could not read, he would often sit at my side in silence while, rather than alienate him further, I summarised each chapter of whatever book I happened to be reading at the time. 'Good wee stories, eh,' he would repeat over and over again as he sat blowing smoke rings skilfully into the air. On one such occasion he cautioned quietly between chapters, 'Here, Weavy, … that Steeko thinks your jist a prick an' he's gonna sort ye oot.' Trying to feign disinterest and mask my increasing worry, I just ignored the warning.

From the outset, I was aware of the hierarchy within the unit which comprised, in descending order, a Glasgow guy called Steeko, the main man, with five or six hangers on in addition to a collection of submissive pseudo gangsters who drooled shamelessly on his every word. There were a couple of guys who generally kept themselves to themselves and for reasons, as yet, unknown to me, were afforded the privilege of doing so, while the rest were just generally ego fodder for Steeko and his gang. Although he was slightly older, Steeko was about the same height and build as me; he had a thick Glasgow accent and a hard looking face, a roadmap to his numerous battles in the past, obviously not all victorious, or at least unscathing. Initially, I was a source of some frustration, mystery and confusion to Steeko – an unwelcome enigma. Since I had arrived in the unit, I would catch him gauging me by a single glance in my direction, and due to my unintentionally somewhat mysterious silence and refusal to mix with anyone, he was unsure how to pigeonhole me. Unable to work me out and obviously tired of trying, with no indications to the contrary, he had now deemed me easy fodder like the other guys he bullied in the unit every day.

Steeko had the timing of his beatings in the unit down to a fine art and as early evening approached it was always a bad time for the vulnerable guys as there was virtually no staff presence. One such time, as I was sitting alone in my room trying to read, admittedly somewhat agitatedly preoccupied with the pending confrontation, Steeko kicked my room door open with a bang and strutted in with an exaggerated swagger; five other guys scurried obediently behind him. My heart was pounding as if it was trying, in anticipation of the inevitable, to escape my chest; I felt really vulnerable. As I lay on my bed he approached and stooped down to my face, 'You're no' so fucken' hard noo, ur ye,' he growled. As I tried to sit up in bed to avoid his smoke stained breath, one of the other guys ran quickly towards me and before I could react smacked a heavy lump of wood over my head. Shocked and stunned by the ferocity of the attack I stumbled onto the floor as the blows rained down on me from all directions and, determined to conceal my pain, in an attempt to protect myself I curled up into a foetal position. Breathless from their exertions, they left me lying on the bedroom floor as they ran from the room hollering and laughing.

With the exception of a dull throbbing pain in my head, I felt relatively physically unscathed as my hands and arms seemed to have deflected most of the blows. However, as I sat up in the bed trying to compose myself I noticed that my book had been torn in half, my shirt ripped open and what few possessions I had, had been rifled from my small bedside unit. Like a simmering volcano, I felt the tears and rage well violently inside me; I felt humiliated, which for me was far worse than any beating I could have taken, and which rapidly evolved into a dark, murderous rage. With tears stuck deep in my throat, almost breathless, I pulled myself to my feet and began running downstairs in pursuit of Steeko. Unable to find a weapon of any kind in my uncontrollable manic state I ran directly to the television room where I knew Steeko and his mates were.

As I reached the television room Steeko happened to be standing at the doorway, holding court as usual. As he was startled and caught off guard by my sudden appearance, I head butted him on the bridge of the nose as hard as I could, the audible impact of which echoed round the place. As he fell backwards I began shouting and screaming, deep nonsensical screams, as I then knelt on his chest before he had the chance to recover and battered my fists into his exposed, defenceless face. With my temper still broken, I shot up, grabbed a solitary dart from the dartboard nearby and stabbed it hard into his stomach while he lay stunned on the floor. The other guys stood motionless throughout as I left him lying groaning in pain.

Nothing was ever said of this incident to me directly and from this time onwards, my stay at the school was hassle free, as was Psycho's. Self-named, Psycho, I soon discovered, was not a real Psycho, but Patrick McFeddres, a vulnerable young guy from Greenock who had enduring mental health problems and understandably, massive insecurities. The facade of being Psycho was a conscious ploy on his part to keep Steeko and his like at bay, which obviously had its limitations. I did wonder, at the time, how his Children's Hearing panel members could have possibly thought that his presence in a place like this could ever be in his 'best interests,' or anyone else's for that matter. When you got to know him, Patrick was a likeable wee guy who had been in and out of local authority care since his mother left him standing in a police waiting room with a broken arm at the age of six. He had never seen or heard from her again; several years later I was to discover that Patrick died, sad and lonely, at the age of 17 from a drug overdose.

The school headmaster, Mr Donald, was a tall, elderly man who resembled a retired military general—straight backed, with a ruddy complexion and full head of snowy white hair, he looked proud and distinguished. A pious disciplinarian, he had an active interest in the running of the school and the welfare of the boys in his charge, centring around the regulation and control of their behaviour. He would conduct our daily school religious services, where he would read from the Bible with great zeal and gusto as we sat regimented before him at pains to disguise our boredom, discomfort and disinterest. I was always relieved during such times that he did not know about me and wee Granty robbing the Chapel collection boxes in Saltcoats some years earlier, as I imagined he would have pursued a lead role in my personal crucifixion.

Other staff members, however, were far less committed to the reformatory task and although some of them were kind and well intended, others, including our housemaster, Mr Alexander, tended to be oblivious, or at least indifferent, to the needs of the boys, opting instead for a less demanding working life. This was, of course, prior to the introduction of audits and minimum standards of care, and at this time staff were normally unqualified, untrained and ill-equipped to meet the complex needs and demands of those in their care: a cross-section of society's most vulnerable and damaged children. Typically, Mr Alexander and the senior members of staff, although not manifestly abusive, devolved a level of responsibility and power to the Steekos of the units and this dominant, aggressive sub-culture imposed its own measures of control. As a result, the school proved a terribly brutal environment for some boys who were subjected to relentless bullying and systematic emotional, psychological and physical abuse.

Sadly, and indicative of the desperation of some lives perhaps, the school still provided a means of escape from some boys' normal living environments. I remember in particular, to everyone's bewilderment at the time, one guy in the unit would refuse point blank to go on home leave and would smash the unit windows and run away to avoid it, always returning as soon as the bus had left to drop people off for home leave. Sexual abuse did not receive the same recognition in the 1970s and for countless child victims it was a case of suffering alone and in silence. Perhaps further reflecting the general culture of indifference, there was certainly no acknowledgement or understanding within the school in relation to such matters. It materialised some years later that this particular guy was being sexually abused by his drunken father and passed to his like-minded friends during his periods of home leave.

As the weeks passed, I missed home more and more despite continuing to receive two letters a week from my maw, which I would take to my room and read repeatedly. I never heard from the guys when I was there and did not really expect to, for this would have been too overt an expression of affection and so I understood. At the same time, I did not really miss them and began to worry more about my pending court appearance as the possibility of borstal was becoming an increasingly worrying likelihood.

Whilst children in mainstream schooling were preparing for their academically orientated preliminary O-level exams, I was assigned to a work party within the school and worked four days a week as a brickie's labourer, with the other day given over to schooling. In reality, however, the classrooms descended into bedlam and were only ever treated as a rest day from the demands of work. In the absence of normal academic tuition, the school nonetheless provided an alternative vocational learning environment; I could mix near-perfect batches of cement for building, foundations or plastering, prepare the required groundwork for construction and cut a brick with a pointed hammer with great precision. On the odd occasion, I thought that maybe my da would have approved of my building skills.

Oddly enough, although I had been categorised as a persistent offender, no reference was ever made to my offending in the school and there was no attempt to intervene, or to improve the social and personal circumstances underpinning this behaviour. Rather, the focus was primarily on encouraging self-control, as if the injection of discipline, both internal and external, would remedy my apparently impulsive, self-indulgent lack of restraint. Thus, when I could evidence an improvement in my presenting behaviour within the confines of the school, I would have demonstrated my readiness to return to 'normal' society, if the mayhem and madness that comprised my ordinary life could be described as such. However, during my time in St Andrews I did learn how to open and start a Mark III Ford Cortina with a teaspoon; make a home-made weapon from a toothbrush and razor blade; pick someone's inside pocket without detection; and to disable the latest shop alarm systems – all practical skills that, in combination with my developed labouring abilities, I could perhaps draw on in later life if required.

Around my seventh week in the school, it was decided that I was ready for a period of home leave and excitedly I wrote to my maw to inform her that I was coming home. The night before my home leave I lay awake, restless. I wondered how things would be at home—would my da start and if so what would I do? Would I be able to keep back from the guys as I could not afford to get into any more trouble, particularly if I wanted to avoid going to borstal for my outstanding court appearance? Also, Mr

Donald would go ballistic if I picked up any more charges. Part of me was wary of going home—it was all very well exercising 'restraint' in a context in which choices were sorely limited; it was another to be plunged back into reality, where the context in which these choices could be exercised was radically different. Still, I was desperate to get home again, this being my longest period so far away from my maw and wee brothers; all the way back, I sat looking out of the train window, willing away the cold looking stations as the train sped down the Ayrshire coast. It was good to have my own clothes on again, two pounds in my pocket and my treasured school letter highlighting that I was on temporary leave from approved school, in the event of being stopped by the police.

CHAPTER 17

Wilful Deviance: Road Map for Borstal

'He's here … he's here, maw!' Billy shouted excitedly as I walked through the front door. 'There's ma big boy!' my maw shouted as she threw her arms round me. My da was in Aberdeen working and whilst this had brought with it some temporary respite for my maw, he hadn't sent any money home for several weeks, creating new and added pressures in response to which she had been forced to borrow money to live on. I discovered later that she had accrued significant rent arrears and had been threatened with eviction.

Jeg, Watty and wee Shuggie called for me the following day and, although initially planning to avoid them, I all too quickly and readily succumbed to the lure of my peers and admittedly it was good to see them all again. Eddie was still in Geilsland Approved School, which had the reputation for being one of the hardest approved schools, where he had been for the past three weeks.

'Good to be free again then, eh?' asked Shuggie as we began walking up towards the Street. 'Free … It's no exactly Barlinnie, it's only approved school,' I replied, cockily with some feigned authority. 'Whit's it like anyway?' asked Jeg with a look of concern on his face, 'cause me and Watty are due to be put in wan soon as well.' Jeg and Watty were still expelled for breaking into the school. 'Aye, you'll be fine,' I lied preferring not to tell them about the on-going pain and isolation I experienced and my solitary existence as an outsider.

We stood on the street corner catching up on old times and the thought of St Andrews disappeared further with every slug of wine. However, my thoughts would increasingly return to my maw and the fact that she had little or no money; I knew she was worried sick about the rent arrears and she did not know when she would get money from my da again. I felt an unshakeable sense of guilt and responsibility towards her. Morosely, I was also thinking of my own situation; although my maw had fussed over me relentlessly, on my return I had felt a sense of dislocation—as if I did not belong in the house. To top it all, Jerry had moved into my bed, which seemed to further displace me, although unintentionaly.

As a welcome intrusion, Watty, rubbing his hands together Fagan-like, said, 'Listen … ah've got a lovely wee turn lined up, plenty o' cash.' Due to his pending Children's Hearing, Jeg declined the offer and began walking home. 'Ah think ah'll jist gee it a miss as well,' said Shuggie sheepishly as he walked away to catch up with Jeg. 'Aye never mind them … let's just dae it,' I said instantly, my senses now dulled completely with the cheap wine, seizing the opportunity to try to fix my maw's troubles, and to strangle the increasingly brooding sense of alienation that my return home and the wine had conspired to create. Watty chattered on excitedly as he began to tell me about a friend of his da's who had apparently just won a lot of money on the horses.

After climbing through the window of the targeted house behind Watty, I was beginning to feel quite guilty, despite the drink. By the look of the house and where it was located, he was obviously just a normal guy who, whether he won money on the horses or not, probably struggled financially like the rest of us. Unable to dismiss the pangs of guilt, I whispered to Watty, 'Remember we're just here for this guy's winnins and nothin' else … straight in and oot, right.' 'Aye, aye, nae problem,' he replied in a concentrated whisper. Moving swiftly through the darkened house we decided to start our search for the money in the upstairs bedroom. Shutting the venetian blinds and closing the curtains, we put the light on and began to search around the room. I felt even more uncomfortable looking at the random displays of ordinariness such as the guy's unmade bed, his slippers, a hairbrush: all reminders of this guy's wearied existence. My feelings of guilt heightened. Conversely, Watty was whistling away quietly at the other end of the room as he began searching through the bedside cabinet.

Some seconds later, we heard a car door slamming shut directly outside the house. Looking at each other in panic, we tiptoed to the window to peek through the blinds. Standing in the front garden, hands on his hips and looking directly up at us as we peered out was a giant of a man. On seeing us, he immediately roared some undecipherable threat, as he then sprinted towards the front door. Rooted to the spot, we could hear him fumbling with his key in the lock, no doubt struggling to open it in his blind rage. 'Quick ,Weavy!' screamed Watty in terror as we heard the front door being violently flung open.

'I'm going to murder you thievin' bastards,' the man boomed as he clattered up the stairs. As we bolted into the back bedroom, we began clawing desperately at the curtains and blinds in our desperation to get the window open, our only way out. The curtains and blinds came crashing down on top of us and tangled around Watty. 'Ah'm gonna kill you!' the guy screamed, now directly outside the bedroom door. Untangling the blind cords from Watty's neck, we fumbled hysterically at the window and as it swung open Watty immediately flung himself through it into the darkness. At that, the bedroom door crashed open with a tremendous bang and splintered under the weight of this guy's boot. His voice seemed to be magnified in the confines of this small space as he came hurtling through it screaming, 'Bastards! Bastards!' With his outstretched hands only inches from me I too threw myself out into the darkness behind Watty.

My fall was cushioned by my fortuitous landing—on top of Watty—who shoved me off him and holding an ankle in each hand, sat on the back lawn of the enclosed garden groaning. 'Ah've broken ma ankle man!' he cried. Before we could get up, the guy's head appeared from the upstairs window, 'Jist wait there till ah get doon!' he screamed at us, a little optimistically I thought, as he then charged from the room. We could clearly hear his hurried footsteps thundering down the stairs several at a time; 'Fuck, quick Watty,' I said in a panic, pulling Watty bodily to the back of the garden, identifying our only means of escape in the shape of a large prickly hedge. Watty screamed in agony as I began pushing him through the hedge as the thorny branches snapped and twisted snake-like around his body. 'Ah cannae get through!' he yelled in desperation as he fought and tore to do so. With one final desperate push, he suddenly burst through to the other side and with the guy now pelting up the back lawn towards me, I threw myself in an adrenaline fuelled abandon, headfirst after him. As the guy wrestled unsuccessfully with the hedge behind us like a trapped, snarling bear, we quickly hobbled to safety, torn and bloodied. Leaning heavily on my shoulder as we made our way down to The Street, Watty turned to me and said through his oddly outraged tears, 'Ahv a good mind to phone the polis ... that guy's a fucken' nutter.'

Some three months after arriving at St. Andrews approved school, I received my summons to appear at Kilmarnock Sheriff Court for the outstanding school offence, a mere two days after my sixteenth birthday. As earlier indicated, the date was to prove quite significant for me as it meant that I could be now be sentenced at court as a young adult, unlike Jeg, Watty and Eddie, who were several months younger than me and who would accordingly be sentenced as children. I had discussed this outstanding court matter with Mr Donald at St Andrews on a number of occasions and he was unfalteringly optimistic that I would not be sent to borstal or a young offenders institution; rather, he was of the opinion that I would be returned to the school, although perhaps under a court order. I did not share his optimism; my experience of the system so far was such that I dared not hope, for fear of having to deal with the worst case scenario, totally unprepared.

In the weeks leading up to the court date, I had not picked up any more charges during my periods of home leave, still recovering from the trauma of our last break-in and life, in general, was definitely quieter than normal. This seemingly positive development, however, could not be attributed to the rehabilitative efforts or successful interventions of St Andrews, as might simply have been surmised by professionals; my placement there still had not acted as the 'gateway for support' it professed to provide, as my feelings of alienation persisted, my attitude to offending had not altered any and my difficulties at home, if anything, had intensified during my brief periods of home leave. Rather, it was due mainly to the fact that Watty was now in the centre for more housebreakings and Eddie was, for most of the time, confined to his approved school.

On the day we appeared in court for sentencing, the public gallery in the court room was packed: with members of our families; some friends; the friends and families of those who were to appear before and after us; not to mention the curious, regular onlookers who discreetly strained to catch a glimpse of the four of us sitting in the dock. My maw sat in the front row, directly behind me, as near to me as she could get. Whilst we were awaiting the start of the formalities, we sat childishly whispering and giggling nervously.

Jeg and Watty were slicked up for the occasion, their turkey like necks protruding uncomfortably from starched collars further secured in position by their ties, which in turn, were stuffed into frayed suit jackets of questionable fit, obviously borrowed for the day. In contrast, Eddie was wearing his approved school sweatshirt, which if not actively suggestive, was nevertheless, a direct cue to the Sheriff that the full range of sentencing options were at his disposal. This was the first I had seen Eddie for several months and he spent most of the time in the dock sitting quietly with his head bowed. 'You awright, Eddie?' I asked him quietly. 'Aye … ah jist want this ower wi,' he returned, somewhat fatalistically and again drew his eyes to the floor. Much to my embarrassment and the amusement of Jeg and Watty, although in keeping with Mr Donald's well-meaning instructions, I was clad in a wee bottle green checked tie and matching jacket, provided by the school. 'You have to present as being smart and respectful, lad,' insisted Mr Donald in his normal unquestionable, authoritative manner as he ran his eye over me before I left the school earlier that morning. In doing so he was plainly oblivious to the further disgrace this dodgy outfit added to my already public shame.

'Whit dae you think'll happen, Weavy?' Watty asked, kick-starting his mantra in nervous anticipation as though suddenly realising the seriousness of our situation. 'Ah don't know, Watty, but ah'm sure we'll be awright,' I replied, trying to calm him down. Returning to his gallows humour, more for his own benefit I suspected, Jeg began to tap his knee with his fingers and hum quietly rather prophetically the tune, 'Working on the Chain Gang.'

As the Sheriff entered, we were ordered to our feet and the now familiar formalities began once again. The courtroom fell respectfully and expectantly silent as Rasputin sat and read over our respective reports. Before sentencing us the court was required by law to have court reports undertaken and, given my age, I required a borstal report, which would focus not only on my personal and family history, but more importantly my suitability for borstal. I read this report some years later and although it recommended that I be returned to St. Andrew's in Shandon, the biographical history omitted anything resembling my own perceptions of my life to date, or the environment in which I had been raised; rather, the social worker's predominant assessment was that my offending behaviour was the outcome of rational choice, thus attributing my apparently malicious actions purely to wilful deviance.

Before sentence was passed the Procurator Fiscal was again invited to outline the offences, which he did fully, with a mixture of panache and dramatic solemnity, as he spoke at length of the cost of this heinous act to the teaching staff, pupils and the tax-paying general public; in short, the unsuspecting law-abiding society, to which we were placed in horrible contrast. Yet again, Mr Hart lacked conviction in comparison to his legal adversary, as he stood and searched frantically through a pile of papers as a precursor to an incoherent ramble which lasted for several minutes, without once referring to us individually or asking the court to consider leniency, given our ages and backgrounds.

As arranged, Mr Donald was then invited to take the stand on my behalf where he spoke with some authority of the difficulties I had faced in my life; the changes in my attitude and behaviour consequent on my placement in the school in the preceding weeks; how my offending had reduced significantly over previous months; and how I was becoming a more positive influence on other boys in the school. 'I have said all I have to say in support of this child and I trust that he will be allowed to return to school with me to continue his rehabilitation in my care,' he concluded confidently and pointedly before leaving the stand. Although I could not recognise fully the child or the rehabilitative process to which Mr Donald referred, I was heartened greatly by his efforts and on sneaking a glance at my maw behind me, she smiled and cocked her thumb positively towards me.

Addressing us over his spectacles, Rasputin began, 'Vandalism is an increasing concern in our society and when it affects schools in such a manner it can be particularly disturbing, especially as it often impacts upon education and staff morale. I have no alternative now but to pass the following sentences. 'Allan Weaver,' he continued, 'you have an appalling record for such a young man … you have consistently refused the help offered to you by your schoolteachers and the social work department and quite frankly you have become an affront to common decency. I sentence you to two years' borstal training.' 'Edward George Nisbet, another young man with no regard for decency and like Weaver, well versed in List D establishments. Unlike him however, you may feel grateful that you have not yet reached the age of 16. I sentence you to two years' residential training [approved school].' 'Walter Wilson', he continued, tearing swiftly through us like a hired assassin, insensible to the effects of his words, 'I sentence you to two years' residential training.' 'James Arthur McCleary …. although you have perhaps been on the periphery of such criminality, you have nevertheless pleaded guilty to a serious offence and you too are sentenced to two years residential training.'

We were too stunned to observe the reactions around us, as we were crudely ushered from the courtroom, and into the cells where we sat quietly, ashen faced; Watty bundled himself into the far corner with his knees pulled tightly into his chest, rocking back and forth. 'Two years fur throwin' a desk through a windae,' said Jeg as he paced manically back and forth, unable to comprehend what had just happened. 'Aye, but remember the watch strap,' I quipped in a failed effort to penetrate the gloom.

Before long, the main cell door was opened by the police preparing for the Barlinnie transfer. 'Weaver, quick outside, we're ready to go,' barked one of the officers. 'Whit aboot the rest o' them?' I asked nodding towards the guys as I walked through the cell door. 'Come on, jump to it, your pals are going to Darvel tonight, you're in with the big boys now son, Barlinnie and then borstal for you,' he said matter of factly. 'Is there any chance o' seein' ma maw before ah go?' I pleaded as he began securing the handcuffs around my wrists. 'Naw, we're too busy,' he replied abruptly as he pulled me by the cuffed wrists to the waiting van outside. Straining my neck to look back, whilst trying to suppress the angst rising within me, I could see the guys standing staring quietly at me through the meshed gate in the cell area; no further word was spoken between us as the heaviness and intensity of our respective situations descended finally upon us, leaving no space even for pretence of anything otherwise. It would be over a year before I saw or heard from any of them again and it would be the last time ever that all of us were together.

CHAPTER 18

Reformative Aims, Brutal Regime

Even though I was only spending one night in 'D Hall', the whole Barlinnie admissions procedure felt far more traumatic without the guys, as I did not have the relative comfort of knowing that they were subject to the same horrible experience as me, nearby. As if to compound my discomfort, it was a blisteringly hot day for May which meant that the dog boxes were far harder to cope with as I stood crammed into the sweltering tomb with three other men, for more than four hours. My chest heaved as I gulped desperately for air. 'Two years' borstal training ...Two years' borstal training ...An affront to common decency,' echoed periodically in my head as I waited, trying desperately to block out any thoughts of what might lie ahead of me.

Borstal training had been introduced in Britain at the beginning of the twentieth century as a reformatory experience for young men who had well-established criminal tendencies and, obviously, for those who were an affront to common decency. It was named after the small Kentish town of Borstal, where the first institution was opened in 1908. It is still hard to comprehend that a corner of the English countryside will be forever synonymous with a regime premised on punishment, discipline and deterrence, and characterised by fear and brutality.

By the mid-1970s, borstal training, which was billed, somewhat idealistically, as an attempt to exert positive influence over the detainees' characters through education, regular work, vocational training and group counselling, was being used quite extensively by Scottish courts, with approximately 400 young offenders aged between 16 and 21 detained in the three Scottish borstals at any one time. Polmont Borstal, near Falkirk, was the principal institution, where every inmate was held in the main allocation hall to undergo a six week allocation assessment. After the assessment period, inmates were moved to one of the four main halls located in another part of the institution, to the semi-open borstal, Castlehuntly, in Dundee, or to the open borstal, Noranside, which was in Forfar. Although I had received a fixed two year sentence, the average time spent in borstal was around ten months; the remission period was the primary incentive for inmates to conform positively to the regime.

While I had spent almost six months in approved school, it had done nothing to prepare me for the harsh realities of life in borstal, which bore no relation to the summary of reformative objectives outlined previously. The admissions procedure mirrored that of Barlinnie and Longriggend and was conducted with the same premeditated brutality—which was no more tolerable with the dubious benefit of previous experience. It must have been a conscious, if unarticulated, method of breaking the spirit of those entering the establishments, as a questionable precursor to reform; it certainly worked with me on each occasion. As I was about to realise, however, each establishment had a slight variation in practice, which, in my experience, became more abusive, the deeper into the criminal justice system you were placed.

Having been processed through the full admissions procedure at Polmont, all new inmates were held in a waiting area pending an audience with the Governor. As I sat on a wooden bench beside the other admissions, clutching my standard issue bedding and toiletries and still trying to take in my surroundings, I was brought sharply back to reality: 'Weaver, report to the Governor ... come on, sharpish, lad!' boomed an officer through an open doorway. With a start, I dropped my bedding and toiletries clumsily on the floor. 'Fucken' leave it, you half-wit ... come on move it,' he continued. My instinctive anxiety about the possible loss of what little I had, was instantly over-ridden by my concern not to aggravate further this already patently agitated officer; I made my way in double quick time, half-walking, half-running, towards the door. 'Quicker, lad, quicker!' he screamed in my ear as I made my way into the Governor's office.

A large, repulsively fat, besuited man sat behind a desk reading what I presumed was my official paperwork. I was hurriedly ushered to a designated point just in front of his desk, where two burly officers positioned themselves so that they stood towering immediately behind me. 'Full name to the Governor, lad!' one bent and bellowed at me unnecessarily. The Governor continued to read as I nervously stuttered, 'eh ... Allan Weaver.' Without warning, the officer on my left punched me hard in the ear, throwing me across the room and crashing me against a filing cabinet. Before I had time to recover from the shock, I was instantly grabbed to my feet by the other officer and dragged over by the hair to the same standing point. 'In future you little ignoramus, you address the Governor as *sir*,' he barked. 'Full name to the Governor lad!' he screamed again. Anticipating another blow, I stood rigid with fear as a searing pain ran through my ear and blood trickled down the side of my face; his voice now resonating off the walls of my head like a cavernous echo. Unperturbed by the events unfolding before him, the Governor continued to read the paperwork nonchalantly, not once acknowledging my presence. 'Sir, Allan Weaver, sir,' I said cautiously, as the tears streamed down my face.

The disciplinary regime of borstal was militaristic in orientation with endless drills, marches and parades and during my early days I would stomp around my single cell in a small circle at night practising my marching manoeuvres in a desperate bid to improve my technique so as to avoid unwanted attention from the officers. As I had experienced on my first day in the place and continued to witness throughout my sentence, violence by officers towards inmates appeared to be the fundamental, if not a publicised, philosophy underpinning the disciplinary ethos. This was the flagship of the reformative experience, where beatings were openly meted out on a regular basis for even the slightest unintended transgression.

Retrospectively, I have wondered at their failure to identify this form of discipline as a continuation of the experiences of many of the inmates' earlier lives and I remain undecided as to whether they thought that such a regime of violent control would reform or recondition us to assume the behaviours they considered acceptable. On the other hand, perhaps the brutality was merely engineered to meet a punitive end in itself. Who knows? So entrenched was the brutality that the chaplain; the visiting committee who were appointed to oversee and monitor conditions within the institution; and all other lay persons attached to the place seemed to accommodate such practices as something of a penal institutional norm. During my first week, I sat before a welfare-type worker and, with the blood still clearly clotted in my ear, was asked chirpily, 'And how are you settling into this big house of ours, young man?'

As the youngest inmate in the borstal at the time, I had little choice but to gauge and try to understand the system as quickly as I could for the sake of self-preservation and, in the process, I soon became hardened to the forced environment. Drawing on certain aspects of my approved school experiences, I kept myself very much to myself and associated with few of the other inmates. I fought with other guys on two separate occasions, nothing particularly serious, but both were with a degree of measured premeditation on my part, and the subsequent, short spells I spent in solitary confinement were a small, calculated price to pay to preserve my continued pursuit of solitude and safety throughout the remainder of my sentence.

Although I was adapting to the regime, I never once lost the yearning for home, to be back with my maw, who religiously wrote to me weekly and who would embark on the long journey to access her awkward 40-minute, monthly visit without question or complaint. However, unbeknown to me, my world on the outside, as I knew it, was continuing to shift and change, both around and without me.

Several months before the end of my sentence, my maw told me during a routine visit that our house had been destroyed by fire. 'It's completely gutted, son, there was nothing left,' she began to cry. I failed initially to comprehend the severity of this situation for my maw—for all of us—as she told me it was due to some kind of electrical fault. In my effort to comfort her I meekly continued, 'But we can get everythin' again, maw, ah'll get a job when ah get oot.' 'Ach, I know son, it was only possessions and at least no-one was hurt,' she responded.

She then proceeded to tell me that we were all moving to Hartlepool as my da had found work down there and the local council had allocated us a house. As usual, she tried to be optimistic and she approached and presented this as an ideal opportunity to provide us all with a fresh start, more out of hope, I sensed, than expectation. Partly because I was unsure as to where Hartlepool actually was, I was apprehensive; once more I found myself entering into a new phase of my life, devoid of choice or control. I would have nowhere else to live, what little possessions I had, had been destroyed by the fire, and I would be released with no more than the clothes I was wearing when I was sentenced, to a strange town where I would know no one.

Despite my own fears and reservations, I willingly bought into my maw's version of events; I thought that maybe my da was trying to change and that this was his way of trying to make the best of a tragic accident; maybe things would be okay. However, several years later I was told that he deliberately torched the house during another drunken rampage but I have no way of knowing whether this is true. Adding to my maw's worries, my elder brother, James, had just recently received a 12 months custodial sentence for seriously assaulting a relative of the guy who stabbed me in the neck, out of pure retribution.

I had no personal contact with any of the guys throughout my time in borstal, although I was kept abreast of events through my maw and sometimes through other inmates who had come across them, or who had heard about them in other establishments. 'Here … are you pally wae that beast, Watty Wilson?' a new inmate confronted me aggressively as I sat in the dining room one morning. I was instantly on my guard on hearing the word 'beast,' which was a term for sex offenders, or someone who committed offences against children or the elderly. Surely not, Watty—tell me you haven't committed a sex offence on home leave, I thought quietly to myself. 'Whit the fuck's it goat to do wae you?' I responded straight off with equal aggression, knowing my response was all important in terms of both my personal standing within this brief exchange and possible guilt by association with Watty and whatever heinous crime he had committed. 'Cause he mugged two auld pensioners, the rat,' he replied matter of factly, as he walked away without further eye contact.

Whilst he was on home leave from approved school, Watty, I was soon to discover, had robbed two pensioners one night as they left a local bingo hall and had just received a five-year sentence in a young offenders institution. The general criminal population has always had a clear moral hierarchy of offences and those against any pensioner, like sex offences, were rooted firmly on the bottom rung and deemed totally unacceptable. The extent to which protection was required for so-called 'beasts' generally depended on how well the individual could fight, which in Watty's case did not bode well. As a result, I knew that Watty would have to be put in protective custody for the length of his sentence, which in effect, amounted to a prison within a prison. I could not hate Watty, or even dislike him for this offence. Knowing him as I did, I knew his behaviour on this occasion was grounded in his compulsion to steal, a trait which has remained with him all his life—as opposed to specifically targeting and terrorising vulnerable individuals, to whose predicament he would have been blindly oblivious. Eddie was also back in Longriggend awaiting sentence for more housebreakings, while Jeg was still in approved school and continuing to commit offences on his periods of home leave; not exactly models of reform and rehabilitation. Perhaps Hartlepool would not be as bad as I thought.

Having spent 12 months in borstal, I sat staring apprehensively out of the train window as it sped through the bleak countryside towards the industrial landscape of the north east of England. Including my time in approved school, I had been away for almost 18 months. I was aware of the physiological changes I had undergone; I was not much taller but I was definitely stockier, I had more body hair, I now shaved twice a week and my voice had deepened slightly. As I had been forced to live on my wits throughout this period, psychologically, I felt more resilient and mature or at least self-reliant, certainly hardened and more cynical—yet these dispositions resided awkwardly in stark juxtaposition to my very real feelings of vulnerability, insecurity and uncertainty. My dislocation from all my previous frames of reference left me confused over my own identity, and I felt cut off from the rest of the world, like a non-person; I did not know how to be either a child or an adult; I did not know where I belonged or even how to be.

Hartlepool lived up to my worst expectations and this particular period in my life proved very difficult. Although my maw fussed over me incessantly, I felt like a stranger in the new house. I was incredibly lonely without the company of anyone my own age; I did not have any friends, I certainly did not have a girlfriend and meeting people was much more difficult than I had ever imagined, particularly as I did not have the courage or the confidence to chat up lassies, even had I been given the opportunity. Even Jerry and Billy were out and about with their new-found friends.

Adding to my sense of unrest, boredom and depression was the lack of available employment; even if my recent borstal training was not an obstacle in itself, the area had higher than the national average rates of relative deprivation and unemployment, which meant that getting work was practically impossible. To pass away my days, I generally read in my bedroom or watched mind-numbing television. My relationship with my da never improved and although he had been off the drink for around six weeks, we kept a controlled distance from each other and never spoke.

To alleviate my incessant boredom and in desperation for something to do, I asked my maw one night if she fancied going to the cinema to see the much hyped film of that year, *Saturday Night Fever*. As if acknowledging my dilemma, she replied a shade too quickly and somewhat theatrically, 'Aye of course, son, I've been dying to see that film for ages.' Standing in the lengthy cinema queue with my maw, I noticed that the main population of film goers that evening were young couples, canoodling away, blissfully unaware of the awkwardness of those forced to stand next to them in the queue, who, like myself, shuffled about awkwardly, trying not to stare. The remainder of the cinema queue consisted exclusively of groups of young, unattached guys, clutching their testicles, punching the air and gyrating in John Travolta, disco-like fashion; I was becoming increasingly self-conscious of standing in this queue with my maw.

To make matters worse, when we eventually got in and started watching the film, there was a scene where a woman started giving her boyfriend a blow job; much to the delight of the whooping audience. Abandoning any attempt to conceal my utter embarrassment, in pure unrestrained desperation to deny the sordid act being played out in front of my maw's eyes, I made a monumental demonstration of turning 90 degrees to face her, as if oblivious to the seemingly never ending scene, and, staring at her intently, asked loudly, 'Do you want anythin' at the shop maw?' 'Its okay, son, I'll get it,' she blurted as she darted from her seat. Not only did we never discuss the matter, we never ever went to the cinema together again.

CHAPTER 19

Strangeways, Strange Days

Unable to stand the emptiness and isolation of my hollow days any longer, I phoned Shuggie, who agreed to come down to Hartlepool for a period as the police were looking for him anyway, for once. Several days later, I was waiting for him at the train station, when he bounced off the train holding nothing more than a carrier bag full of drink. 'You'll no' be stayin' long then, eh?' I quipped, relieving him of a can of beer, my first drink since being released from borstal. 'Ya wanker, ah thought you hud turned intae a grass or somethin', hidin' doon here oot the road!' he shouted affectionately around the station. 'Aye, but keep it quiet will ye,' I replied in the spirit of things, although inwardly I was overjoyed at his arrival.

Naturally, we automatically headed for the nearest pub, where we sat reminiscing but after such a long time without alcohol, its influence took a rapid hold. 'Any decent turns aboot here, Weavy, ah didnae even get a chance to get to the broo before ah came in case the polis were waitin' fur me,' he interrupted the drunken banter. Having just spent my own fortnight's Giro on us both in the pub, it sounded a plausible enough and rather seductive, well-argued proposition to me. And so, within a short time and with no thought of the possible consequences, Shuggie and I embarked on what turned out to be my last ever housebreaking, which proved more calamitous, more farcical and more mindless than anything that had gone before it.

After a drunken, rather half-hearted rummage through an empty house in a pretty affluent area of the town, we left completely penniless, although not entirely empty-handed—I was proudly sporting a heavy pair of cricket leg pads whilst Shuggie was the fine new owner of a cricket bat and a Bing Crosby record. Rather considerately, the latter was supposedly a present for his maw from Hartlepool, 'Ma maw fucken' loves Bing Crosby,' he said clutching the record adoringly under his arm. As I clumped down the road with my pads on, like a wee reject from Lords Cricket Club, a police car suddenly arrived on the scene and screeched to a halt before me. Some way behind, no doubt checking the Bing Crosby tracks on the record, Shuggie obviously saw the events unfolding before him, dropped his ill-gotten gains, loyally walked up the nearest garden path and escaped into oblivion—again.

Having spent two days in the cells at Hartlepool police station, I was taken before the local juvenile court charged with burglary and a public disorder offence, of 'resisting arrest'. However, rather than actively resisting arrest, I had been genuinely just unable to move properly when the police grabbed me because of the ill-fitting cricket pads strapped to my legs; instead, I was dragged unceremoniously into the back of the police car like something out of a *Carry On* film—and what a carry on. I also suspected that the latter charge was due in part to the fact that I would not tell them who my accomplice was.

Unlike Kilmarnock Sherriff Court, the juvenile court had far less pomp and ceremony and instead of a Sheriff, three lay people presided over the sentencing decision. In a well spoken voice and not unpleasant manner, the chairman of the bench addressed me directly, 'Well, young man, we see you have just completed borstal training in Scotland several months ago.' Tutting in disapproval, he added, 'and not a very successful rehabilitation at all, we see ... have you got anything to say before we move to sentence?' Standing nervously before him I knew that they had two main sentencing options: a fresh full term period of borstal, known as a 'fresh whack,' or a borstal 'recall,' which meant that I would be returned to a borstal for a period of four months only. In my normal, monosyllabic manner, I replied submissively, 'No, sir,' thinking that this was still preferable to legal representation by Mr Hart or his English equivalent.

Unable to face my maw, who sat alone in court, for the first time ever I felt truly ashamed of my behaviour; it had not been about money, or food, or a drunken rage or revenge. It had been a puerile, senseless, unnecessary act which caused untold further grief to my maw, not to mention the innocent victims whose house had just been mindlessly raided. Maybe the social worker compiling my original borstal report had been right all along about 'rational choice', although he would have been hard pushed to have found anything rational about this latest escapade.

Putting his papers aside and leaning slightly towards me the chairman cleared his throat, 'Against our better judgement, perhaps, we have decided to consider this criminal infringement a minor relapse on your part, young man. We therefore sentence you to a term of borstal "recall".' Having received the lesser of two evils and unaccustomed to such sentencing compassion, I replied, 'Thank you, sir.'

Those youths sentenced to borstal in the north of England were initially taken to the borstal allocation hall in Strangeways Prison, Manchester, to await transfer to borstal, the full process normally taking around six weeks to facilitate. Strangeways was infamous within the penal system, not only due to the appalling conditions within the prison but also for its formidable reputation for violence and brutality, both of which were publicly highlighted several years later in the well-publicised prison riots of the mid-1980s. Not to be outdone by its Scottish counterparts, the admission system in Strangeways was equally difficult—again particularly for young offenders who, by virtue of their age and vulnerability, tended to fall victim to more overt methods of maltreatment by prison officers. By now, however, I was more hardened and prepared for the reception process.

After my transfer from Strangeways, I spent around ten weeks in a semi-open borstal named Hatfield in the north of England; the regime was far more relaxed than anything I had experienced in Scotland and as such stood in direct contrast to my experience of Strangeways, which had a far harsher impact on me than anything that had gone before.

In Strangeways, borstal boys spent over 23 hours a day alone in their cells, subscribing to the relentless, grave routines. At half-past six in the morning, the lights were switched on and we each had to tuck our mattress down the side of the bed frame, flat against the wall on wakening to prevent us from lying on our beds at any time during the day. For the remainder of the time, we were forced to sit on a solitary hard chair in our cells all day, with no stimulus, until our supper of tea and dried oatcakes was given to us around 6.30 in the evening, after which the mattress could be returned. This solitary existence inevitably resulted in prolonged periods of brooding introspection, in which I became increasingly full of bitter self-loathing, for having wantonly sacrificed four months of my life for a Bing Crosby version of 'White Christmas' and a pair of oversized cricket pads. Whilst my own responsibility for my situation was inescapable, at the same time, I bitterly regretted contacting Shuggie.

During this period of confinement, I also developed alopecia, manifesting in large random bald patches over my head, and infected, weeping cold sores on each corner of my mouth, which made it difficult and painful to part my lips, aggravated yet further by my enforced silence. In addition, I lost a significant amount of weight as the pre-steamed food was served to us in our cells, and, by the time the rest of the prison population had been catered for in the dining hall, was always cold and inedible.

Although my subsequent days in Hatfield remained uneventful and agonisingly slow, compared to Strangeways they were relatively more structured by involvement in work, or even playing football at weekends, and although we maintained weekly contact through letters, I desperately missed my maw's visits, In fact, I had no visits throughout my borstal recall because I had insisted that my maw did not come to see me as it was too far for her to travel and too costly. I suspected that my da was back on the drink, which was later confirmed to be the case, when my mother wrote to me some three weeks before my release to inform me that my da's work had fallen through and we were returning to Saltcoats. Although my release signalled yet another period of uncertainty, I took solace in the return to an element of familiarity, even if I remained unsure what shape my immediate future would take.

After almost two years, I arrived back in Saltcoats with my bag of letters which I had received in borstal, and which I had carefully preserved, unwilling and unable to let them go; the clothes I was wearing; my discharge grant, which consisted of one week's state benefit allowance; and nowhere specific to live; I was not yet 18. Since returning from Hartlepool some weeks earlier, my maw and da, along with Jerry and Billy, had been living with my sister, in what had become her sorely over-crowded tenement, whilst they awaited allocation of local authority accommodation, and so initially, with no alternative, I oscillated between sleeping there, on the couch, or staying with my other sister, who was recently married.

With no academic qualifications or significant vocational skills and a criminal record in place of a *curriculum vitae*, I, perhaps somewhat fatalistically, was not hopeful of finding work in the economic climate and the depressed employment market to which I had returned and into which I had felt I had few hopes of breaking. During this period of the late-1970s, unemployment figures were at their highest for decades due to a national economic decline, from which Saltcoats and the surrounding areas have never really recovered. Apprenticeships, even for those who had academic qualifications, were hard to come by and local factories were either downscaling or closing. Being Catholic was a further disadvantage as the scarce employment opportunities which did become periodically available in factories, the local power station, or even within nationalised industries like British Rail, tended to sway towards Protestant applicants; one's religion was readily identifiable from the application forms which firstly sought to ascertain what school you had attended. On the other hand, youth training schemes had been recently introduced and these low paid programmes, which were ultimately limited in their capacity to assist the participants to progress into full time or permanent employment, in the absence of any governmental will to target the structural causes underpinning the employment crisis, were being almost exclusively targeted towards unemployed working class youngsters in an attempt, no doubt, to keep the unemployment figures down.

From where I was standing, it all looked pretty bleak and uncertain; without a stable living environment and no sign of work, and the prospect of endless, meaningless days ahead of me, resuming contact with the guys so soon after my release felt like the only means of escaping the monotonous, debilitating existence that lay ahead. It could have been worse I suppose; Eddie was then serving three years for a number of housebreakings and was in Glenochil Young Offender Institution with Watty, who was still in the early stages of his five year sentence; Clicker was in some other penal institution serving nine months for assault.

Jeg and Shuggie came up to my sister's house to see me several days after my release. Jeg had been released from approved school around three months earlier, he too had been unable to find work and was living again with his parents in Anderson Drive. He had been charged and convicted of several minor public disorder offences since his release and had been subsequently fined. 'Ah hear you joined a cricket team when you wur doon there,' quipped Jeg, as if unsure how to be in my company again, given that we had not seen or heard from each other for over 18 months.

Jeg looked physically different. He was now three or four inches taller than me and, unlike me still sporting my baggy, all-too-last-season trousers, was now reflecting the latest fashion trends with drainpipe trousers, pointed shoes, that I suspected initially were perhaps still his Longriggend shoes which he had customised for effect, his hair slicked into a carefully groomed side shed and a ginger fuzz lying pathetically under his nose, which on closer inspection I discovered was indeed not a rash, but a moustache of some sort. 'Aye, well at least a don't model part time fur a gay magazine … Christ, Jeg whit happened tae you?' I enquired teasingly at the sight before me. Maintaining a rather pretentious manly façade, we shuffled about awkwardly in a macho perversion of a mating ritual, bantering deliberate misrepresentations idly back and forth, unable to express our obvious feelings of warmth at our reconciliation.

Within hours however, the earlier awkwardness faded as we embarked on the first of our many pub outings together. On my arrival, I was greeted like a prodigal son, and at first, I was overwhelmed and taken aback at the attention I received from most of the younger people in the pub, as I stood at the bar drinking whisky, courtesy of just about everyone else present, despite completely despising the drink. Heroically, I forced down one drink after another on the grounds that it was my da's favoured drink and somehow felt that this translated into a public communication of my own manhood. If I could get this odious beverage down my neck without visibly reacting, I was a man to be reckoned with.

Amid the raucous noise, I was approached by an older guy who I vaguely knew, 'Here get that intae you, wee man,' he said handing me a slither of material which resembled a tiny corner of sellotape. 'Whit is it?' I asked him, focusing one drunken eye on this substance balancing precariously on my index finger. 'A wee acid tab man, take it an' chill!' he shouted back at me over the music as he disappeared into the crowd. Before the popularity of the more commonly used recreational drugs in the 1980s, LSD was strictly the prerogative of weird pop stars, drop-outs and hippies. For this young Saltcoats guy, however, any deliberations over the relative moralities of this particular drug use were instantly over-ridden by a drunken 'fuck it', as I swallowed it, washing it down with the infinitely more legal and socially acceptable, but certainly more repugnant tasting, whisky.

LSD was discovered by the Swiss chemist, Albert Hoffman in 1938, and remains one of the most powerful, pharmaceutical, hallucinogenic drugs known. It was the Beatles who, in famously describing the psychedelic effects of LSD, wrote the song, 'Lucy in the Sky with Diamonds' immortalising the LSD experience with poetic allusions to a 'boat on a river with tangerine trees and marmalade skies'. That imagery bore absolutely no relation to my particular 'trip,' which was substantially more akin to a murky, threatening swamp and menacing grey clouds. Ignoring the loud incessant chatter bouncing off the walls and the exaggerated expressions and incomprehensible gestures of the people around me, I sat, locked deep within myself, as soon the heavily patterned, textured pub wallpaper slowly began to breathe into being and sway to the rhythm of the music with a malevolent life of its own.

Sitting in a panic and inwardly feeling significantly less manly than I had a few minutes before, I frantically and discreetly attempted to make sense of this surreal state of being, as the large round ashtray on the littered table began to wink at me, while the cigarette ends themselves took on a life form, as they too began to move slowly back and forth to the beat of the music. Amid an arc of exploding colours, that would have present day advertisers rushing to their technological accoutrements in a frenzied fit of inspiration, I picked up a small chrome Zippo lighter from the table and with great precision held it inches from my right eye. With a slight turn of the lighter, scenes from my life as a young child were played out as if displayed on a small television screen, as I looked on, smiling; cine film type images in which I ran about innocently with tousled hair, kicking a ball relentlessly.

Tilting the lighter slightly in another direction, I could see more modern and disturbing images, of my maw sitting alone in a chair in the living room of our Dalry Road house while livid crackling flames licked upwards in a menacing dance, all around her; when she turned to face me she had the same big ugly bruised head I had seen in the hospital, after my da had beaten her; then, with her wounds weeping, she began to cry for me with her arms outstretched in my direction.

With another tilt of the lighter, the frame shifted again and I watched myself being battered into the back of a police van by two police officers, wearing bloodstained butchers' aprons and then all of a sudden, I was being frogmarched around a borstal exercise yard, while an eyeless officer, his face contorted with rage, slapped and kicked at me repeatedly. As I reached to lift my glass from the table, a rainbow of colours, stars and flashes burst brightly upwards from the glass; my jaw hanging open in wide-eyed astonishment as I followed the coloured dancing images with my eyes whilst they disappeared up towards the smoky ceiling.

Someone was shaking my shoulder firmly. 'Weavy, Weavy … you okay? You're well oot ae it, man …. I told that big wanker no to gie you Acid,' Jeg's voice boomed in my ear, the sound crossing multiple worlds to reach me, as I turned vacantly to face him. Jeg's cornflake freckles danced independently all over his face as he spoke; the wee scrawny baby red ferret lying under his nose writhed about and smiled at me as his lips moved in a parody of speech. Looking from the ferret towards the crowd, I noticed that everyone in the pub was now making their way over to me, pointing and laughing, only their eyes were blackened and sitting deep in their shrunken, skull-like heads. I began crying for my maw as I sank deeper and deeper into the chair.

'So you're Weavy,' a clear authoritarian voice asked above the prying skull voices. To my right a tall, bearded guy with long brown hair, parted in a middle shed, towered over me. His frame was a silhouette against the cloud of cigarette smoke and splashing bright pub lights. He had a full length leather coat on giving him a serene, divine like appearance. It was Jesus; open mouthed, I sat staring intently up into his darkened eyes. I then noticed that his coat was sleeveless and he had two wee deformed fingers protruding from each shoulder instead of arms.

'Shuggie, Jeg!' I cried desperately, 'They dirty Romans schopped his arms aff when they crucified him an' naebody even cares!.' 'Shuggie, Shuggie … its Jesus, ah've just spoke to Jesus!' I shouted again demanding Shuggie's attention. 'Whit are ye sayin man, whit is it?' replied Shuggie shaking me by the shoulders. 'It's Jesus man, Jesus is in here,' I said to him, incredulously pointing to the man who stood before me. 'It's only Big Chris, ya mad man, he's just moved into this area fae Glesga,' replied Shuggie, trying to calm me down. 'But somebody's cut his fucken' airms aff,' I argued. 'That's cause he's wan o they Thalidomide guys, ya daft bastart.'

Having heard the full exchange and getting into the spirit of things, Big Chris leaned over and, touching me on the shoulder with one of his fingers said, 'Arise, my son, and go forth.' Chris Graham had moved to Saltcoats from Glasgow just after I had been sent to borstal. The natural growth of his arms had been affected when his mother had taken the prescribed drug, Thalidomide, during her pregnancy in the early 1960s and he had two fingers protruding from each shoulder area instead of arms. Before I had the chance to get to know him properly, Shuggie sold him a stolen bottle of whiskey, around three months after my release from borstal. He drank himself into a stupor alone in his bedroom and choked to death on his own vomit.

CHAPTER 20

Sins of the Children Visited on the Parents

Given our ages now, limited alternatives and obvious lack of direction, we drifted inevitably towards the pub culture; once we had paid our respective dig monies to our landlords, we would proceed to spend the remainder of our Giros in the pub. It was during the early stages of this newly adopted lifestyle that I really became aware of the reputation that both myself and the guys had acquired locally.

I had always been conscious of other people's reactions and behaviours towards us, my vigilance in this regard intensifying with every custodial sentence I had received, but I noticed now that relative strangers would at least give a dry nod of recognition, whilst others more willing to suffer us would, for their own reasons, blether away superficially, or make a fuss of us and buy us drinks. However, this show of acknowledgment did not appear to emanate from the respect, albeit misplaced, normally bestowed on recognised criminal gangs or networks; rather, people were perhaps frightened, certainly wary and did not like us very much as people, due to our propensity for trouble, which was, admittedly, on occasion, spontaneous and unprovoked.

On reflection, this only served to marginalise us further from everyone else and solidify the subculture we had created during our early days in The Street. That said, the sociological explanations of our evolution as a recognised crew were unimportant to me; I was just glad of the attention and enjoyed the notoriety which fed into and nourished my insatiable *alter ego* and longing to be recognised. I could not have known at the time, however, that I would be held hostage to this for years to come, as with this identity came inevitable expectations and consequences.

As incongruous as it may now seem, this period in which my personal and public identity was developing also heralded a change in the nature of my offending pattern. Despite, or perhaps because of, my own life circumstances, I was experiencing something of an internal morality shift, a shift which had started some years previously. The growing discomfort and disquiet that I had begun to feel about rummaging through other peoples' houses no longer sat easily with me and the thought of disadvantaging those who were already disadvantaged or violating peoples' personal spaces had become, by now, intolerable. Although some of the guys continued to engage in housebreakings, I steadfastly refused; I no longer wanted to be associated with an activity which I now recognised as basely opportunistic and exploitative.

Several weeks after my release from borstal recall, I met a lassie called Maureen McKee who had been raised in The Street, where she continued to live when we first met. Foregoing the normal rules of courtship, due mainly to my own inexperience in such matters, we tended to snatch time together in between my destructive encounters with the guys. However, as time progressed, I found myself feigning excuses, like so many of my museum excursions some years earlier, to enable me to spend more and more time with her. Contrary to everyone's well intended advice and cautious warnings, we married on 29 June 1979, a mere two months after I had left borstal; I had just turned 18 and Maureen was still 16.

Although we were very much young teenagers in love, who pledged their undying and endless love for each other until the end of time, with hindsight, I think in some way we subconsciously viewed this as a means of escaping our own lives, and we no doubt thought that this transition would provide us, in some way, with a passport to adulthood and all that that entailed, which in our youth we could not have hoped to envision. Whilst neither of us was in any way deluded by the prospect of adulthood, knowing from our own experiences that it was not without its own burdens and difficulties, it, perhaps for me at least, seemed to promise a level of stability, certainty and predictability, even control over one's destiny, that I desperately craved. It must be said, however, that our relationship developed and Maureen proved to be en extremely warm, honest and loving wife who was my rock for so many years to come.

Following our marriage, we moved in with Maureen's mother in The Street and, despite our youth and naivety, we tried where possible to engage in the everyday chores of married life. Meanwhile, life for my maw and da still wasn't exactly the perfect model of domesticity that I appeared to be seeking for myself. Although they had recently been re-housed, in Maxwell Road, of all places, my da's drinking was spiralling out of control and he was becoming increasingly fixated with his illusions of my maw's fictional infidelity, relentlessly torturing both himself and my maw in the process. As she began to spend more time alone with my da at home, I was becoming progressively more anxious about her safety and although she would occasionally leave him behind and stay with my sisters for brief periods of respite, she always returned home after several weeks, despite my outrage and protestations.

Testing my long suffering maw's stamina and endurance still further, Jerry and Billy, now 17 and 15, were getting into more trouble. Both had, by now, spent brief periods in Darvel for continued truancy and Billy was subsequently sent to St. Mary's Approved School in Glasgow. Unlike myself however, he could not reconcile himself to his approved school fate and continually absconded; after several weeks of staying with various friends in Saltcoats or sometimes sleeping rough, he would be caught by the police and returned kicking and screaming to St Mary's. His lifestyle on the run was a source of worry for us all with his constant offending.

During one particular period of unauthorised absenteeism from the school, the police arrived at my maw's door one morning looking for him. 'Come on, Ellen, we're here to get Billy and then we'll leave you in peace,' said one of the uniformed officers in a rather resigned tone, no doubt sick of chasing this wee scrawny runt all over Saltcoats every couple of weeks. Predictably, if not understandably defensive my maw genuinely and in no uncertain terms, informed them that she had no knowledge of Billy's whereabouts and had not seen him for several days. An argument ensued between my maw and the police officers, who by this time had surreptitiously engineered their way into the hall. 'Look, I have no objections to you searching the house, but don't you dare suggest that I know where my son is,' she repeated indignantly to the advancing officers as my da, fortunately sober, now intervened.

As voices rose and tolerance levels on both sides of the divide shifted, the loft hatch, directly above them was flung open and to the amazement of my maw and da, Billy's face appeared, only to be rapidly followed by the rest of his wee body as he was immediately hauled from the loft and dragged unceremoniously to the waiting police van outside. The police returned some time later and charged my maw and da with harbouring Billy. Despite their initial shock, at being unnecessarily charged with offences which were at best bordering on the pedantic, given the circumstances, and at worst a travesty of justice, nobody was particularly worried as it was fully expected that the charges would be dropped. As such, I was not overly concerned that I was unable to go to court when they were cited several weeks later; as the police were by then looking for me for an offence of assault. Both my sisters accompanied my parents instead.

Presiding over their trial was the family Sheriff, Rasputin, who apparently guided proceedings to an unnaturally swift guilty verdict as my maw and da sat before him bewildered. To everyone's utter astonishment, Rasputin made open reference to their sons' repeated offending behaviour and court appearances and without offering any form of explanation or justification, remanded them both in custody for pre-sentence reports, despite the nature of the charge and their absence of any previous convictions. The stunned silence in the courtroom was pierced by the wails of my sisters, who could not believe what they had just heard. 'Order, order in this court, will someone please stop that infernal noise!' Rasputin bawled, pointing to my sisters who by now were sitting in the public gallery sobbing uncontrollably. Unable to comprehend what had happened, my maw and da were taken immediately from the dock to the cells below.

When I heard of what had transpired, I was immediately engulfed with an overwhelming sense of horror and I began to sob, painfully, as my emotions proceeded to rampage quickly back and forth, between an inward facing guilt and an outward facing hatred, colliding in the middle to form an unstoppable rage. I thought of my maw being dragged through the humiliating and degrading admission process at Cornton Vale, having no reason to think that it would be in any way different to that practised in the male institutions. Likewise, I was even in turmoil at the thought of my da, for all his faults, his misplaced pride, machismo and ingrained need for power and control—to have all that taken away from him so brutally in a single act of having to strip naked and be examined by strangers.

It was all so unjust and too agonising to consider and my hatred for the police and the courts, particularly Rasputin, for acting in such an inhumane manner towards them, spiralled into almost obsessive proportions with no means of outward expression. In abject misery, unable to eat or sleep, I paced the living room floor like a deranged soul, wanting to pounce on someone, anyone, and tear them to shreds with my bare hands as I thought continually of my maw sitting in a cell in Cornton Vale; truly the worst, most disempowering experience of my life.

Following an appeal by their lawyer, they were released by the High Court some four days later and both given minor fines for this offence by a different Sheriff, which, despite their innocence, was the best possible outcome in the circumstances. In distinct and deliberate denial, and as a consequence of being hounded by my tortured thoughts of her experience for years to come, I could never talk to my maw about this incident.

CHAPTER 21

Blood and Violence Within Prison Walls

I was almost 20 when Maureen's da began getting me work with him on building sites as a trainee steel fixer, a semi-skilled trade, which to begin with gave me a sense of purpose along with the first chance in my life to earn money through legitimate means. Maureen and I had by this time moved into our own council house which, coupled with the prospect of work, despite the sporadic and short term nature of the opportunities available, nevertheless afforded me a degree of stability, and presented as something of a safety net that would help me try and settle down, cut down on my drinking and see the guys less.

I could not have been more wrong however, as the construction industry, and in particular steel fixing for some reason, was very much permeated by a hard drinking, masculine culture, which generally entailed working away from home for weeks at a time. In addition to this, the construction trade and, in particular, steel fixing in Ayrshire in the early 1980s, was at times something of a distinct manifestation of a fundamental and all-pervading sectarianism. I was one of the few Catholics in the trade during this period and although nothing was ever said overtly, I still detected a thinly veiled, underlying hostility emanating from a certain few individuals. This only served to add further to my feelings of displacement and restricted any concrete sense of belonging, which, retrospectively, I was desperately seeking, to reinforce my changing sense of identity in the light of what I then perceived to be my new responsibilities and transition into adulthood.

Perhaps because we were so young and immature, life at home would inevitably have been difficult for me and Maureen and, on a number of levels, we still seemed to be children desperately trying to negotiate an adult world. I did not know how to be in a relationship, how to be a partner, or run a house—and, to all intents and purposes, I had only ever had my da as a male role model. After several months, sometimes weeks, I would leave a job and go on a cycle of seeking out the guys, drinking heavily and becoming involved in pub fights. Looking back, with no external recognition of my attempts to embrace my responsibilities and my confused sense of self in the midst of all this, in my discouragement, I was reverting to the identity and behaviours which I knew would afford me a level of respect, status and, perhaps, a sense of self that at least I, and those around me, recognised.

During this period the Maxwell Road mob obliged by reappearing on the scene, resulting in numerous gang fights fuelled by an endless artillery of baseball bats, hammers, bricks and bottles which ultimately resulted in a number of custodial sentences. With Eddie and Watty still in prison, I was spending most of my time with Jeg, Shuggie, and occasionally Clicker (who had now fathered two children and seemed hell bent on continuing to sow his seeds), plus a few other guys, including two of the Herkiston brothers, Jim and Tam. A third brother, Kevin Herkiston, drifted on to the scene at a later date.

The Herkistons were roughly the same age as us, they had attended the same school, had experienced broadly similar upbringings, and they had all served sentences for violence; it was a match made in hell. Jim and Tam in particular were terrible bullies at times and they were the scourge of the neighbourhood amongst the smaller weans throughout their school days. Towards the latter part of their schooling they went through a phase of ambushing primary school weans, holding them down and drawing thick framed glasses, moustaches and goatee beards on their faces with a black permanent marker pen. For a couple of weeks the scheme was full of miniature Rolf Harris look-a-likes and it was hard not to laugh out loud when you saw them all toddling away Didgeridoo-like, on their way to school together. The wee Rolf Harris clones became extinct, however, when an irate father went to the Herkistons' door and battered one of their older brothers in direct retaliation for the humiliation of his son. Following a number of further custodial sentences, the Herkistons both moved to London with their families around 1995, where Jim now continues to live a law abiding lifestyle, and Tam (Herky), who drifted in and out of various addictions over the years, was kicked to death in a public park in north London in July 2007. The perpetrators were never apprehended.

At this time in my young marriage, I was appearing in court with a degree of regularity, for violent and public disorder related offences, which primarily resulted in the imposition of fines. Court appearances had become such a common occurrence for me that the judicial and penal process, by now so familiar, had lost their capacity to instil fear and trepidation in me, and to some extent, had lost any semblance of legitimacy. With little or no money, I necessarily opted, most of the time, to serve a short custodial sentence as a direct alternative to payment, which led to brief periods in Barlinnie's D Hall, the 'Jakey' Hall. Lying in Barlinnie, listening once again to the desperate screams of the psychotic and alcoholic prisoners undergoing their forced withdrawals, only served to heighten my increasing feelings of worthlessness.

Given the extent of the trouble we were in during this period, the police were never far from the scene and they regularly indulged themselves in their own quasi-legitimate practices, most often at our expense. 'Stop and search' was a particularly favoured practice in which they would stop us in broad daylight and huckle us into the back of a van to be half-stripped and searched for stolen goods or weapons, while they also checked for outstanding warrants in the hope that some matter had, for some reason, escaped their somewhat over-zealous attention.

I was of the opinion that these practices were not essentially an attempt to prevent or detect crime but a method of goading us; reinforcing their own power and control, which in effect only served to underline my feelings of loathing towards them. It was a commonly held belief, and thus an accepted axiom, that their behaviour was far more destructive and abusive than it appeared to those unversed in police relations, unlike our own which was deemed illegal and thus unacceptable.

One night in particular I was staggering home alone quietly through an area of wasteland after a full day's session in the pub when a police van drew up suddenly beside me. 'Whit have you been up tae, Weaver!' one of the officers shouted at me aggressively as he leaned through the open window of his van, with his well rehearsed opening line for a scene in which our delineated roles and lines had long been over-played. Never one to disappoint, I offered him the reaction that he had predicted and provoked; turning to the sneering face before me I hit back with, 'Whit the fuck's it got to do wi' you?'.

As if on cue they both jumped from the van doors, one radioing for 'back up' as he did so, and rushed towards me. I was unable to react or defend myself due to my drunken state, as they proceeded to punch me until I fell down to the ground where I tried to curl up tightly to protect myself. Obviously having acquired a degree of success against this tactic, one of them took out his truncheon and battered me hard over the leg with it as I hurled abuse at them throughout. During this melee, a police dog patrol van drew up and as I lay on the ground I could hear the dog handler opening the van doors. I then looked up to see the two police officers stand to one side as the dog handler walked towards me with a snarling, slavering Alsatian dog straining at the leash in its efforts to get at me.

'So who's this toe-rag then?' the handler asked rhetorically as the rabid looking dog began snapping at my feet viciously with its bared teeth as he was held at a tormentingly, strategic distance. 'Right, get up and run ya bastard,' he said as the dog, with a deep menacing growl had now sunk its teeth into my shoe and begun shaking it hard from side to side. 'Get that thing aff me … get it away!' I shouted in panic as I tried to loosen its grip from my shoe and as I dragged myself backwards from its reach, the beast tore the shoe from my foot. 'How fast can you run then?' he threatened as he continued to walk the snapping, snarling dog towards me at the same pace that I was desperately trying to scurry away from it. As they laughed, one of their radios crackled into life requesting urgent assistance elsewhere and, just as suddenly as they had arrived, they all made their way back to their vehicles without saying another word as I lay battered and shocked on the ground. I still have not got over my fear of dogs to this day.

Despite the madness of my own world, I would still make an almost daily pilgrimage to my maw's to make sure she was okay; my relationship with my da continued to be marred by an irreconcilable distance as his behaviour towards my maw was one that I was unable and unwilling to forgive or forget. Ironically, when I was out drinking in certain pubs in Saltcoats, some of the older guys would make a fuss of me because I was my da's son and tell me how good a guy he was, 'Aye he wis a hard man awright your da … huv a whiskey, son,' they would say as I stood consciously trying to crush a misplaced, bizarre pride. Was it because he was a hard man? Was it because he was so well liked and respected? I wasn't really sure, but in the hazy pub setting, I did not question it too much. Elaborating on this theme, older guys in the dank, smoke filled pubs would proceed to tell me at length about my granny Weaver, who was apparently a local money lender in her day and how, fighting like a man, she and her posse ruled the town with a detached coldness that made the later Thatcher-led government, look almost warm and fuzzy. This of course appealed immensely to my perverse sense of status and belonging and again in some way glorified, justified and legitimised my own public image and lifestyle.

Despite my conflicting emotions however, my maw's safety was always paramount and I tried endlessly to get her to leave my da. 'But I've nowhere to go, son,' she would often say in resignation, as she would never even consider the thought of 'burdening' me or any other family member, which almost proved fatal for her.

One Saturday evening, just prior to my twenty-first birthday, Billy, who was now around 16 years of age, and his mate went up to my maw's to make sure that everything was okay as my da had been drinking particularly heavily during this period, for no more reason than in any other period that had witnessed a downturn in his self-control.

When it was only my maw and da left in the house, I suppose an unofficial rota was negotiated between us all, wherein the unwritten rule was that someone would have to visit or establish contact with my maw every day or two to ensure that no harm had come to her.

Although he was puzzled at finding the house empty and in darkness, Billy was about to leave under the assumption that her unexpected absence probably indicated that my maw was at one of our houses. On his way out of the house, however, he and his friend looked at each other as they heard a strained, muffled groan from my maw's bedroom. Unsure what to expect, they crept apprehensively into the room and looked about the place. 'Billy, quick ... quick,' his mate shouted in unrestrained panic as he discovered my maw's body lying naked behind the bed at the far end of the room; she had been battered with an uncontrolled viciousness that was almost incomprehensible; she was in shock, and drifting in and out of consciousness. So severe was the beating that she was hospitalised for a week and we were told later that she would almost certainly have died if she had not been found when she was. The police briefly interviewed her several days later in hospital but did not appear too interested in pursuing this 'domestic'—their attitude not having altered much since they had left our house with her gasping for air in a dark, airless cupboard some years previously.

While my maw was still in hospital, I had been down at the house several times looking for my da, my hatred boiling and deepening. Fuck it, I thought as I scoured the house and his local pubs looking for him; he had gone too far this time and I just wanted to kill him. I was driven by a combination of factors: as I knew that my maw would always return to him I wanted to prevent it from happening again; I also wanted to show him that he could not just do this anymore and that he was no longer the big man; but mainly I was driven by the lust for sheer revenge.

The night before my maw's return home I went again to the house, drunk; I needed the drink to dull my senses and to ensure that the deep fire of my hatred burned with the same white fury with which it had simmered all week. Seeing the lights on, I began to hammer on the locked door. 'Ah know you're in there, open the door, ya shitebag!' I shouted in a rage. Unable to kick the heavy door open, I heard him turn the key as he drunkenly ranted his threats and curses from behind the door; in my mind, I suspected that he was welcoming an inevitable confrontation which he thought he could easily deal with. And then he was standing before me in the open doorway, his face contorted with hate, his eyes, wild and challenging, boring into mine, as he voiced once again that slurred statement I had heard so often since the age of 13, 'Here's the big fucken' hard man, eh.'

Without a further word said, I lunged forward and head butted him as hard as I could and, before he could fall from the sheer impact of the blow, I grabbed him by the throat, dragged him out through the front door and threw him violently to the ground. Instinctively, he curled up into a protective ball and screamed, 'Leave me alone, ya bastard!' I stood over him, swaying slightly from the mixture of alcohol and adrenalin, with a half-brick in my hand; I had waited for this moment since early childhood as thoughts of my maw's naked and battered body washed over me, the torrent of abuse she had been subjected to over the years, the fear and hardship she was forced to endure. However, this wasn't the way I had imagined it, with him lying in a foetal position, defenceless and crying at my feet for mercy. I was rendered speechless, motionless and began to feel physically sick. Despite the intensity of my complete loathing towards him in the build up to this, I turned my back and left him lying there.

CHAPTER 22

Lone Wolf Surprised by His Reflection

I was in the pub with Jeg, Shuggie and Herky several weeks later having a heavy drinking session and feeling more morose than normal. 'Ur you still thinkin' aboot your maw?' Jeg asked me repeatedly, knowing that I was clearly preoccupied with something. This of course was partly true but I also felt increasingly trapped in this lifestyle and could not see a way out. I had since recognised the violence and its trappings, in terms of reputation or so-called status as, progressively, holding less and less meaning for me; I had no job and little prospect of one, any decent one anyway; I loathed the way I was treating Maureen and did not want her to be my maw and me my da. In short, I hated my life.

As I sank deeper into my whisky glass in despair, I was informed that a guy by the name of Bobby Fairhead was going round the pubs looking for me and telling anyone who was either bored enough or scared enough to listen, that he was going to murder me. Apparently, I had set about one of his brothers outside a pub in recent weeks, which I, of course, had no recollection of, not having diligently maintained a scrap book of fights, past and present. Unsure if it was through sincerity on his part, or for dramatic effect, although I suspected the former, I was told he had pulled a flick knife from his inside jacket pocket, swished it open and growled to this guy, 'Tell Weaver he's fucken' getting' this whenever ah see him'.

Fairhead must have been in or around his mid-thirties, a tall heavy set guy with a fighter's face who always reminded me of the fictional television character, Grizzly Adams. He was from a neighbouring town and had a reputation for violence born, in part, from having completed a seven year sentence for attempting to murder someone a few years previously—with a flick knife of all things. He was a bully who enjoyed living on this reputation.

'Come on, we'll head somewhere else,' Shuggie piped up nervously as he stood up and gulped at the last of his pint in his desperation to leave. 'Aye, let's go, we don't need hassle wae this guy and we don't even huv a blade between us,' added Herky pulling on his jacket, his nerves outdoing Shuggie's. With his side shed still groomed but moustache continuing to fail him, Jeg theatrically whipped a plastic comb from his pocket and, looking like Errol Flynn's retarded cousin, said, 'Right you three just hod him doon when he comes and a'll comb his hair intae a middle shed.' This eased the tension momentarily as we laughed loudly; nevertheless, this guy's public threats and humiliation tactics were not lost on me and I knew that I could not lose face by trying to avoid him; I had a heavy problem.

Later the same night, and definitely the worse for wear, we staggered out of the pub; as we were leaving, I did not really notice who the man was who had entered the small pub foyer, and by now the guys were outside as I was trying to manoeuvre around this bull of a man to join them outside. With my back to him I suddenly heard a shout, 'Weaver, ya bastard!'

Turning to face him, my heart missed a beat as Fairhead stood before me with his open knife. As I stepped quickly out to the street, he lunged from the pub after me and swung the knife in a crude arcing motion at my chest. I darted back from his reach in a panic as he swung the blade at my face in a quick slashing motion, missing me by inches as I continued to back away from him and the area of his reach. As he braced himself for a third attempt, Jeg ran at him from behind and hit him over the head with a bottle. Dazed, unsteady on his feet and still clutching his knife, he staggered back holding his head as Herky then jumped on his back. Instinctively, I quickly bent down and retrieved the unbroken bottle, a large heavy soft drinks bottle, and running towards him, battered it again over his head. This blow rendered him less conscious, and he eventually fell to the ground.

My fear now subsided, I felt nothing but an insatiable and profound rage as I sat on the guy who embodied everything that was locking me into a life I wanted no part of, and with this fuelling my frenzy still further, I battered the bottle into his face several times as he lay unconscious on the ground. Amid the screams of the passers-by, I grappled for the knife still held in his hand as the guys tried to pull me away. 'Quick ,Weavy, come on, let's get tae fuck!' screamed Jeg as he and Shuggie finally dragged me off Fairhead's broken body.

Acknowledging the seriousness of our situation, Jeg, Shuggie and Herky had long since left for home, however, I could not see a way out of this one, knowing that I had committed a serious offence and in front of a number of witnesses. The police were also looking for me for several other offences, so I knew a prison sentence was inevitable; in resignation and with an overwhelming sense of emptiness I thought, to hell with this, I'm staying for more drink.

As I sat alone in a pub later the same evening, still stained with Fairhead's blood, a mob of uniformed and plain clothes police officers barged into the pub and marched hastily towards me. I did not have the energy, or indeed the inclination, to resist arrest as they grabbed me from the chair, threw me face down on the floor and handcuffed me as everyone looked on aghast. 'You've went too far this time, Weaver ya animal,' growled one of them in my ear as he kneeled on top of me with his knee fixed firmly into the small of my back. As my limp body was dragged unceremoniously from the pub, I felt almost relieved.

Following a brief trial before a jury, I was convicted of assaulting Bobby Fairhead to his severe injury and permanent disfigurement. He had a fractured skull, 20 stitches securing a number of lacerations on his head, a broken jaw and he had required an operation to prevent the loss of an eye. Shuggie was never charged with this offence and immediately before trial all charges against Jeg and Herky were dropped due to a 'lack of evidence,' despite the witness accounts presented at trial which were equally damning of them. Nevertheless, I was glad for them both as I knew that, in many respects, I was the main perpetrator and if they had not been there to support me, and Fairhead had been left to his own devices, the ending could have been radically different.

I felt regret at my pending imprisonment and of course the distress I was continuing to cause my maw and now Maureen, who despite our difficulties, remained fiercely loyal to me; obviously seeing something in me that I could never have recognised then; she firmly believed that I had the capacity to change. Fairhead was portrayed at the trial as an innocent victim of a senseless, irrational, unprovoked attack, and the fact that he had publicly sought me out and subsequently tried to stab and slash me with a knife, as he had done before to someone else, was barely acknowledged. Although still angry with Fairhead and the situation I believe he created, I was privately remorseful for the horrendous injury I had inflicted on this man and knew that nothing could ever justify this.

Thanking the jury for their service the Sheriff turned to me in the dock. 'Weaver', he deliberated, unimaginatively, as I stood to be sentenced, 'you were clearly the ringleader of this gang who acted like a pack of unmerciful baying wolves and the public deserve protection from you and your like.' For this offence and the other outstanding offences, at the age of 21, I was given a three year custodial sentence.

Long since desensitised to the admissions procedure, and now categorised as a long term prisoner, I was herded through to the halls and allocated a single cell on the third floor landing of the notoriously violent B Hall in Barlinnie Prison. When the cell door clanged shut behind me, I sat numbly on the side of the bed as if spiralling into an abyss of hopeless despair, as I felt a small part of me starting to wither inside. I wondered, resignedly, what my life consisted of, where it was going, where it was all going to end. I had now served my penal apprenticeship having spent time in assessment centre, approved school, remand institutions, borstal and borstal recall, culminating in a cell in Barlinnie Prison. Having experienced penal institutions since mid-adolescence, I had done enough time to know that if you voluntarily hand over your autonomous self, your will, your desire for self-determination and your individualism to the systemic institutional life, time passes more easily. In this manner, it was imperative to my survival that I switched off from life emotionally in many ways and concentrated on day to day survival within the prison regime.

For the first couple of months I tended to associate with guys I had met during previous sentences and we were placed in the same prison workshop, which I welcomed, at first, because it provided elements of both company and safety, particularly as prison life amongst the younger adults tended to revolve around cliques and gangs. Within a brief period, however, I began to find the incessant gang related talk of violence and the planning of future turns increasingly banal; it seemed that everyone I spoke to was either related to the notorious Glasgow gangster, Arthur Thomson, or worked for him. It all seemed so affected, so pretentious and entirely pointless and inane—some guys were clearly out to impress others with their countless, thinly-veiled-fabrications of hard life, hard man tales which they would deploy on the gullible or willing as a means of cementing their own position in the Darwinian pecking order of things.

On the other hand, there would be those who *were* actually involved in this type of life, or at least on the periphery of it, who failed, in equal measure, to recognise the futility of their existence—their participation in a life without direction and without purpose—and the more I began to listen and to understand this, the more I felt that I did not belong either there or amongst this company. I felt further alienated from the prison population following an incident which occurred fairly early on in my sentence.

As I was standing in the busy toilet area one evening, washing at a sink, with two prison officers as per standard routine standing supervising proceedings, a guy marched quickly into the toilet area with a large iron bar in his hand. Seeing this, everyone, including the two prison officers, quickly vacated the toilet area, leaving him to his obvious mission. Entirely planned, the guy proceeded to kick open the door on one of the three separate shower cubicles, and shouted 'You're getting' it ya fucken' grass!' as he began battering this bar over the unsuspecting guy's head. Awash with blood, he then dragged the guy from the shower cubicle and continued to batter his naked body with the bar as the victim cowered and pleaded for mercy, his screams reverberating around the full hall, as the blows repeatedly hammered into his body with a dull thud after thud. As quickly as he had entered the toilet area, the perpetrator then threw the bar into a corner and marched back out as this guy lay unconscious on the toilet floor, seeping blood.

Reflecting on events in my cell alone later that night, I was surprised at being struck by the savagery of this assault; after all, I had been brought up with and exposed to violence all my days and had inflicted it in no modest manner myself. I was now well versed in the full criminal justice and penal systems and I was doing time for a serious assault, battering a man unconscious with a bottle — so what provoked this reaction in me I wondered? Was it that I was now more clear headed, being out of my own oppressed environment with time and space to think? Every offence I ever committed since the age of 14 or so had been committed whilst I was heavily under the influence of alcohol or was driven by some form of rationale — distorted or otherwise. Did that make a difference? Perhaps my understanding of my own behaviour and associated reasons held more legitimacy than what I perceived to be the reasons underpinning the behaviour of my imprisoned peers — their seemingly mindless maintenance of a certain lifestyle? Was it also in part to do with the perpetrator's almost sadistic disregard for the victim's pleas for mercy? Was it everyone's seeming indifference or even their complicity in this attack? Was it a reminder of the stark realties of this lifestyle? Perhaps it was a combination of all these these factors.

Although mingling with those I knew in the workshops, as with previous sentences I had served, I sought to keep myself to myself whenever I could. However, in Barlinnie this appeared to take on more significance and as opposed to merely opting for this prison lifestyle as a method of getting through my sentence, this approach afforded me the opportunity to explore my developing inclination towards more personal understanding. This was not a hippy-type, New Age bent towards personal growth and development, nor was it akin to discovering oneself through a religious, epiphanic 'road to Damascus' experience. Rather, it was just about trying to take advantage of both the opportunity and the available means through which to try and get to know myself better as a reflexive individual, and which heralded the beginning of a slow and challenging process.

I began to visit the prison library, albeit one which was extremely limited in its ambitions, with less of an ordered grouping of books and more a random collection of lost, found and donated works. Nevertheless, I became an avid reader, preferring to spend time in my cell reading as opposed to partaking in recreation time or time in the exercise yard. I also devised a rigid physical training regime which I would undertake daily in my cell. I listened to the topical debate and discussion channels on my radio and, through the use of library books, I also taught myself yoga and would practice meditation techniques for hours on end.

The initial dreaded solitude of prison life soon became an ally to the point where I longed for the end of the days spent in the busy prison workshops, favouring instead the peace, tranquillity and, paradoxically, the freedom for thought and exploration afforded me through my cell. This orientation towards self-imposed discipline and structure as a means of maintaining my mental and physical health and as a measurement of my own levels of control, within a system designed to reduce autonomy, has remained with me throughout my life.

Maureen wrote to me almost daily and religiously attended our regulated monthly visits, which were held behind glass screens depriving prisoners of any intimacy or even basic human contact, reinforcing one's isolation and distance from the outside world. My maw of course also maintained contact throughout my sentence and, not wishing to impose on the limited time and contact Maureen and I had together, would only visit occasionally. Although I was glad of the visits, they were always difficult and a painful reminder of a life ostensibly lost.

Several of the guys passed through on their way to short term prisons or halls and one day, while being escorted, single-file, from the main hall to the dining hall for breakfast, someone began shouting at me from the other hall as they were being escorted in the opposite direction from the dining area. 'Weavy, Weavy!' continued the shout as I scanned the passing line for a familiar face. 'Weavy, its Eddie!' came the shout again as I turned to see a gangly six foot three figure waving towards me. 'Eddie, is that really you?' I shouted back unable to believe it was him as I had not seen him for around five years when we were near enough the same height. 'Ah goat another two year fur housebreakins!' he shouted as he was marched away into the distance.

Watty had been released some months earlier and was now in the Barlinnie remand hall. Several weeks after his release he held up a shop at knifepoint and escaped with around £70; he was caught in a pub next door to the shop with the knife still in his waistband and for this he would subsequently receive a seven year sentence. As prisoners in the remand hall were generally isolated from the main prison population, I did not see Watty during this period although he managed to engineer the smuggling-over of the occasional letter, known as a 'stiffy', to update me on events. I also received several other letters from guys in Saltcoats who were in other halls to update me on events outside, but I found that I was becoming less interested in the news about these guys or the fights they had been in or who had been battered and so on and, latterly, I would not even read them.

CHAPTER 23

Crossroads but no Signpost

Having spent around 15 months in Barlinnie, I was moved to Dungavel, a semi-open prison in the Lanarkshire countryside, now a detention centre for those seeking political asylum. Dungavel housed around 100 prisoners in dormitory accommodation, all long term prisoners, most of them lifers, who were now approaching the end of their sentences. The regime, as you would expect, was far more relaxed, although I desperately missed the privacy afforded me through my single cell in Barlinnie which had enabled my daily routines of exercise, reading and meditation. However, two particular events occurred in Dungavel which significantly influenced and further supported the process of change I had detected unfolding in myself.

The first of these began with my enrolment in education classes. I naturally gravitated towards studying for my English O-level which provided an excellent means of escaping prison life, albeit temporarily, and which reminded me how much I was drawn to the essential creativity of this subject and the licence to be expressive that it afforded. I would find a quiet area of the prison and pore over my recommended reading and work to develop my literacy skills for hours on end in preparation for my preliminary and final exams. When I was eventually informed that I had achieved an A grade pass I felt not only an immense feeling of self-satisfaction and unprecedented achievement at passing my first formal exam, but it released in me an overwhelming desire, indeed a hunger, to pursue more educational challenges, which I would subsequently realise in the coming years.

Within several months of arriving in Dungavel I was moved from making suitcases in one of the main prison workshops, to the garden details, where I met and worked with a guy who was into the thirteenth year of a life sentence: Donald Lake. When our disparate worlds collided, Donald was in his mid-forties, balding, around five foot eight inches tall, and sporting a hardened battle-scarred face few would voluntarily argue with. Donald had been born and raised in one of the Glasgow housing schemes but moved to the East End of London in his early twenties, where he became involved with the London 'firms' as some kind of enforcer. Sent to Glasgow to 'collect' on an unpaid debt in the early 1970s, Donald kicked in the door of a high rise flat, shot some guy in the head and then threw his lifeless body over the fifth floor balcony. Since he was never one to talk openly of such things, I discovered this from a number of other prisoners who had served time with him in Peterhead Prison.

It was immediately apparent on seeing him that Donald had an enigmatic aura about him; not one to suffer fools gladly, he did not mingle with other prisoners, preferring to keep his own counsel; he had been involved in the Peterhead prison riots and hunger strikes and he was well known and respected within the system. People, including prison officers, really only conversed with him at his invitation. For some unarticulated reason, Donald took a liking to me and as we stood together in a large industrialised greenhouse tending to our tomato plants, like old men in an urban allotment—an almost absurd scene that could never have been actualised in any other setting in life—he would enquire about my past, family, relationships, the guys and my experiences of custody. As the days and months passed, I would be encouraged to consolidate, elaborate and convey my thoughts in relation to each of these subjects.

Like the wise old Temple Master in the cult 1970s television drama, *Kung Fu*, Donald would dissect every account given and challenge me gently on a number of issues: 'So tell me, whit are yae gonnie dae when you get oot and this guy you set aboot has another go at you?' This was not only a means of ascertaining my thoughts in relation to this potential scenario, but in his own way was a conscious effort to prepare me for some of the realistic dilemmas I would almost certainly encounter on my release: 'Ah've no' really thought aboot it that much a suppose,' I replied with a degree of honesty. 'Well, don't you think you should?' he continued; the manner of the question was utterly unassuming but the importance and relevance of it was lost on neither one of us.

In addition to this, by drawing together similarities between our two lives, he began to talk tentatively about his own experiences, his earlier beliefs, values and influences and how they conspired over the years to result in his life sentence—but more importantly to me, how these had then changed during his years in prison. Unlike anyone else I had ever conversed with in prison, however, Donald proceeded to talk candidly about his lifestyle, his 'wasted life,' the stark realities of his life of crime and how this differed massively from the way it was often sensationalised and immortalised in books and films.

Donald also spoke insightfully and at great length of the perceived needs and pressures of certain people in certain environments to pursue status in a culture where people were judged solely on their aggression and masculinity and in so doing he was speaking directly of both our situations whilst reinforcing certain conclusions I was already in the process of drawing in my own mind. By way of emphasising and exemplifying certain points, he would assign me 'homework' in the form of insisting that I engage with certain prisoners and listen intently to the way they spoke and how they defined their lifestyles, experiences and aspirations, which on so doing proved his point exactly. He was an immensely interesting and intriguing character who had lived the life I had perhaps at one point aspired to and it was in some sense because of this, in part, that Donald was able to provide me with the framework to continue analysing and understanding the futility of my own criminal life experiences and thought processes.

On reflection, therefore, somewhat bizarrely, my first experience of pro-social modelling was embodied in a Glasgow gangster who was serving a life sentence for shooting someone in the head on the orders of a London East End criminal gang. Several weeks before my release Donald was moved to Penninghame Prison, an open prison in Dumfrieshire where lifers served out the remainder of their life sentences before release. 'Make this count,' was all he said to me as he shook my hand and looked at me intently before turning to leave Dungavel in his normal quiet and unassuming manner.

I was released in July of 1984, having spent two years in prison and on my release I was subject to a brief period of post-sentence community-based supervision. I did not really mind this as Margaret was once again my allocated supervising officer, who I knew would not make any great demands of me. Although overjoyed at the prospect of my release, having literally counted every passing day in prison, I was also apprehensive about my imminent and inevitably uncertain future; feelings which tended to follow me after every period of custody.

Unlike other times, however, I knew that something inside me had changed during this particular period of imprisonment; I was beginning to view my life differently. In addition to this, I was equally conscious of the paradoxical fact that whilst I had undergone the beginnings of a process of change within the confines of an institution, on the outside, whilst broader changes may have occurred in the wider world itself, many of the people and situations in my former world had not changed and I was unsure how, or if, I could realistically navigate this. None of the guys, the only real friends I had ever had in my whole life, had appeared to change in this sense and for the last two years, they had still been living the same lifestyle I had left behind at the start of my sentence.

Watty and Eddie were in prison yet again and, given the relentless cycle of their imprisonment in the preceding years, and the nature of my brief communication with them in prison, there was certainly nothing to suggest to me any form of change in their thinking or attitudes that might reflect my own. Jeg, Shuggie and Herky appeared to remain firmly committed to a life on the conveyer belt of drinking, fighting, turns and subsequent short term prison sentences. My brothers Jerry and Billy were getting into far more trouble. Jerry was in fact just about to start a 12-month sentence for his part in an assault. My maw was still living with my da and his pattern of behaviour, if anything, had worsened in relation to my maw. My job prospects, other than short term sporadic work on building sites, were pretty bleak. Picking up my relationship with Maureen, which seemed to offer the only semblance of sanity and stability, was difficult initially, given the time we had spent apart and of course the chaos we had experienced in our relationship through my behaviour, prior to my imprisonment. Where was Donald Lake when I needed him, I often thought to myself during the early days of my release, as the life I had left behind two years ago was waiting—almost unavoidably—to welcome me back.

The guys came up to my house a number of times during the first month or so after my release but I rarely went out with them, knowing that sooner or later I would become involved in some fracas or other, which I was desperate to avoid: 'Come on, Weavy,' said Jeg trying to encourage me, 'Ye need a right good drink, man.' On the odd occasion that I did go out with them, we went to the pub, and our small company quickly expanded into a big crowd, insatiably drinking in tales of recent battles and skirmishes. Once again, I found that I was the centre of attention for all the old reasons.

Feeling increasingly uncomfortable with it all, and much to the disappointment of the guys, I would make my excuses and leave after several drinks. The problem posed by Donald about what I would do if I met Fairhead and he had a go at me also preyed on my mind as I honestly did not know how I would react. I knew that a further act of violence on my part would only result in a longer prison sentence and besides, my need for status and recognition within this subculture had diminished significantly; such a confrontation would now only leave me more exposed and less prepared to deal with this situation. My feelings of vulnerability to unwanted police attention were heightened around a month after my release when I was stopped by the police during the day in a busy street, slammed against the side of the police van and searched. Disappointed at not finding a weapon and failing to discover any outstanding court or police matters, one officer whispered menacingly in my ear, 'Just remember we're watching your every move.' Christ, I was hardly Machine Gun Kelly.

As if acknowledging the general difficulties I was encountering and my obvious efforts to distance myself from the guys, Margaret Clark, during one of our early meetings, tentatively asked whether I would be interested in helping her as a volunteer with a group-work programme with youngsters subject to supervision. 'Just come along and give it a try,' she said detecting my apprehension and showing far more confidence in me than I myself possessed at that time. However, I always had time and patience for young people and I was acutely aware of the pitfalls for youngsters blindly stumbling along the path I had myself trodden. Even then, I was clear that I knew something of what they were experiencing. I liked the idea of it, certainly, but was a bit daunted by the fact that it was a bit of a move to the 'other side'. Still, Margaret convinced me; this was before the advent of criminal disclosures and during a time in which there remained some belief in the process of change and rehabilitation and which recognised the dual benefits that could be gained by someone from my background and with my experiences working with such young people. By contrast, in current practices there prevails a culture of fear, risk and blame so any potential benefits for both clients and volunteer ex-offenders are ignored in favour of a wider abstract concerns about risk.

Nevertheless, between sporadic periods of employment on the building sites, I went along to the Ardrossan social work office one evening to begin the group-work programme with Margaret, still unsure of what to expect and with my reservations in tow. When I arrived at the office, Margaret was already sitting in the room with eight boys, all aged around 12 or 13, who, as if conspiring to add to my apprehension, fell silent as I walked into the room. Margaret's attempts at formal introductions were soon abandoned as the boys having momentarily weighed me up, as boys of that age do, resumed their arguing and swearing. 'Here, big man, huv you any fags?' asked a scrawny looking wee boy. 'Naw … and anyway they stub your growth, wee man,' I replied in a rather poor attempt to strike up some kind of rapport with the youngster. 'Smart bastard, eh', he snarled squaring up to me, no doubt thinking that I was yet another authoritative pain in the arse adult swanning in, and probably right back out, of his life. If only he knew. Trying desperately to diffuse a difficult start I replied, 'Sorry, wee man, naw I don't have any fags, ah don't smoke.' This being a more acceptable response he said to me with an outstretched hand, 'By the way, the name's Albert.' 'How you doin' Albert, ah'm Allan,' I replied shaking his hand.

Albert and the rest of the boys were all under social work supervision for a combination of truanting and offending and had each been referred to the group work programme by their social workers. Differing from my own experience, thankfully, this ten week issue based programme was a concerted effort by the social work department to address directly the problems faced by these youngsters and to divert them from residential care where possible. How they expected to realistically achieve the manifold task of undoing a decade of damage in ten weeks struck me, even then, as a little ambitious. Although they were encouraged to do so, the boys rarely spoke about their difficulties in the group setting and tended to give me abbreviated insights on a one-to-one basis, which did not surprise me greatly when I thought back to how I myself and the rest of the guys were at that age.

On reflection, I felt quite uncomfortable, initially, whenever any of the boys began talking about their own difficulties; which occurred more frequently as I got to know them better. I could not really offer them any profound words of wisdom as I was not confident or sure how yet to use my own experiences within this setting. However, it soon became apparent that merely demonstrating a willingness to listen to them, whilst respecting and treating them as individuals was more than enough for them at this particular point and as time passed and my confidence grew, I tentatively began to offer little snippets of advice.

As I bonded with the boys individually and realised that the programme was not going to be a panacea for all in terms of their so-called delinquent behaviour, it was upsetting to think of them lying alone in the secure admission room in Darvel Assessment Centre or, even worse, being processed through Barlinnie and Longriggend like branded pieces of meat. I found working with the boys to be extremely demanding, but captivating and energising; I felt that it provoked something that had lain dormant, unnoticed and as yet, still unidentified, within me; importantly, it gave me a sense of worth and self-respect which I had never really experienced before. 'Well I think it's safe to say you've found your vocation, Allan,' said Margaret on completion of the group-work programme, with the smile I had not witnessed since she appointed me football captain of the Probation Team, evoking a parallel sense of pride in me.

Like my stolen visits to the museum some years earlier and in any case seeing them far less, I did not tell any of the guys at this point about my voluntary work with Margaret. However, standing in the pub with Jeg and Shuggie one night, Jeg rather nonchalantly threw into the conversation, 'Ah hear you're getting' fitted fur a wee tank top and a pair of cords, then.' Trying to remain unperturbed and refusing steadfastly to enlighten them for fear of ridicule at joining the 'system', I replied, 'Aye, its aw part of this supervision thing ah'm still on … it's a right pain in the arse.'

CHAPTER 24

Meeting My Beautiful Boy

I was still working away on the building sites now and again and with no particular sense of purpose beyond obtaining an income, my thoughts always seemed to turn to the next group work programme starting; it was not long before I had competed three separate programmes with Margaret. I had been out of prison for well over a year and in addition to this, had incurred no further charges during this time, something of real significance given my offending history, and I continued my, albeit restricted, contact with the guys. All of these differing dynamics coursing through my life at this time acted like external reinforcers of the progress I felt that I had made. I was beginning to see the possibility that there was another way of being for me and, for the first time, I liked and respected the man I was becoming.

Then, the most significant addition to my changing responsibilities occurred, which heralded the most poignant shift within me; Maureen became pregnant. At the age of 24, my initial feeling was one of elation as somewhere deep inside me I had always longed for the prospect of fatherhood, but, at the same time, I had fearfully suppressed this as I had always felt unready to care for, love and nurture a child as I could hardly take care of myself, never mind a baby; my own baby. I was also particularly conscious of the destructive elements inherent in my own relationship with my da and was always determined that this would not be a feature of my relationship with any child of mine.

My second emotion was one of panic. *Was* I ready for this? How would I know if I was? How does being ready for this entire new world of responsibility and selflessness manifest itself? Could I cope with the responsibility? I did not know the answer to any of these questions. Although wary and apprehensive in case I would fail my child in some way, increasingly I could not disguise the growing waves of pride and absolute joy inside me. Neither did I want to.

As the local employment opportunities for steel fixers were becoming increasingly limited, I had no alternative but to work further and further afield, ultimately ending up on location in various cities across England. Although this situation was not ideal, on one level I welcomed the distance it allowed me to maintain from the guys,

Saltcoats and the seemingly never ending potential for further trouble. Whilst in a practical sense, it provided me with the opportunity to earn money for the coming baby, it simultaneously entailed leaving home, with Maureen pregnant, and prevented me from undertaking any more group-work. It also placed me directly in the macho, drinking culture which characterised the building trade during this period, with no readily available means of escape. Once again, I found myself entering into a lifestyle which was not of my own choosing, which I felt I did not belong to and which divorced me, at least physically, from the things that meant something to me. As a result, I immediately began to feel unsettled; it was as if I had come so far, only to swap one kind of prison cell for another.

After several months working in and around the London area, I had a chance of more lucrative employment; but which again could only further my feelings of self-imposed exile: as a steel fixing supervisor in Saudi Arabia. In reality, I knew that this meant that I would be away for the birth of my child, which was now only around six weeks away. I was also uneasy about moving to a country where public floggings, amputations and beheadings were a prominent part of their savage 'justice' system, where other cultures and religions were viewed with deep suspicion; and where, of course, the sale, possession and use of alcohol were strictly illegal. However, the money was a form of compensation and, more importantly at this stage perhaps, such a move would render impossible the daily temptation I had to overcome, of just downing tools, packing my bags and returning home. In October 1985 I flew out to Khamis Mushett on the west coast of Saudi Arabia where I was to live and work for the next five months.

Whilst working in Saudi Arabia I received a telephone call on 27 February 1986, to inform me that Maureen had just given birth to a baby boy. I was wildly euphoric at this news and I was bursting with a pride I had never before experienced; I relished the thought of fatherhood and bringing up my son, of just being with him, loving him boundlessly and unconditionally and giving him all the things in life I had never had. I now just wanted to go home.

As if awakening from a beautiful dream. however, I was hauled unwillingly back to the stark reality of my life; my former life; with a nauseating jolt, when I received further word from home during the week after my son's birth. A more serious feud had erupted between some of the guys and the Maxwell Street mob and to make matters worse, Eddie, who had been recently released from prison, along with his brothers, had joined up with the Maxwell Street mob for some unknown reason and had been at my door in Saltcoats looking for Billy.

After all we had been through together, I felt totally betrayed by Eddie and I could not understand his motives; I was particularly incensed that he had been at my house in Saltcoats along with a number of other guys, knowing that Maureen and my new born baby were there, which directly and unavoidably involved me in this whole affair. Adding to my concerns, just days before I was scheduled to fly home, the feud had escalated and consisted of running gang fights in the streets, doors being kicked in on either side, cars torched and a petrol bomb flung at the house of a very dear and trusted friend, as well as several serious assaults. Following one such incident, Billy and several of his friends had been arrested and remanded for seriously assaulting one of Eddie's brothers.

The day came when I returned home—a time I had for so long yearned for, when I would meet my son, Paul, for the first time. Maureen, Paul and I had only been together a short time when Jeg, Shuggie, Herky, his brother, Kevin, and Tam Black, who had just drifted onto the scene with something of a salacious interest in events, came to the door unexpectedly with a large plastic bag full of drink and each carrying a weapon, an indirect reference to the escalating trouble. Falling in through the door in a loud, raucous manner, Jeg hugged me and with his breath stinking of drink shouted, 'Aye, a jist knew you'd be back!'

'Fur Christ' sake, Jeg, the wean's tryin' to sleep,' I replied, trying to extricate myself irritably from his drunken grasp.

'Right,' immediately retorted Tam Black, 'when ur we gonna do they bastarts?'

Spinning to face him I spat out, 'So when the fuck did you become a hard man, Tam?' offloading my anger and frustration at the entire situation in which I was being unwillingly cast in the lead role. It was alright for them I thought, but it wasn't they who would be left to do the prison sentence if this thing wasn't resolved or if it escalated even further beyond control. They left a short time later, their departure far more subdued than their arrival.

Despite my initial attitude towards them, the guys would still come regularly to my house and update me on events and the taunting that was now going back and forth, which as always, only serves to inflame such situations and add to the hype. It was becoming increasingly obvious to me that things were due to kick off again, no matter how hard I endeavoured on each occasion to diffuse the situation with the guys. I was unsure as to how to proceed to secure the best possible outcome for everyone, and after much deliberation, I decided that I would confront Eddie to see if this could be straightened out.

With this as my primary objective, I borrowed my sister's car one night and decided to wait outside his door for him under the cover of darkness. I did not fear any of these guys physically but I feared the fact that, unlike me, they seemingly had little to lose. I, of all people, knew the implicit danger in that. Knowing Eddie's unpredictability and increasing propensity for violence, I put a baseball bat in the boot of the car and a Stanley knife in my waistband as I headed for his house, still unsure how this would unfold, but prepared for any eventuality in my desperation. As I sat alone in the car outside his house, my thoughts of diplomacy were fast diminishing as I began to resent deeply the situation Eddie was putting me in; I should be home with my wife and wean but, as it stood, he was a threat to them and to my attempts to move towards a different way of life and perhaps an all-out attack on him was the only realistic way to end this.

As I sat brooding with my destructive thoughts, a taxi pulled up directly behind me and I heard Eddie's voice as he and three other guys got out. As they walked towards my car, I slumped slowly down in the seat, following their every movement in the car mirrors, as I quietly wrestled the knife from my waistband. Disaster threatened as a range of scenarios, including the prominent one of being forced to slash and stab my way to safety, raced through my head. Fortunately, for all perhaps, they were oblivious to the car and walked directly past it to get to Eddie's house; with an element of relief and growing frustration, I made my way home, no further forward.

Feeling under mental siege, I would pace the floor, alone, in the early hours of the morning. On occasion, I paced with Paul in my arms and I would hold him close to me, all the time blowing on and kissing his tender baby cheeks, with no one else on earth existing in those precious moments bar me and him, whilst wondering alternatively how I could escape this madness. I was still anxious to avoid further trouble and I knew that any decision I made could have a significant impact not only on myself but also on my family; in addition, for the first time ever, I had so much to lose and my will to fight was for what I had, not for this. I was totally unaware however, that my immediate fate was already decided and beyond my control.

CHAPTER 25

Back to Barlinnie—Barricades Not Required

Within weeks of my return home from Saudi Arabia, Maureen and I were awakened from our sleep late one night by an incessant banging on the front door and someone shouting in a muffled voice through the letter box. 'Weavy,… Weavy, it's me' Kevin,' came a drunken voice from outside the door as I approached it warily from the inside. As I opened the door, Kevin Herkiston fell in with a Samurai sword in his hand; a surprisingly popular weapon of choice in the west of Scotland.

'For fuck' sake, Kevin, whit ur ye up to … ye nearly gave us a heart attack,' I said. He brushed past me as I stood somewhat ridiculously at the open door with nothing more on than my underpants.

'Ah'm gonnae chop him up,' he slurred at me in reference to Eddie, as he now stood swaying on his feet in the middle of the living room waving the sword about. It would have been hilarious in almost any other context.

'Calm doon, Kevin, Maureen and the wean's upstairs and she's worried sick,' I replied trying to appeal to his more sensitive side. 'We'll go roon in the mornin' an' sort them aw oot … jist me and you,' I concluded in my obviously unsuccessful effort to placate him as he then turned and rushed from the house with his sword pointing purposefully towards the night sky. The Last Samurai? Not quite; we had one more here. I had no idea what I should do. I got dressed and paced the room trying to think of an appropriate course of action as I knew that Kevin was capable of almost anything when it came to drunken violence; Maureen, at this point, just sat quietly on the chair in bewildered disbelief.

Within an hour of Kevin's rather surreal visit, I looked tentatively out of the blinds as nearing police sirens broke the stillness of the early hour silence and with some incredulity watched as a police van and two police cars stopped suddenly outside my door. I stood at the window, utterly bemused as around six or seven police officers jumped from their vehicles, ran up my garden path towards the front door and began banging on it, bringing me to my still confused senses. My stomach lurched in horrible familiarity at what could only come next, although why, I did not know. 'We know you're in there, Weaver, open the door!'

At this time, I was concerned to keep Maureen and, by implication, Paul well away from any troubles, so I told her to wait in the living room as I went into the hall to open the front door. 'Weaver, fucken' move it!'

'Aye awright, calm doon, calm doon, there's a wean up the stair in here!' I shouted while I began to unlock the front door. As I did so, it was kicked hard from the outside, the force of it throwing me against the hall wall, instantly clarifying any fantastical illusions I may have harboured that they had merely arrived to make enquiries. Piling in, several of the officers grabbed me and threw me face first against the wall. Although still unable to comprehend what was happening, I could only focus on Maureen as she stood screaming at the living room door, while Paul lay crying in his cot upstairs.

'Ah've got a wean in the hoose, ya cunts!' I bawled at them as they snapped the handcuffs around my wrists.

'Right, get him oot tae the van,' intervened one of them in a quietly assertive tone as he tried to calm things down.

With Maureen standing at the front door crying, I was dragged down the path and thrown in the back of the police van. I was soon to discover that Kevin had gone along to one of the Maxwell Street mob's house, smashed the front window and climbed in waving his sword above his head. There were only two women and a three-month-old baby in the house when he smashed his way through it like a drunken psychopath waving his Samurai sword. As they cowered screaming in a corner trying to protect the baby, Kevin went on a rampage swiping at every piece of furniture in the living room with his sword. Not content with this, he then made his way to one of the bedrooms as he slashed and stabbed at the bed, scythed at the baby's clothes and cuddly toys, before chopping the cot into small pieces. As Kevin continued to wreck the house, the women fled in terror with the baby in their arms.

Kevin's actions filled me with horror, given that the wean in the house was around the same age as Paul and I thought initially that I was being coerced into being a prosecution witness in some way, given the actions of the police. Within hours of my arrest however, I was to discover that the two women, obviously influenced by others, informed the police that Kevin's brother, Herky (Tam) was an accomplice, along with a third person, who they said resembled me, and, in addition to this, the two attending police officers, who actually apprehended Kevin alone in the house, subsequently gave statements stating that they had seen me and Herky in the house along with Kevin and that we fled the scene when they arrived. We were all charged with hamesucking, malicious damage and breach of the peace. Not only was I *not* involved in this incident in any way, but I had actively tried to disarm Kevin to prevent him causing trouble and, just prior to his arrival at my house, I had been asleep there with my wife and my *own* baby.

Following a sleepless night in the cells, Herky, Kevin and I were handcuffed and taken to Kilmarnock Sheriff Court in the back of a police van. Although Kevin acknowledged the situation he had put me and his own brother in and apologised profusely. Little else was said between us, as Herky and I struggled quietly to come to terms with this nightmare; I felt my whole world crumble around me. I had moved on from this lifestyle and felt physically nauseous knowing that I had been fitted up and that a long term prison sentence was a distinct possibility.

Following a brief court appearance we were remanded in custody to await trial; Herky and I were remanded in Barlinnie and Kevin was remanded in Longriggend as he was under the age of 21. I did not have the same internal defences as I used to, having begun the process of moving away from this lifestyle and I felt like a child again as I experienced every painful moment of the admission procedure yet again; and then *again* when Herky and I were taken over to C Hall: the remand hall. In addition to this, I was worried about Maureen and what impact this would have on her and our baby and the fact that I was not there to help her.

For the first two weeks of my remand, I never conversed at all with my cellmate and just lay on my bed, staring at the ceiling. As I lay there, I was consumed with rage and hate, directed mostly at the police, whose actions I found far more despicable, than anyone else's, however, I was not long in succumbing to a complete sense of hopeless resignation. Perhaps selfishly, I had written to Maureen and told her not to visit as I did not feel I could cope with the heartache of visits and, having seen weans running wild and neglected in prison visiting rooms over the years, I always vowed to myself that no child of mine would ever go near a prison. However, this only exacerbated my feelings of loneliness and despair.

After several weeks in Barlinnie I received a visit from my lawyer which in itself was unusual and, as I was led over to the agents' interview area, I allowed myself to think briefly that he would be here to inform me that this injustice had been rectified and that I could go home, I could begin work again and perhaps even resume my voluntary work with Margaret. I was sadly mistaken. Instead, the lawyer had come at the request of the Procurator Fiscal who offered us a plea bargain; he wanted

Kevin to plead to all charges, Herky to malicious damage and breach of the peace and me to the breach of the peace.

'It's a good deal, Allan,' said the lawyer smugly, leaning back in a self-congratulatory manner as the plastic chair creaked under his weight. 'A good deal? Ah wisnae even fucken' there!' I replied angrily as he looked taken aback at my complete lack of gratitude. Where was this deal struck, I wondered briefly: did we merit a mention over a lunchtime Chardonnay or was it in a dingy courthouse corridor as they walked quickly in opposite directions without breaking stride?

'Well you know how these things work … they have two police officers locating you firmly at the scene of the crime and if you go to trial they will produce countless photographs of the damage done to the baby's belongings, the damage to the cot and of course stress how these two defenceless women fled for their lives with the baby,' he said more seriously now as if irked at my response.

'So whit's the likely outcome for me?' I asked dispiritedly.

'The Fiscal basically wants Kevin and by the sound of things you'll probably get a fine, whereas if you go to trial and lose, you could be looking at four years,' he said as he shuffled the case papers in front of him without looking at me, presupposing a foregone conclusion. I knew I had little way out and with no time to really think things through and with no faith in the man who sat before me, I agreed to the deal, as would Herky and Kevin. At our court hearing the following week, Kevin was sentenced to 20 months imprisonment, Herky received a nine month sentence and I a three month sentence. So much for the fine, I thought; the lawyer could not even look at me as I was led from the dock.

Returning to Barlinnie's 'B Hall' after such a long time out of the prison system, and having tried so hard to move on with my life in so many ways, I struggled badly to cope, which was compounded by the unjust circumstances of my return: the unfairness of it all. I felt that no matter how hard I tried, my liberty now seemed to be at the mercy of others and completely beyond my own control. To make matters worse, Billy appeared in court and received a three-year prison sentence for seriously assaulting one of Eddie's brothers, with his co-accused receiving prison sentences totalling 12 years. My future just seemed to get bleaker by the day.

During this particular time in Barlinnie, I came across very few people whom I had met during previous sentences, rendering the main prison population something of a relatively unknown entity and, as such, Herky and I just kept ourselves to ourselves. Whilst this strategy may have proved effective previously, as there seemed to be a number of guys inside who were friendly with Eddie, in addition to some of the Maxwell Street guys, the atmosphere was becoming noticeably tense between us in B Hall. The mounting pressure unmistakeably peaked during exercise when they walked around the exercise yard opposite us, in almost perfect synchronicity, staring meaningfully in our direction with an animalistic fascination usually reserved for the opposite sex or a voracious opponent. Herky and I were becoming increasingly and necessarily worried, as there were only two of us and we had no recourse to any form of strategic backup.

After slopping out one evening, I made my way along the landing and as I approached Herky's cell, I noticed him standing at his open cell door, holding his head, as blood seeped through his fingers. 'Whit the fuck happened?' I asked rhetorically, knowing that it had only ever been a matter of time before one or other of the guys made a move on us.

'They bastards slapped me ower the heed wae a blade,' he said pointing across the landing where Eddie's jail pals were standing smirking. 'They said you're getting' the same at exercise the morra, Weavy,' he added in a panic.

On reflection, they must have been able to sense my dispirited vulnerability and they were ready to pounce like snarling hyenas; for some it would have been plain to see that my heart was no longer in this lifestyle and I certainly had no desire to adopt the prison persona I so readily did at the beginning of my other sentences by way of settling in and ensuring, in some sense, an element of self-protection. We had little time to talk further as I was forced along to my own cell by the prison officer and locked up for the night with the threats reverberating in my mind and my own tormenting demons relentlessly plaguing me.

What the fuck do I do here? I thought as I paced the cell with the tension of a hunted animal, knowing I would be slashed or stabbed the following day. I had the option of requesting 'protection', which would have meant I would be taken from my cell and placed in a neighbouring hall with the grasses and sex offenders to be protected from the mainstream prison population, which of course was never a realistic option; my pride came before my safety and I would rather they attacked me and cut my heart out with a rusty knife. With no weapon at all at my disposal, I stood on a chair in the early hours of the morning, rather pathetically sharpening the edge of my plastic comb on the cell bars, more out of desperation and a need to distract myself from my racing thoughts than any form of offensive strategy, as I tried to prepare myself for the inevitable.

When the cell doors were unlocked the following day for exercise, I rushed along to Herky's cell, only to discover that he had been taken into protective custody during the night. Although angry at the time, I could never have held this against Herky as I shared his fear and desperation and knew that I might have perhaps followed him but for my own masculine pride. Alone, vulnerable and determined not to lose face, I made my way out to the exercise yard and slowly began the ritualistic process of walking in a circle around the small yard. I felt the eyes bore into me as I walked this solitary path, wrapping my fingers round my plastic sharpened comb for comfort as I braced myself for the assault. This in itself was a form of mental torture and with the dread and anticipation rising by the minute, I would have welcomed an attack, any form of attack, as the beads of sweat ran down my face and down my back.

As we were being herded back in to the hall, after what seemed an eternity, I gulped in an enormous, quiet sense of relief thinking that I had survived what for me was the most vulnerable situation I had been in. As we all made our way back up the metallic staircase to our respective landings, I suddenly became aware of three or four guys, directly in front of me, coming to a sudden standstill with their backs to me, then closing ranks to prevent me moving any further. I did not need to see their faces to read this situation; within the very moment that my brain registered an ambush, I felt a hard blow on my left cheek from behind and as I heard the blade tear through my flesh, the blood immediately began to spurt from my face.

Turning instinctively to face my assailant, I gave no thought to any further danger as I grabbed the guy by the hair, rapidly head-butted him twice in the face and as the two of us tumbled down the stairs, the riot bell rang noisily through the hall. The gawping prisoners at the bottom of the landing stood aside as we both fell awkwardly at the foot of the stairs; my rage and prolonged tension catapulted me to my feet quicker than him, and as I reached down, I grabbed his hair, pulled the comb from my pocket and began gouging it into his face, screaming aloud with a primeval rage as I tried desperately to rip his face open. No-one intervened and as I caught sight of a number of prison officers running towards us, I continued to hold his hair and then began rattling my foot into his face again and again and again as he screeched in pain. In that moment I knew full well that I had only seconds left both to survive this and to make sufficient impact to prevent further recriminations.

I was still kicking his face and head as the prison officers pounced on me and pinned me to the floor. It was pandemonium as I struggled, writhed and kicked under the officers in an attempt to reach this guy again, as he was helped to his feet nearby and led away meekly by other prison officers. Saturated in my own blood, I was dragged along the landing and thrown into one of the ground floor punishment cells, still shouting and screaming. I threw myself at the cell door like a madman as they slammed it behind me and began kicking and punching it. I also began laughing hysterically in an adrenalin-fuelled high. Despite my face hanging open, in my own mind I had won; I had humiliated the sneaky cowardly bastard in front of everyone.

'Is that the best you can do, ya bunch of fuckers?' I screamed at them in defiance from behind the cell door until I was drained of all energy. Soon, feeling nauseous through loss of blood, I lay down on the floor in silence, no longer able to stand or speak; I knew that I would be badly scarred as I tentatively put four fingers into this gaping face wound. Within a short ten minute window, I had experienced a range of conflicting emotional extremes: fear, hate, rage, elation and desperation; now, I just felt emotionally dead and physically drained. Some time later, and with the blood now well congealed, I was taken from the punishment cell over to the hospital wing; it took 25 stitches to pull my face together. Fingering the stitches gently, I knew that I would carry this unsightly scar on my face for the rest of my life.

CHAPTER 26

More than One of Everybody

As if I had been undeservedly stealing a private moment with my wife and wean during my first hours of release, our peace was soon invaded when Jeg, Shuggie and the now annoyingly regular Tam Black arrived at the house. 'That's some scar, man,' said Jeg with the subtlety of a sledgehammer as he stood peering inches from my cheek. 'Fuck it, get this can doon ye,' said Shuggie, disrupting the inspection as he thrust a can of lager towards me. 'Aye, an we'll sort they bastarts out later,' piped Tam Black predictably, as he too began scrutinising my scar.

Maureen by now was mulling about the kitchen with Paul in her arms and, when I caught her eye, I could see only sadness. It was a sadness that mirrored my own; I knew that I was no longer part of that historical quartet whose heads had once protruded from their cell doors singing the chain gang song, with no cares beyond the immediacy of the moment, but I looked the same. There was no shared language to communicate the mixed loyalties, and feelings that churned within me that would make any sense to these people who on so many occasions had been a lifeline for me. Making an excuse, I refused the can of lager and managed to get them to leave promptly without causing offence, stating that I would catch up with them in several days time once I had spent time with Maureen and seen that my maw was okay.

Once again, my release from custody brought with it more uncertainty and confusion, and despite my longing to be back with my family, any feelings I had were tinged with the colours of my heightened anxieties. I was conscious of the fact that avoiding the guys for lengthy periods of time and actually staying out of trouble was no longer enough and whilst the injustice of this and the apparent futility of my endeavours had brought me so much pain on so many levels, I did not particularly desire revenge for what had happened. As it turned out, the guy who slashed me would be dead within six months of his release from a drugs overdose and for my part, I did not want to become embroiled in anything further, particularly not through my own volition. I was just yearning to escape this madness, but I felt increasingly entombed and wedded to a fate in a way that I had never anticipated would transpire. I knew that if I remained in Saltcoats, despite any efforts on my part to distance myself from current events, I would inevitably end up in serious trouble within weeks, possibly days. With this realisation came the knowledge that it was time for me to go. Saltcoats people were not going to let go of the 'me' that they had known for so long, despite the fact that I was trying to shed my skin, and let another self surface. The process that I had begun would need to be continued elsewhere.

Perhaps sensing my desperation, my contacts in the building trade came through for me and I was offered a job on a building site in London within two days. Although it was perhaps the only realistic means of escape open to me, the prospect of moving still threw me into something of a personal turmoil. I would have to leave home again, albeit under different circumstances, but nevertheless I wanted to be with Maureen and Paul; I was worried about Jerry being left behind in Saltcoats and though I felt that I wanted or needed to move on in my life, I still felt that I was running out on the guys, in some respects, which on reflection represented some kind of misplaced loyalty as they were no longer significant people in my life. Despite the dilemmas I experienced, I packed up and left for work in London at the age of 26, and within two weeks I had found fairly suitable accommodation and arranged for Maureen and Paul to join me, where, with the building boom in full flight, we intended to live permanently.

London, or perhaps it was the distance from Saltcoats and everything that it entailed, afforded me a new way of life and, with it, a completely different outlook. At first, it was difficult to find suitable long term accommodation but, following a brief period living with a guy I knew, then a period in a bed and breakfast, we obtained our own council tenancy in Stamford Hill, North London. Although we were housed in a large inner city housing estate, resplendent with the attendant social problems normally associated with these working class ghettos, such as poverty, general disadvantage and, ironically, crime, I nevertheless felt at peace. With no external pressures and relative anonymity, I no longer had to live on edge, or carry a weapon, or think about what people were saying or doing. Nor did I have to live up to peoples' distorted and misplaced expectations and so, as a result, I began to revel in family life.

Maureen fell pregnant shortly after we arrived in London. Unlike the apprehension and doubts over my own ability to rise to the demands of fatherhood when Maureen was pregnant with Paul, I was overjoyed at the prospect of another baby and now firmly confident in myself as a father. Allan, my second son, was born in London on 29 August 1987, within the sound of Bow Bells and I took great pride in the fact that he was both my namesake *and* a genuine Cockney.

Within months of Allan's birth, my maw finally came to the end of the line with my da and she left him and moved into a Women's Refuge in Port Glasgow. 'I'm okay, son,' she said when we spoke on the phone, 'I'm not going back to him … it's over,' the resolution in her tone was unequivocal and I knew that my da had already had the last of his last chances. I was immensely relieved for her sake and safety but I was still pained as I knew she was finding the whole process extremely difficult and unsettling. I also knew that to have arrived at the point of leaving, to walk away and start down the road that she had embarked on by doing so, was just the beginning of the process for her.

My own anger and frustration at her unwillingness to leave him over the years were perhaps a failure on my part to understand fully the dynamics of abuse. On reflection, she exhibited the classic signs of an abuse victim, including: the endless *hope* that things would get better between her and my da and that the abuse would stop; *shame*, that she would be letting both him and us down by leaving; and *denial*, blaming it on the drink, 'He doesn't behave like that when he's sober,' she would often say in his defence as I insisted that she leave him; all the while, no doubt loving the man. Unfortunately for her, however, it took years of repeated victimisation before she accepted the reality of her situation.

I had rarely seen my da in the preceding years and in trying to gain some insight and understanding of his abusive behaviour, I considered the fact that he himself had grown up in a violent household and that this was perhaps some form of learned behaviour and an expression of his own insecurities. However, I too had experienced a violent household but, conversely, the sheer horrifying brutality seemed to instil in me from an early age a determination *not* to behave in this way. Rather than resort to violence, I would relate to relationship difficulties by internalising my anger and brood silently for days, which perhaps was an alternative form of abuse, I don't know. Like my maw, I guess that deep down I too had hoped that my da would change. I also hoped and on occasion I suppose, yearned, for some form of acceptance from him, to be loved like a son, as I now loved my sons. However, since I was so fiercely protective of my maw and perceived in some way as a direct threat to him, this was always unlikely. Despite the changes in my life over the years, I have consciously maintained a distance from my da since my maw's last savage beating, although admittedly, I still ache periodically in my private moments for the relationship that never was and for the grandfather-grandchild relationship between him and my sons that might otherwise have been.

In 1991, after around four years in London, we received a telephone call informing us that Maureen's mother, Susie, had died unexpectedly. To those who knew her, and particularly for Maureen, her da and two brothers, the loss was immeasurable. Maureen could not settle in England after this and, after much discussion, we decided to return to Saltcoats to live. This decision was not taken lightly, given the way our lives had unfolded over the last four years or so and we both knew we had much to lose. I had been in regular well paid employment since moving to London and felt valued in many ways, increasingly ending up as foreman with supervisory responsibilities including, on occasion, hiring and firing the workforce on the sites.

My increasing distance from the guys was another factor, although we had maintained contact, and several times I actually found them employment alongside me for brief periods. However, despite our shared history, I no longer felt the same bond; we had less in common and no longer shared the same values. In addition to this and more importantly perhaps, I no longer needed or desired the notions of toughness, reputation or status that I had previously embraced. My sons were the centre of my universe, and drawing on my own experiences, I was particularly conscious of the impact my attitudes and behaviours would have on them; I knew that I would have to be a positive male role model in order for them to grow into well adjusted, healthy young men. All of these factors combined to facilitate a change in my whole identity and it was with some trepidation that I wondered to what extent this change could be sustained through my return to Saltcoats.

Life in this small seaside town had continued without me; the particular trouble I had left behind in Saltcoats some four years earlier had long been replaced with several other destructive conflicts. Eddie had maintained his well established pattern of imprisonment; and Watty, following yet another brief period of freedom, had received a ten year prison sentence for armed robbery just prior to my return. The rest of the guys had not changed much and, having eventually been forced to make way for the younger guys in town, they had drifted into lives characterised by tenuous relationships, heavy drinking, sporadic work and occasional trouble.

With nowhere to live on our return to Saltcoats, we moved in with Maureen's da in New England Road (The Street), my life now having turned full circle. Although I had very much settled down and had not been in any form of trouble since leaving Saltcoats, some people were still wary of me and associated me with my old life, either trying to avoid me in any way possible for fear of trouble, or wanting to talk endlessly about the 'old times' and everything that that entailed. Either way, people tended to have their own perceptions of me over which I had no real control and in which I had little interest. On the other hand, my reputation, I knew, afforded me an element of protection, particularly among younger, so called up-and-coming guys in the town, (not to be confused with that newer breed—the Yuppie) and guys whom I had previously had run-ins with. This ensured that I was pretty much left to my own devices, which suited me perfectly.

On my return to the local building sites, I began a series of mundane, low paid jobs which were all that was available at this time, as the construction industry desperately tried to fend off the vertigo that it was encountering, as it stood precariously on the brink of a recession.

Being at home however, allowed me to re-establish my voluntary work with Margaret Clark, which gave me a necessary and welcome focus during increasing periods of unemployment. Perhaps because of my own experiences in life, I re-engaged in my voluntary work with the same zest that I had brought to it whilst I was still under supervision and although I continued to find it challenging and, at times difficult, I increasingly felt that I had an aptitude and passion for this type of work. I later extended my voluntary work from working with young people on the brink of entering residential care for various reasons, to include volunteering in a mental health support group and a children's befriending scheme.

The ultimate irony, however, was my involvement in the evolution and maintenance of the New England Residents' Association, developed as a forum through which to voice the views and concerns of residents of the Street (the locus of my earlier rampages) within a larger community residents' association, Saltcoats Neighbourhood Access Project (SNAP). Never a day passed without someone seeking me out to complain about the state of their window frames, their fencing or the lack of lampposts in the Street, to name but a few regular examples, and, diligently I would raise these issues at the community residents' association.

On one such occasion, as I spoke to a toothless old guy who had come to my door, I had to suppress a wry smile as he muttered, 'It's these weans an their fucken' baw, Allan,' his roll up cigarette dangling precariously from his mouth as he spoke.

'Whit … dae yi want a game, Jimmy?' I teased gently.

'Naw, naw, ahm too fucken' auld for that noo,' he replied seriously, 'It's aw day and the baws never oot ma gairden,' he said, as he stood unconsciously scratching away at his arse.

'They're only weans, Jimmy, an' it keeps them oot o trouble … and anyway we were the same when we played aboot here.'

'Aye, but at least we could get cheap fags fae yous,' he said indignantly, in a tone reminiscent of a West of Scotland send-up of old man Steptoe, the classic television rag-and-bone man.

'Ok, ah'll huv a word wi them … aboot the baw, Jimmy, no the fags,' I concluded much to his satisfaction. The weans in question, of course, included my own two sons who by now were aged five and six; Paul and Allan would play football in the same local park where we had played for hours on end many years earlier and this was one of the few places where local weans could play in the area. With this in mind, I set about securing funding from the community association to buy a set of football strips and along with another guy in the street, Davy Hughes, we formed a young football team, SNAP Colts.

At this juncture, Davy was a single parent raising his three small weans in the Street; he was slightly younger than me and with his tousled ginger hair and matching beard, he scarily resembled the late Robin Cook MP (and at one time Foreign Secretary), the general impression aided, no doubt, by his avid interest in politics and, in particular, local politics. Together, we assembled a team of weans (including our own), from in and around the Street who tended to be overlooked, for a number of reasons (not all of them defensible) by the more established youth teams in the area and entered them in a newly formed district league. For training purposes, we even managed to secure a games hall—in my old school, St Andrews, of all places.

As word spread, we soon had a number of older boys from the scheme turning up at training nights; as most of these guys seemed to have little else going for them in their lives at this point. We would often forego the more traditional training practices and hold hugely popular impromptu five-a-side tournaments for weans of all ages. The initiative proved, almost instantaneously, to be an overwhelming success (and definitely more conventional than the Probation Team that I had played for as a child). Davy and I ran a number of teams over the next ten years, winning countless leagues, cups and tournaments in the process. We also embarked on countless fundraising activities which enabled us to take the teams to compete in tournaments in England, Belgium and Holland.

As important as SNAP proved to be for the local boys, it was just as important to me. As a wean, one of my earliest, less destructive means of escape from the darkness of my world had been the ability to lose myself, uninterrupted, in that small, grassless New England Road park with a ball, dreaming of playing for a professional team as I kicked and practised with such heart. Whilst that passion and those dreams remained locked in the heart of the boy and were of course, never realised, it was with unending pride and satisfaction that I watched several boys from our team, including my own two, actually progress to play and/or train for professional football teams in later years.

CHAPTER 27

Know Me Better Now?

With the recession in the construction trade biting hard, I decided to return to school at the nearby Ardrossan Academy, to sit two higher grade subjects in English and in Modern Studies as an adult pupil in 1992, in the hope that this would enable me to access alternative employment, particularly in the care sector. Although several other adults began the classes with me, they soon withdrew for various reasons, leaving me as the only adult, apart from the teacher, to attend classes during the day with the children studying these subjects.

For the first month I struggled to adapt to this environment, feeling awkward, embarrassed and painfully out of place, being the only adult and one with a large battle scar emblazoned crudely down his face, which understandably seemed to draw the eyes of some of the children. I was also painfully conscious of the fact that the last time I had been in a secondary school I had departed drunkenly from a side window in the dead of night leaving behind a trail of utter devastation, and that the last and only time I had studied for an exam had been in prison. As a result, therefore, I was always worried about being ousted and escorted from class in the event that any police checks were undertaken, given my extensive history of offending. Adding further to my discomfort, I bumped into the guys one day who inadvertently fuelled my apprehension by asking me teasingly if I was still fighting at 'play times'; I felt like a fucking knob. With a dogged determination, however, I stuck with it and grew to really enjoy the academic challenge.

My interest in politics and associated cultural debates helped me to immerse myself in the Modern Studies subject and of course, I relished the opportunity to develop my knowledge of English literature, my former English teacher, Mrs Robertson, having laid the foundation for this, perhaps, so many years previously. Shakespeare's tragedy, *Romeo and Juliet*, comprised part of the English literature studies and the behaviour of the Capulet and Montague families intrigued me greatly as the celebrated tales of deceit, revenge and violence reminded me starkly of eerily familiar themes, which, it must be said, were rarely viewed through the same romanticised lens. I was equally interested to observe the dynamics within the class and in particular between the teacher and pupils which bore, for whatever reasons, no resemblance to my own earlier experiences. For the most part, the pupils were respected and encouraged positively to work their way through the subject matter and I could not help but wonder how things might have been for me had I had the opportunity to engage in this style of learning as a schoolchild. The following year I sat my exams and passed both subjects.

With even less desire to return to the building sites, spurred on by my recent academic achievements and continuing voluntary work, I applied for entrance to the social work course at Strathclyde University in 1993. This course, alongside its sister course at Glasgow University, was notoriously difficult to gain entrance to, given the sheer number, as well as the experience and quality, of applicants and the few available places. I was also acutely aware that my extensive criminal record and custodial sentences would pose something of a barrier, or at least be disadvantageous, to my progression in this chosen career. Whilst I did not allow this to deter me from applying, I was unsure how my past would be received, or indeed how I could even begin to talk about this in such a context.

Despite my feelings of self-doubt and apprehension however, within a short period of time I was invited along to the university for interview and as I only had two highers, as opposed to the three required for acceptance onto the course, I had to sit an entrance exam in preparation for my interview, which I subsequently passed. Nonetheless, it did little to ease my growing unease as the interview date approached.

I found the interview extremely difficult as I sat uncomfortably wearing a suit and tie before a panel comprising a senior social worker and two academics from the social work course. Although they seemed agreeable enough at the beginning of the interview, when formal, elementary introductions were announced, it rapidly transpired that they were considerably uninterested in the significant personal changes that I had managed to make, and the commitment that this had required from me in the face of so much adversity. It seemed irrelevant that I had not offended for some six years; the enormous efforts I had made in respect of my recent academic achievements, my participation in, and variety of, experience in relevant voluntary work, even my active involvement in my local community, which had long been renowned for its high incidences of crime, poverty and disadvantage seemed to be of no real consequence. Rather, they focused predominantly on my previous convictions and, selecting them at random, requested that I account for them.

'So can you tell us about the issues and your thoughts leading up to your involvement in the serious assault, perhaps?' they asked as though I had the option of saying, 'No. Next question, please'. With the tie tightening round my parched throat and the shirt sticking to my back, I squirmed in my seat wondering how these people could possibly understand the wider context of such behaviours, yet somehow I managed to navigate their questions and talk about my life within this specific culture This included the pressures and influences inherent in the world I had inhabited and how, in many respects, whilst recognising that I had both will and responsibility, I was socialised into this way of life so the decisions and choices that I had made could not, and should not, be divorced from that restricted context.

Whilst I was surprised by the approach and orientation of their enquiries, I understood their need for thoroughness, but, at the same time, I had not been quite prepared for the intensity of their examination of my past deeds. I felt an unprecedented level of exposure talking about my past in such a way, with people who seemed to me to have little understanding or desire to understand. I was totally drained as I left the interview, feeling defeated and profoundly dispirited; it had been scheduled for 40 minutes but had in fact continued for well over an hour. I had always known that my involvement in criminality would have presented as something of a concern. However, I had expected them to have some interest in, if not understanding of, the dynamics of the processes of change and the unique insights and skills that I might possess, that would perhaps be of significant value to the people who used social work services.

I received a letter shortly afterwards confirming my worst fears and informing me that my application had been unsuccessful, although I would be put on a 'reserve list' and it would be re-considered in the event that any further places became available before the actual course started. Feeling rejected, dejected and uncertain as to where my future lay once more, I returned to work on the building sites and cursed myself for having dared to hope, for ever thinking that I had a realistic chance of escaping the charade of my mundane existence.

Despite my trying so hard to move on with my life, no one was willing formally to take a chance with me; it was alright while I was volunteering my services, but nobody seemed to be prepared to venture beyond that, to put their money where their mouth was, as it were and give me more responsibilities. What more do I need to do? What more can I do? I thought, as my feelings of disappointment turned to self-pity and then to resentment at the thought of being labelled and excluded once again. Within a month of my interview however, I received a letter informing me that several places had been made available and that I was now accepted onto to the course.

It took some time for me to accept that I was actually a university student. This was a social status historically filled with so much prestige and seemingly so distant from my own world and experience, implicitly laden as it was with a multitude of possibilities and opportunities, that for the first several months I was completely overawed by everything this institution symbolised. Strathclyde University's academic history was seemingly autonomous and largely uninfluenced by time and change, which I saw mirrored in the sheer splendour and grandiosity of the university building (formerly Jordanhill College) itself. While representing one extreme end of the social spectrum in relation to the institution's population, I was particularly conscious of the fact that the last formidable building I had been affiliated to, albeit involuntarily, that had so impressed itself upon my mind, and which was similarly steeped in much history and tradition, and whose imposing physical structure had an equally symbolic presence in the community in which it stood, had been Barlinnie Prison.

My class comprised around 50 mature students, most of whom seemed, to my mind then, to be middle class, post-mid-life-crisis do-gooders, embarking on more 'meaningful' second careers, having realised that it was not just a myth that you could not actually live *through* your children. Once more I felt I had little in common with the people around me, only this time, due to my background I felt like an impostor, a fraud, as if somehow, I should not be there—who did I think I was? This feeling remained with me throughout the course. As a result, drawing on the skills I had honed so well in prison, I generally just kept myself to myself.

The course itself and the subject matter were diverse and interesting and I felt prepared for the academic challenge that I knew was ahead of me as I had learnt through my past studies, that, although I was not outstandingly academically gifted, I could achieve sufficient grades through preparation, diligence, grim determination and hard work. However, my feelings of being an outsider were often exacerbated and reinforced in discussions surrounding how social work practice related to and impacted on people lives. The quasi-theoretical interpretations conflicted with my own life experiences and understanding. When a debate raged about whether a client in adversity should or should not receive financial assistance within the theoretical context of 'learned helplessness' and creating 'dependencies', I could only sit quietly for fear of being discovered as I thought of my maw pleading with Margaret Clark for money to feed us as my da had drunk the money.

I felt particularly exposed when discussing the area of 'offenders' as there had been a shift within criminal justice social work from the so-called rehabilitative, welfare orientated approach to understanding and working with offenders to that of choice, accountability and responsibility; the focus was now placed on correcting the 'problematic' thinking that offenders exhibited, which led to their deviant behaviour. The ensuing formulaic interventions, to my mind, lacked compassion and insight, and tended to objectify the offenders on whom these approaches were imposed. This jarred completely with my own experience of the fundamental basics of the process of change.

After one such lecture, reluctant to expose myself, I chose not to raise the issue in front of the full class and so I waited behind to discuss certain points with the lecturer. I felt strongly that there was too much of a shift away from addressing the social and cultural causes of crime and that the suggested interventions were too prescriptive and therefore failed to deal with the root causes. The discussion progressed to a heated exchange of views after which the lecturer suggested that I concentrate on specialising in one of the other areas of social work such as community care, or children and families, as I was apparently failing to understand the fundamental concepts of criminal justice social work. Disillusioned, I left university that day pondering my future, as I was now questioning the very reasons I had wanted to be a social worker: to work with people who offended.

Despite my feelings of alienation at times, determinedly, I persevered and completed the course successfully obtaining my Diploma in Social Work in 1995. Opting to undertake a further academic year, I graduated from Strathclyde University in 1996 with a Batchelor of Arts Degree in Social Work. Maureen, Paul, Allan and my maw attended my graduation ceremony and as I walked up to accept my degree, I could hear them cheering loudly from the audience. My feelings at this point were somewhat conflicting as I somehow felt that I had deviously penetrated the system through the back door, yet part of me was bursting with personal pride and an overwhelming sense of achievement. I was the only one in my family to make it beyond secondary education, let alone graduate from university with a degree.

As I rejoined my family, my maw grabbed me, the way she had when I was sent to approved school when we were at the children's hearing some 20 years earlier, only this time she was crying with happiness. 'Ah'm that proud of you, son,' she said through her tears as she clung to me; and this time, I hugged her right back. My maw's pride and joy were not lost on me and I was overjoyed to have been able to make her feel this way; I felt that I had in some way made amends for the worry and distress I had caused her over the years. Likewise Maureen, who had also accompanied and supported me through so many dark periods of my life, hugged me tightly.

Following my graduation, I was interviewed for a post in criminal justice social work in the former Strathclyde Region, by a panel of senior social workers representing the former Strathclyde Regional Council. Unlike the other newly qualified applicants, my interview questions bore no relation to my university experience or the personal qualities I could bring to the post, but again focused predominantly on my offending past. It was with a look of some resentment, almost, that one of the interviewers asked me directly, 'So do you see yourself on this big white horse now, curing people of their offending behaviour?' Choosing to treat this insult with the contempt it deserved, I ignored him totally and sat silently waiting on the next question.

Whatever his reservations may or may not have been, I was successful in obtaining the position and I began work immediately as a criminal justice social worker. Amongst other duties, my work predominantly entailed supervising people who were subject to probation and parole licence and writing reports for courts and the parole board. Part of this process necessarily entailed visiting people in prisons, and, at first, I found this aspect extremely difficult as it threw up so many memories of my past and reinforced to me that I was now firmly part of the *establishment*, as I saw it then. Now, I enter the likes of Barlinnie through the agents' (lawyers and social workers) area, as opposed to through the front gate in handcuffs, which, believe me, not only allows for a speedier exit, but is significantly less hassle.

Social work for me became something of a labour of love. I relished the work for the challenges that it brought with it, but also because not only was it something that I felt passionately about, but I felt I had so much to offer, had I been able to draw on my life experiences, as at first, I hoped I might. However, it was with some frustration that I could identify the same issues emerging that some people, and particularly younger guys, were experiencing, which had led to, and sustained my own involvement in offending behaviour for such a lengthy period.

Yet, the approaches employed to address offending did not resonate with my own experiences of change; current criminal justice practices primarily depend on using methods of intervention which aim to correct offenders' 'deviant' thinking and through this process it is expected that they will then take responsibility for their various forms of anti-social behaviour, with limited cognisance taken of their own understandings of themselves and their individual circumstances. However for me, change had come in the form of people who believed in me, who could envisage different possibilities for me than I had dared to imagine; in the opportunity to gain self-worth and status through employment via legitimate means, replacing the illegitimate opportunities that had been the sole option for me previously.

Still, nobody asks offenders what needs to be done to support them to change and certainly no one asked me what I thought in this context. From childhood, males in this particular part of the world are almost encouraged to see themselves differently from wider society, from the cultures they inherit, to reject images of weakness and vulnerability, in a denial of intimacy or sensitivity, conversely emphasising more culturally defined masculine characteristics such as aggression, toughness and an unwillingness to express emotions, resulting almost inevitably in some of the thoughts, values and beliefs that supported the behaviours that I had engaged in and which I saw being repeated in front of me. To my disappointment, I was never encouraged to use aspects of 'self' in a professional context and indeed if my experiences of the social work course were anything to go by, it would be actively frowned upon. As such I refrained, therefore, from overtly discussing my past with clients, which I found frustrating as perhaps the use of my own experiences might have given my role, advice and understanding a degree of credibility in their eyes.

I was certainly conscious of the pro-social impact that Donald Lake, the life-sentence prisoner, had made on my life and how in many ways he nurtured, encouraged and facilitated the process of change that was shifting within me. Not only because of the proximity of his experience to my own, which lent legitimacy to what he had to say, reaching me in a way no social worker could have had the capacity to do at the time, but because he watched, listened and believed in my capacity to change— even in the absence of any visible external indicators. Too often now in current criminal justice practices, there is an overwhelming preoccupation with risk which can unravel the work that such practices are fundamentally attempting to achieve, and in turn can erode the concepts of faith and trust, the basic tenets of any constructive relationship, be it personal or professional.

On a more simplistic level, the use of self and elements of self-disclosure were actively encouraged on the social work course and in general practice when discussing, for example, experiences of single parenthood, unemployment, or bereavement. However, when applied to offending, this does not pertain, for reasons that have never been fully or convincingly expressed, and which, to my mind, creates in itself, inadvertently or otherwise, a sense of 'them and us' which does little to address the issues I myself experienced for so many years including exclusion, alienation and rejection. Ironically, I still find myself in the position where, to all intents and purposes, I have to deny my past and, thus, deny too the very experiences which not only spurred me on to pursue a career in this field, despite so many hurdles, but which also underlie, illuminate and enhance my ability to communicate and engage with the people with whom I work, in order to be accepted as a real 'professional.' This aside, some of the people I continue to respect and hold dear in my life, outside my immediate family, are those who could still be characterised as 'offenders,' or 'ex-offenders.'

I began studying on a part-time basis at Edinburgh University through work in 1998 and two years later I graduated with a Master of Science Degree in Advanced Social Work Studies in the Criminal Justice System. The following year I passed the Social Work Practice Teachers' Course and began the supervision and teaching of social work students, making me the most highly qualified social worker in my local authority area of employment at the time. Eclipsing any thoughts or desires for promotion, my relentlessness in this regard was driven more by the desire for perpetual self-improvement and the personal challenges this presented. However, behind this bent was the constant need to prove myself; although I practised with integrity and was always accountable to the wider organization, I never felt that I truly belonged, or rather that I had a right to be there, and that in some way, constantly progressing in my career would provide me with a sense that at least I had earned my place. Likewise, at the same time I was aware that if I could prove myself through external credentials, it would in some sense compensate for my past and make me beyond reproach. My determination, abilities and achievements were subsequently recognised professionally when I was promoted to the post of Senior Social Worker (since re-titled Team Leader) in 2002.

Of my crew, some have drifted away from offending behaviour over the years; others remain on a continuum between minor sporadic offending and a more conscious commitment to that lifestyle. To talk of differing levels of insight or intelligence as precursors to change would only trivialise the issue. Despite my early experiences I have never felt that there was a fundamental, unbridgeable difference there. That said, I knew then, as I do now, that I did not belong in that world. Within that world which I once inhabited, recognised and embraced, I still felt a sense of otherness, like a displaced, nomadic tribesman with no place or time to really call my own; as for many other people, it was a life I had inherited. Unlike the guys, however, I created and grasped the opportunities to gain self-worth and status through more legitimate means, like family, employment and education. The transition from that lifestyle, in which my identity was entrenched, if not my spirit, was a long painful process and one which, to an extent, I have never been allowed to fully travel.

I am still held accountable for my offending behaviour and always will be in specific contexts. In certain circles I am still known and feared for the person I was and the reputation I acquired 25 years ago, and this evokes a range of emotions inside me which sit sometimes comfortably, sometimes uneasily, beside each other. Some of the things that I have done have caused some people immeasurable pain, and for that I feel sincerely remorseful. Simultaneously, I cannot regret this part of my life, that part of myself, as to do so would unravel the multiple identities I embody. This continuing process of reconciliation with my past and the law-abiding adult, father and social worker has made me who I am today.

Epilogue

My maw finally divorced my da in 1986 and went on to live a full and active life before her death in 2003. Regrettably, she died a slow and agonising death from cancer and in many ways I still struggle to come to terms with this. However, I remain eternally grateful that she lived long enough to see me succeed and transform my life and I knew that this and my formal graduations were amongst the proudest moments of her life. As she was slipping in and out of consciousness for the last days of her life I never got to tell her just how much I really loved her, but I think she knew.

Maureen and I separated in 2004 and subsequently divorced after 25 years of marriage. This was an exceptionally painful time in my life, our lives, as we had shared and experienced so much together. However, we had both grown latterly in different directions and a failure to accept this reality would have merely proved destructive for us and those closest to us. We remain good friends and it was with great pride on my part that Maureen recently qualified as a social worker, and she is now working with a local children and families social work team.

Since receiving his two year residential training sentence in 1977 when we all appeared at court together, Watty has ended up spending most of his life in prison with one long term sentence immediately following another. He is presently in Shotts Prison in the latter stages of yet another ten year prison sentence for armed robbery.

Jeg went on to serve a number of short term custodial sentences as an adult. He was a heavy drinker and continued to involve himself in petty offending over the years. After renting a television and video and selling them, Jeg was arrested for fraud and appeared at Kilmarnock Sheriff Court in 1995. He somehow managed to persuade the Sheriff to defer sentence for two weeks to enable him to return to court with the full cost of both the television and video. He has been living somewhere in north London ever since.

Eddie has remained living in Saltcoats and has lived a criminal lifestyle since childhood. He has served several long term prison sentences over the years, mainly for housebreaking and latterly for violent offences and continues to involve himself in offending behaviour. We bump into each other occasionally and spend what brief time we have together reminiscing about the past.

Shuggie served several short custodial sentences and continued to appear in court for minor offences until the age of 30. In 2004, he was found not guilty on a charge of attempted murder, a definite change in his previous pattern of offending. He lives in Stevenston with his wife and young son and I still see him occasionally.

Living in Saltcoats, Billy is a committed husband and father of two who has worked hard over the years to provide for his family and has not been in trouble for a number of years.

Jerry floated in and out of trouble until his mid-twenties. In 1991, he found Jesus Christ and has been a devout, committed Christian ever since. I was honoured to be best man at his wedding in the year 2000 and he lives happily with his wife and children in Saltcoats.

Still staying in Saltcoats, I occasionally see my da although we do not speak and he has never known my children. To this day, he still speaks abusively about my maw to anyone who will listen, yet despite this, I continue to feel saddened periodically at what could have been.

My two sons, now aged 20 and 21, are law-abiding, healthy young men who are constructively pursuing their dreams. Paul is a professional footballer and presently attends college studying sports psychology and Allan is undertaking a football scholarship in Missouri, USA, also studying teaching and the fundamentals of theatre. I am immensely proud of them both; we have always had a strong, loving relationship.

As for me, well I met Beth, fell in love and we married in April 2007. She lovingly cajoled, demanded and bullied me into re-starting this dormant book project after it remained relatively untouched following the death of my maw. To me then it symbolised little more than a painful reminder of the past. However, Beth recognised the value in the book and refused to take no for an answer so although hesitant initially I dusted down the worn pages and slowly got to work. Looking back, it is difficult to imagine at times how a story like this can have any tidy or irrevocable ending and I still shudder periodically in my private moments when I think of some of the things I once did. All I can say is that some life events, and yes fate I suppose, took a remarkable turn at some point and although still struggling at times at memories of the past, I now have a new life with my family around me and I am happy, settled and content. And I wake up looking forward to every day as it comes along and can only wonder at times what the future might hold.

I'm Still Standing

~ Bob Turney

The autobiography of a **dyslexic, alcoholic, ex-prisoner**. When this book was first published, Bob Turney had given up crime, was studying for a degree at university and was generally rehabilitating himself through voluntary work.

Later Bob became a probation officer working in a Youth Offending Team (YOT). His progress from down-and-out 'ex-con' to respected citizen is charted in this highly successful book which contains his life story up until 1997. The next instalment: *Wanted!* was published by Waterside Press in 2005.

'A truly remarkable book' *Prison Writing*

'I have always been rather against the idea of prisoners after discharge becoming professional former prisoners. They should, it seems to me, learn the lessons of imprisonment and move on to fresh lives with new occupations and new interests. Bob Turney is an exception and as **Lord Longford** points out in his introduction, has devoted his life after prison to helping other people with problems of drink and drugs. There seems no doubt he has done a great deal of good. I would wish to commend his book for general reading': **Sir Stephen Tumim**

'The good news is that Bob Turney has a lot to say. The bad news is that until he spent eighteen years in the prison system, he didn't have it to say. As a child and as a man he underwent immense traumas, tramped the streets, succumbed to addictions, lived in gaols and hospitals and, became institutionalised. His experiences - his hopes and fears - are shared by many people held behind prison walls': **Dr Deborah Cheney**

June 2002 | 160pp | P/back | ISBN 978-1-872870-58-8

✇ WATERSIDE PRESS

Going Straight
After Crime and Punishment
~ **Angela Devlin** and **Bob Turney**

Looks at a range of offenders who have changed their way of life. They include **famous, notorious, creative** and ordinary people who were prepared to talk about the turning point in their lives - the events which caused them to leave crime behind.

The book comprises interviews with people **whose experiences have been raw, demanding and sometimes 'close to the edge'**. Their candid explanations about how they rebuilt their lives - often full or remorse for their victims and determined to repay something to their communities - are illuminating. The interviews include

- ex-burglar **John Bowers** (later editor of the prison newspaper *Inside Time*)
- former violent criminal **Frank Cook** (a sculptor and author)
- ex drug-dealer **Peter Cameron** (a successful artist: see his work on the cover of *Going Straight* and also of the Waterside Press publications *Introduction to Youth Justice, The Longest Injustice* and *Human Rights and the Courts*)
- Great Train Robber **Bruce Reynolds**
- actor **Stephen Fry**

- former gangland gunman **Bob Cummines** (now Chief Executive of Unlock)
- **Cameron Mackenzie** (Glasgow villain turned minister of religion)
- *Plus* several women offenders
- a self-made millionaire
- a one-time compulsive gambler
- someone involved in The Troubles in Northern Ireland
- *And* a number of other people who preferred to safeguard a precious new life by using a pseudonym.

Going Straight has been reprinted several times: it has proved to be of interest to a wide range of readers including researchers, students, prisoners and ex-offenders.

April 1999 | 272pp | P/back | ISBN 978-1-872870-66-3

☆ WATERSIDE PRESS

The Criminal Justice System
An Introduction
~ **Bryan Gibson** and **Paul Cavadino**

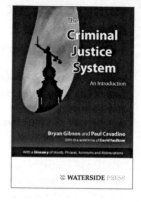

A comprehensive and accessible overview of the CJS, its framework, institutions, practitioners and working methods—that will be of interest to readers seeking an up-to-date description of this important sphere of public life.

An informative, practical handbook which describes the wide-ranging developments and changes that have taken place in relation to crime prevention, public safety and the punishment of offenders.

- Investigation, arrest and charge
- The police and policing
- The Crown Prosecution Service
- The courts of law
- Trial and sentence
- Appeal and review
- Due process
- Judges and magistrates
- Law officers
- The Criminal Defence Service
- Advocates and legal representation
- Victims and witnesses
- The Youth Justice System
- The Probation Service
- HM Prison Service
- Imprisonment and parole
- Independent Monitoring Board

- The private sector
- The voluntary sector
- Strategy
- Criminal policy
- Cabinet committees
- Partnership and working together
- Community justice
- Restorative justice
- Constitutional affairs and human rights
- Interpreters
- Accountability, oversight, inspection and monitoring
- Guidelines, codes, protocols and Best Practice.

- *Plus* - now includes a **Glossary of Words, Phrases, Acronyms and Abbreviations**

Highly acclaimed since first published in 1995, *The Criminal Justice System* covers the entire spectrum of the criminal process against a backdrop of the Common Law, legislation and human rights—from investigation and arrest to trial, sentence, release from prison and parole, as well as key modern-day reforms such as the **Ministry of Justice** and new-style **Home Office**.

3rd Edition | May 2008 | 240 pages | ISBN 978-1-904380-43-6

⚝ WATERSIDE PRESS

Lightning Source UK Ltd.
Milton Keynes UK
UKOW030622130113

204791UK00003B/16/P